P9-DMB-572

3-

John
Gielgud

Books by Ronald Hayman

The Collected Plays of John Whiting (editor)
John Gielgud

John Gielgud

by

Ronald Hayman

Random House, New York

It has not been possible to trace the copyright holders for all the photographs. The publishers apologize for any omissions in the acknowledgments and would be glad to hear from any of these copyright holders.

Copyright © 1971 by Ronald Hayman

All rights reserved under International and Pan-American Copyright Conventions. Published in the United States by Random House, Inc., New York. Originally published in Great Britain by Heinemann Educational Books Ltd. London.

ISBN : 0-394- 46486-9
Library of Congress Catalog Card Number : 73-159348

Manufactured in the United States of America

987654321

First American Edition

Contents

CONTENTS

Acknowledgments

My biggest debt of gratitude is of course to Sir John Gielgud himself, first of all for entrusting me with the book and then for being so extremely co-operative. He has not only put his scrapbooks, letters and personal papers at my disposal, he has been very generous in taking time to talk to me about his past and to read through three successive drafts of the book, making detailed suggestions each time.

Secondly I am grateful to my friend Richard Bebb, who has spent a great deal of time playing Gielgud recordings to me from his large collection and has been a valuable and constructive critic throughout the process of writing and rewriting.

I am greatly indebted to Dame Peggy Ashcroft, Irene Worth, John Perry, Hugh Beaumont, and to John's brother and sister, Val Gielgud and Eleanor Ducker, and to Richard Findlater for both talking to me about him and for reading through early drafts of this book and making useful suggestions. I am also grateful to all the other friends of John's who have given me interviews during the two years I have been working on the book: in chronological order, Basil Dean, George Howe, Glen Byam Shaw, Emlyn Williams, Gwen Ffrangcon Davies, Kitty Black, Rodney Ackland, Richard Clowes, Isabel Jeans, Dame Gladys Cooper, Alan Badel, Fabia Drake, Rosalie Crutchley, Enid Bagnold, Michael Benthall, Barbara Jefford, Alan Dent, Dame Edith Evans, Anthony Quayle, Robert Flemyng, Sir Laurence Olivier, Sir Alec Guinness, Peter Brook, Harry Andrews, Sir Ralph Richardson, Christopher Fry, Ariadne Nicolaeff, Sir Noël Coward, Michael MacOwan, Marius Goring, Margaret Webster and David Storey.

Paul Scofield and Athene Seyler have been kind enough to write to me about John, and John Carleton, Headmaster of Westminster School, has not only answered my queries about the school but sent me excerpts from a manuscript notebook kept by Dr H. Costley-White, who took up his appointment as

ACKNOWLEDGMENTS

Headmaster there in September 1919. I am grateful to Mrs Costley-White for permission to quote from these.

I am obliged to Mr Jonathan Mayne for his help in tracing the typescript of the late Hallam Fordham's unpublished book about the Granville Barker Lear, to the author's mother for permission to draw on it, and to Muriel St Clair Byrne who loaned me the typescript of Kate Terry Gielgud's notes on her son's performances.

I am grateful to Gwen Watford for allowing me to quote from her letter about John's Angelo and to Richard Burton for sending me his two articles in *Life* and *Playboy* about the *Hamlet* John directed.

Finally, I should like to express thanks to my publisher, Edward Thompson, who made the book possible and has since been patient and encouraging, and to my wife, who has not only typed all the drafts for me but cooked innumerable meals which formed a very pleasant accompaniment to innumerable conversations about John.

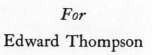

For
Edward Thompson

1 An Edwardian Childhood

One afternoon in 1887, Arthur Lewis, a fashionable Conduit Street haberdasher, and his wife Kate, who was Ellen Terry's eldest sister, received a telegram from Mrs Leonard Messel, who had invited them to a dinner party that evening. Could they bring one of their girls to the party to fill the place of a guest who was ill? They took the eldest of their four daughters, nineteen-year-old Katie, who had 'come out' as a debutante the previous year.

It was a big party and she was taken in to dinner by a tall dark man who had arrived late with his blonde American wife. Katie was shy and she did not catch his name when they were introduced, but his opening remark made her forget her shyness. 'I have often seen you from afar at the Lyceum. But you were always in a box, I in the pit.' Though Kate Terry had given up an extremely successful stage career in 1867 to marry Arthur Lewis, her four daughters had been brought up to take a passionate interest in the theatre, and all through dinner Katie talked eagerly about plays and actors with the charming stranger. She noticed that he used his hands more than most Englishmen do, and she was intrigued by his long square-tipped fingers. Was he an artist? Many of the friends he mentioned were painters or sculptors or worked in the theatre, and later, when their hostess asked for music, it was he who went over to the piano.

When a painter friend of her father's slipped into a chair beside her, Katie was anticipating a whispered conversation all through the usual 'music after dinner'. But there was something about the dark man's playing that commanded attention. Schumann, Chopin, Brahms, Schubert, Sullivan and Wagner. He played by ear, but expressively and authoritatively. 'That's what it is to have Polish blood in one's veins,' whispered the painter. But the party was over before Katie had another chance to talk to the Pole.

Five years went by before she met him again. Arriving with one of her younger sisters at a house party in Devonshire, she found that one of the other guests was Frank Gielgud, who had now been a widower for two years. He took Katie for long walks and talked about Evelyn, his dead wife. 'How I wish you had known her. You would have been a friend after her own heart.' He also talked about his own career. While he was working in the Bank of England, he had made a number of Jewish friends through going to musical parties, and eventually Leonard Messel, a stockbroker (and great-grandfather of the designer Oliver Messel) had offered him a position in the family business in the city. Frank would have preferred to be an artist but at least the job provided him with a steady income.

His grandmother, Aniela Aszpergerowa, had been a well known Lithuanian actress, and on the banks of the river Memel, in Lithuania, there was a castle, Zamek Gielguda, which belonged to the Counts Gielgud until the revolution of 1831. The eldest Count Gielgud, a Polish general, died in the revolution and his younger brother was banished. He came to England where his son, Adam, was born. He was to make his career in the English Foreign Office and he was Frank's father.

Frank met Kate Terry, Katie's mother, and after he had taken Katie to several tennis parties, he invited both her parents to be his guests in a box at Covent Garden to hear *Tristan und Isolde*. More tennis parties followed, then a charity ball, at which he proposed to Katie, though neither of them was very much in love with the other. She had a close and devoted relationship with her father, who had implanted in her a deep need to feel she must always be of service. Now she saw how she could devote her life to this lonely, gentle, charming man, six years her senior, who wanted and needed her companionship. She promised to speak to her father. By six o'clock the following evening they were officially engaged. The wedding was arranged for two months later so that they could have their honeymoon during the holiday his firm had already arranged for him.

They spent the first ten days of their married life at the Bull Inn, Streatley, and the rest of the holiday in Scotland. In mid-August, Katie took possession of her husband's little red-brick house in Earl's Court Square, staffed by an elderly cook and a parlour maid. Their first child, Lewis Evelyn, was born in June 1894, and their second, Val, in April 1900.

In March 1904, when Katie was thirty-five and eight months into her third pregnancy, they moved into a much bigger house on the corner of Gledhow Gardens and the Old Brompton Road.

The French windows in the ground-floor drawing-room over-looked a square with a large garden, where the children could play. A steep staircase led to a bedroom, a library, a dressing-room and a good spare room. The second floor had two big nurseries, another room and a bathroom, while the third had two maid's rooms and a boxroom-playroom. But it was a cold house and there was never enough hot water. All the bedrooms faced north and Frank allowed fires only in the day-nursery and the drawing-room.

After two sons, Frank had set his heart on having a daughter, but in April, a third son, Arthur John, was born. Katie would have preferred him to be called Arthur James, but John was a traditional Gielgud name. Unlike his brothers, Jack (as he was always called as a boy) was blond with blue eyes and an innocent expression. He had sunstroke as a baby and Katie was inclined to treat him as if he were more delicate than he actually was. Engaging a nursery governess to take care of his two brothers, she devoted the next three years of her life to looking after him. Then in 1907, when she was thirty-nine, her only daughter, Eleanor, was born.

After the birth, Katie went through a period of illness and had to employ a nanny to look after little Eleanor and the other children. She was a sensible, intelligent woman, well-read and much travelled, who was to stay with the family for five years, exercising a healthy influence on the growing children. Some-times she would quarrel with the maids – usually there was a staff of five – but she hardly ever disagreed with Katie about the way the children ought to be brought up. All four of them were extremely fond of her, though there were spanks if she wasn't obeyed.

According to his brother Val, Jack's talent for acting was already being developed through his childhood technique of playing up the myth of delicate health in order to get his own way. 'Mother wouldn't like me to do that. I might get sunstroke.' 'You're feeling tired, aren't you dear?' 'Oh yes I am.' But Nanny could tell the difference between a pain in the stomach and a piece of nursery play-acting. The three younger children shared a night-nursery and Eleanor remembers that Jack would some-times wake up screaming in the middle of the night. Sometimes Nanny would sympathize; sometimes she would put him in a cold bath – 'to cool his ardour off'.

On the whole, family life was fairly happy. If Frank was

something of a martinet, Katie would usually side with the children when she felt he was being too strict with them. Whenever she could, she would avoid household rows by getting them to conform to his discipline, hustling them punctually to the breakfast table in the mornings. Jack would wake up to find her shaking his shoulder and saying 'I've turned your bath on.' Dragging himself out of bed he would stumble sleepily to the bathroom, where she would be sitting in her long white dressing gown beside a bath with only a few inches of tepid water in it, 'for fear it might run over,' she would say.

Frank and Katie lived their married life very much in the Edwardian convention of good manners. Later on when Jack, as a schoolboy, read *The Forsyte Saga*, he was surprised to find how much of his parents' life was reflected in it. With her Victorian upbringing and her Edwardian sense of duty, Katie devoted her life entirely to husband, family and household. She was always enchantingly kindly and polite, efficient and busy as a housewife, punctilious and imaginative about Christmas and birthday presents.

Frank, too, loved having the children around him. He would invariably spend an hour with them each evening when he came home from the office. Sometimes he would sit without saying a word while Katie sewed, also in silence. And almost every evening he sat down at the upright cottage piano in the day-nursery to play to them. In the drawing-room there was also a big Bechstein at which he played after dinner and on Sunday afternoons. He was a keen concert-goer and took the children with him as soon as they were old enough to the Queen's Hall, where he had a season ticket, and the Albert Hall, where he always chose the hard seats above the organ loft. He gave Jack Bernard Shaw's *The Perfect Wagnerite* to read before he had ever seen an opera and played him motifs from *The Ring*.

Eleanor seemed to be the most musical of them and there was talk of a musical career for her. She practised every morning before breakfast on the Bechstein in the cold drawing-room but it was very discouraging for her to spend hours working at a difficult new piece, only to find that Jack, who had inherited his father's gift for playing by ear, could effortlessly rattle off a plausible imitation of it.

Katie was not at all musical and on the whole she was less intellectual than Frank. As a girl she had attended French classes and lectures in anatomy and medicine. One of her friends was a surgeon and she was fascinated by the medical profession. She would have been an excellent nurse and, as it was, she was very good at nursing the children when they were sick. She was also interested in writing and achieved some success with her short stories, some of which were published in periodicals like the *Pall Mall Magazine*. Throughout her life she was an energetic letter-writer, taking great pleasure in her unfailingly regular correspondence with her friends and family. One of the main interests she shared with Frank was the theatre. They went almost every week, buying half-crown tickets in the pit or sitting in the dress circle when they had more money to spend. One of Katie's friends had an invalid mother who was interested in the theatre but could never go. For her, Katie kept a notebook in which she wrote perceptive reviews of the plays she saw.

There was a certain streak of bohemianism in both Jack's parents but they did not indulge this side of their natures. Like all respectable middle-class Edwardians, they had a strong sense of responsibility. The pattern of their lives was based on punctuality, politeness, self-discipline, a 'cutlet-for-cutlet' exchange of visits with relations and friends and a determination to set the right example to their children.

The Terry family played a large and glamorous part in the children's lives. Their great uncle, Fred Terry, would often come to Sunday lunch with his wife, Julia Neilson Terry, and would regularly press golden sovereigns into the children's hands. Frank liked him, though they had little in common. Fred Terry was rather a Philistine, interested in gambling, horse-racing and golf. But Frank was very fond of Julia Neilson's mother, and of Katie's Aunt Marion, who often came to the house. Ellen Terry was a less frequent visitor but John remembers her vividly as a charming, vague, benevolent old lady, always fumbling in an enormous bag for things she couldn't find. She had first appeared on stage when she was nine and married the painter Frederick Watts when she was sixteen. After being Sir Henry Irving's leading lady since 1878 and going into management on her own in 1903, she married again at the age of sixty and then made only occasional appearances on the stage. She would come to Gledhow Gardens on Katie's birthday and on Christmas Day after lunch with presents for the children. Frank had an enormous admiration for her and for Irving (who had died in 1905) and Jack loved to hear him talking about them. But Katie found her aunt's restlessness rather distracting and did not care for her son and daughter, both born out of wedlock. So Edith and Edward Gordon Craig were never invited to Gledhow Gardens, and Jack saw less of Ellen Terry than he would have liked.

There was also something of a delicate situation between her and her eldest sister, Kate, Katie's mother. She was a very frequent visitor at Gledhow Gardens and the children were taken once or twice a week to call at her rather gloomy house in West Cromwell Road. Having given up the stage, she talked more like a dowager than an actress, and Jack never heard her pronounce an opinion on either of her actress sisters, Ellen or Marion. But she often took Jack to matinees. They nearly always sat in a box and at the Haymarket Theatre they had the Royal Box. During the intervals they would be sent tea by the management. At the curtain calls he would see the stars giving a special bow in his grandmother's direction, and often Kate would take the boy behind the scenes to meet them in their dressing-rooms. After she died, he bitterly regretted the hours he had spent in her company when he could have asked her about Charles Kean and the theatre of the 1850s in which she had been trained as a child actress.

He was particularly excited when she took him to plays starring his Great Uncle Fred or either of his Great Aunts Ellen or Marion. He saw Marion Terry in a revival of *Pygmalion* with Mrs Patrick Campbell. Both Frank and Katie considered her a better actress than her sister Ellen, and she must have been an excellent comedienne, but she played very little Shakespeare, though Frank thought very highly of her Rosalind in *As You Like It* for Frank Benson at Stratford-on-Avon. Jack was always surprised, though, to hear his father say that the best actress of the period was not a Terry at all, but Mrs Kendal.

Altogether Frank was ambivalent towards the Terrys. A frustrated artist himself, he admired them as keenly as he disapproved of them, respected them as much as he resented them. He enjoyed their visits to Gledhow Gardens, but he was liable to complain that his sisters-in-law bored him and that his mother-in-law ate all the best tit-bits at Christmas.

His father-in-law, Arthur Lewis, had died in 1901 after losing most of his money in the slump of 1898, when Frank had to lend him money he could hardly afford. After living stylishly in Campden Hill, Kate Terry Lewis was now reduced to a depressingly narrow house, with only transient dailies and a deaf maid to look after her. She spent a great deal of time with Jack, who still remembers travelling with her in one of the first cars, an electric brougham. They were driving down Chiswick High Road when they were caught in a violent thunderstorm. Nervous that they might be electrocuted, they stopped the engine and sat there in the open car while large hailstones spattered down on them.

Vehicles always made a vivid impression on Jack. He remembers driving in a four-wheeler cab over the Serpentine Bridge to children's parties, with Nanny beside him carrying canvas bags containing brush, comb and dancing pumps. And he remembers freezing on the upper deck of a horse bus in spite of the large mackintosh lap-robes attached to the seats. It was snowy weather, and after the bus had stopped outside St Mary Abbot's in Kensington High Street (where his parents had been married) more horses had to be added to drag the bus up Campden Hill.

Lewis and Jack were the more attractive-looking of the four children and though their parents tried hard not to show any favouritism, it was impossible for them to conceal their preference altogether. Katie's relationship with Jack was always so close that, with Lewis away at school, it was inevitable that Val and Eleanor should gang up together, forming a rival alliance. And when Val and Jack were sharing a bedroom, Val would make his little brother warm his bed for him by climbing first into the cold sheets.

The boxroom became known as 'the top room', and Val gained possession of it for an elaborate game he played with toy soldiers. With his eight hundred rifles and sabres and his forty guns, wars were fought for days on end, first with Lewis, later with Jack and Eleanor. But Jack never enjoyed the game as much as the others did, and secretly he had designs on the room himself. He was becoming very keen on painting and thought the attic would make a good studio. Sometimes he would disturb the tactical positions of Val's and Eleanor's soldiers and spread his pastels around the room. In revenge, Eleanor would sit on them, smudging the colours.

When he was seven, his mother bought him a toy theatre for Christmas. It was three feet wide, painted in cream and gold, with a red velvet curtain, which could be pulled up and down. From then on he played soldiers with Val only on condition that Val would join in his theatre game. Toy soldiers were made into actors, costumed in plasticine farthingales and ruffs and daubed with gold paint. Jack also recruited the passengers from a toy station he had been given. Furniture, including a miniature grand piano, was borrowed from Eleanor's doll's house, and Jack took sand from the canary's cage to create the effect of an Arabian desert. Clever with his fingers, he used cracker-papers and various odds and ends for his scenic effects, lighting his scenery with a collection of pocket torches.

In the theatre game which the boys improvised, Eleanor had the role of Lady Jones, their rich patron. She was also the one regular member of the audience and occasionally she would act as box office manageress, selling tickets to other children. (Thirty years later, during the second world war, she was to work in the box office of the Globe Theatre.) Parents and servants were coaxed upstairs as often as possible. The productions were elaborate, but though Jack and Val agreed in advance about the main outlines of the plot, all the dialogue was improvised at the performance. Nothing was ever written down until afterwards, when they reviewed their own productions. As well as costume melodramas, thrillers and romantic society dramas, they put on plays making fun of their Terry relatives, especially Great Aunt Marion, who had a quavery voice. Their favourite scene was on board ship, with Grandmother Kate seasick and shouting for her deaf maid.

The children started playing this theatre game seriously when Jack was eight and they were still enjoying it when he was fifteen. Katie kept one of the notebooks in which they recorded details of their productions. The title page reads: 'The New Mars Theatre, in Trafalgar Square, W.1. Erected between April 1912 and March 1913. A list of plays produced between 1913 and 1919. Under the joint management of V. H. and A. J. Gielgud.' The titles include *Lady Fawcett's Ruby*, *Kill That Spy* and *Plots in the Harem*.

2 School

In 1912, Jack started at Hillside, a preparatory school at Godalming, where Val was now Head Boy, as Lewis had been before him. For Gielgud Minor, as Jack now got used to being called, boarding school at the age of eight was something of an ordeal. There were girders running across the dormitory, and new boys had to be initiated by swinging on them, hand over hand, from one row of beds to another, while the other boys flicked wet towels at them, or threw sponges. Another most unpleasant experience was to be shut into the tunnel-like cupboards under the window-seat of the library by boys who would then sit on the seat, drumming on the doors with their heels.

Jack's drawing improved, and when he ran out of news to put into his letters home, he filled up the space with crayon and ink sketches. His best subjects were Divinity and English; Maths was his worst. He enjoyed singing at the Sunday services, fancying his shrill treble as he made it ring out above the other voices, and he enjoyed his first chances of acting in front of a real audience. In one production of *Alice in Wonderland* he played the Mock Turtle and in a later one he was a successful Humpty Dumpty.

It was when he was about ten that the desire to be an actor first seized him. He had always enjoyed dressing up from the box of hats and costumes which Katie had collected for the children. But the decisive moment seems to have come when he was convalescing from a childhood illness in the private garden of the school. He draped himself in a tartan rug and marched up and down the steps from the terrace to the lawn, hoping not to be seen, yet conscious of his dramatic grace and swagger.

In these years at boarding school, he spent very little time in Gledhow Gardens. His parents took furnished houses in the holidays – by the seaside at Easter and in the country for the summer. At Berkhampstead they rented a rectory where Cowper had once lived, with a yew-hedged garden, and at Steyning a vicarage. They also went to Tadworth, Beaconsfield and Uckfield. But neither of his parents felt very much at home in the country. They did not like outdoor sports, they neither swam nor shot, rode nor fished. Frank enjoyed long walks, but he liked everything in the house to be arranged more or less as it was in London, so, weeks in advance, the luggage would be carefully prepared. Katie took everything with her, down to the pots and pans.

They all cycled a lot on holiday and they spent time reading, sketching, walking and listening to Frank playing the piano. They played tennis and croquet, went for drives in the dog-cart or the brake, and the children played soldiers or cowboys in the garden. Katie was good at preparing picnics, feeding her family

well but economically, as in London. They would go away at
the beginning of August and stay for six weeks. Frank only had
two weeks holiday but for the rest of the time he would commute.
The children took it in turns to meet him at the station when he
arrived back every evening from the office in London.

During the 1914 summer holidays, war was declared. The
Gielguds had taken a house at Crowborough for the summer and
Katie read the news in a paper she bought on the railway journey
with the two younger children. (Val was at Rugby having
mumps.) When term started again at Hillside, casualty lists were
read out every few days. The headmaster and his brother, who
had also been a master at the school, both left for the front, where
the brother was killed quite early on. Lewis, too, got a commission
and was sent to France, where he was badly wounded. Frank and
Katie were allowed to go to Le Touquet to visit him in hospital.
Frank came home exhausted as soon as his son was off the danger
list, but Katie made herself so useful in the hospital, doing jobs
for the nurses and writing letters for the men, that she was
allowed to stay there for eleven weeks.

Meanwhile at school Jack was entrusted with the role of
Shylock. At the age of eleven he stage-managed *The Merchant of
Venice*, introducing some scenic ideas of his own, incorporating
the wall he had fallen from last term as Humpty-Dumpty. With
screens on either side of it, it provided a street along the back of
the stage and an extra exit.

By now his letters were becoming remarkably articulate and
his sense of humour was already developing. At the age of eight
and a half he had already been able to send home a detailed and
vivid account of a bonfire party. By the time he was eleven, a
certain sophistication was starting to emerge from behind the
schoolboy jokes and the schoolboy language:

> Mice seem to abound in this place. One was hunting for crumbs all
> through litany this morning. You might send this epistle on to Val, as
> I can't be fagged to write all this to him again. The Doddite Magazine
> ought to be coming out soon. Val has not contributed this time. I have
> written a detective story skit with a moral in verse. Quite original. Que
> penses-tu?

This letter ends with a creditable ink sketch of himself as a
bearded Shylock in a broad-brimmed hat and ankle-length coat,
clutching a parchment in one hand and a long kitchen knife in
the other.

None of the Gielgud children could swim and John says he was 'always a funk at games', though by the time he left Hillside he had managed to win his second eleven cricket colours, scraped into the second eleven for football and played rugger for the first fifteen. But he moved awkwardly; his legs were undermuscled from hip to knee and overmuscled from knee to ankle. He was happiest in his last year when, as Head Boy, he was appointed scorer for the first eleven at cricket, as Val had been, and kept the scorebook in his minute, neat and very mature handwriting. He was also cast as Mark Antony in the school production of *Julius Caesar*.

Lewis had won a scholarship to Eton before the war and Jack now sat for the examination, but his hopes of following his brother were foiled by his maths paper in which he only got four per cent. A few months later he tried for a scholarship to Rugby, where Val was, but failed again, and after Val's descriptions of the discomforts of life there, he was not altogether sorry. He finally won a scholarship to Westminster.

By now he was very keen on music. His favourite record was the Bach Double Violin Concerto. 'It's a very nice record you're always playing,' his unmusical mother said, 'but what a pity the two violins don't catch each other up.'

In September 1917, aged thirteen, he started his public school life as a weekly boarder at Grant's House, or 'Up-Grants' as the Westminster boys called it. Coming home every week-end was very unsettling for him. There were also Zeppelin raids almost every night of the week. Shaken awake when the warning sounded, the boys would race across the school yard in their dressing gowns to shelter in the Undercroft of the Abbey, where the effigies are now shown. He became more and more upset and homesick. Soon he was writing to his mother asking whether he couldn't become a day-boy. He could always have lunch at school but be home by five, he said, in time for the evening meal. He would be able to settle to his prep better at home than he could at school 'with the distractions of other chaps' and he would get more reading done. But Katie now had no servants and at first she resisted his entreaties, even when he offered to make his own bed and clean his own boots. Genuinely unhappy, but also determined to get his own way, Jack bombarded her with letters, playing up the horror of the nightly raids. Still she resisted his pleas and now he began to work himself up to a point of near-breakdown. By the end of November he was writing to his mother four times within two days. 'All I feel inclined to do is either cry or shriek and it's so awful trying to fight against it.' 'I still feel vilely rotten. Woke up this morning with a deadly fear of waking up, getting up, the day, the house, the work, the play, the meals and the going-to-bed-again. I shiver and shake and think and worry. It is too beastly. One can't enjoy a moment.' The masters were sympathetic and the school doctor gave him a tonic, which did not help.

But in spite of all this hysteria he managed to do quite well at work. He had been put in the Upper Fifth, three forms from the bottom, which was good for a boy of his age, and at the end of his first term he came top of his form, so it is understandable that when he went home for the Christmas holidays his parents remained firm. He had to go back to start his second term as a weekly boarder. But in March they gave in, and for the summer term he was a day-boy.

Living at home again he was much happier. Ivor Montagu, a friend who lived nearby, picked him up in the mornings. Often they would come home from school with John on the step of Montagu's bicycle, their tailcoats and satchels flying behind them and their top-hats stuck firmly on their heads. After taking another examination in the following September, at the start of the new academic year, Jack was elected a non-resident King's Scholar.

Now he usually went to school by underground. When Frank had taken him to kindergarten, he had always followed the same route, crossing the same road at exactly the same paving stone each day. But now, going to school on the underground, Jack would get out at different stations, giving himself as many variations of his walk as possible, stopping to look at theatre posters and finding new short cuts.

He became very interested in Westminster Abbey, fascinated particularly by the cloisters. Hoping he would have an excuse to avoid other classes and people he didn't like, he joined the art class. The art master encouraged him and though he found the life class boring, he produced some good sketches in charcoal, pencil and pastel of the Abbey and cloisters, already developing a good sense of perspective and a keen eye for architectural detail.

At home Val had been given the old nursery as his study and the top room was now given to Jack. He installed his paints, his books, his gramophone and his beloved toy theatre, spending hours designing and constructing ever more elaborate scenery for it, getting up in the middle of the night when ideas came to him. He did a great number of detailed studies of imaginary stage sets and brightly coloured costume designs. Admiring Beardsley, Dulac and Arthur Rackham, he imitated them freely. And he delighted his mother with a very colourful birthday present – *The Lady of Shalott*, written out in the form of a missal on brown paper, each verse set in its own frame, with tiny landscapes, figures and flourishes meandering around and between the lines.

As the idea grew in his mind that he would like to be a scenic designer, he spent more and more time sketching and painting, working in pencil and in ink, in poster colours and water colours. His output was enormous. The faces in his costume designs are all very sketchy and altogether his drawings show little interest in the human figure—more in the pose than in the body – but he had an extraordinary love for visual detail. Eclectic though he was in design, in composition and in choice of colour, the contrasts of texture are very well contrived, the elaboration of detail is minutely painstaking and the results are nearly always pleasing. Whether or not he could ever have become a successful designer in the theatre – and I think he probably could – he was developing a sure sense of visual style which was to be invaluable to him. As a director he has been able to work very closely with designers, while his eye for costume has been almost equally valuable to him as an actor.

The majority of Jack's friends at Westminster were Jewish. He hated the antisemitism that was fomented by the inevitable segregation of the Jewish boys at prayers and meals, where they ate specially cooked food. One of his closest friends was Arnold Haskell, already a balletomane. Frank had taken Jack to see the Diaghilev ballet at the Alhambra. He saved up his pocket money to go again and again. He spent hours with Haskell standing in queues for ballets, where their top-hats and high stiff collars caused sniggers. John has never forgotten the opening performance of *The Sleeping Princess* with its superb Bakst decor and four leading ballerinas. Ballet tickets were tickets of admission to a magic world: *Carnaval*, *La Boutique Fantasque* and *Prince Igor* all enchanted him. Lopokova and Tchernicheva became his idols and Karsavina was still dancing.

He also spent hours queueing to see plays from the pit. He still remembers the buskers and the long waits while the queue moved slowly towards the box office, the clink of the metal admission-plaques given out by the attendant, the rush to get a good place on one of the front benches and the disappointment when a paper slip fluttered out of the programme to announce that one of the stars was indisposed. He was deeply impressed by the power his favourite actors wielded – the way a star like his great uncle Fred Terry could bring a hush over the entire audience just by dropping his voice. But though John was almost conscious of wanting to appear on the stage himself, he did not study their acting with an eye to imitating it. He was more aware of the audience's reaction to the way they made effective entrances – invariably greeted by applause – and the way they took their curtain calls.

Of course it was always exciting to be taken backstage. Lewis Gielgud was in love with Mary O'Farrell. She was the third leading lady in *Peg O'My Heart* by Hartley Manners, whose wife, the famous American actress Laurette Taylor, had created the part very successfully, but the air-raids terrified her and she went back to the United States, to be replaced first by Moya Mannering and then by Mary O'Farrell. Lewis, who had been invalided out of the army, took his young brother to see the play from the pit. A. E. Matthews, already in his forties, was playing the male romantic lead. Afterwards they went to see Mary O'Farrell in her dressing-room. Jack and Val were afterwards to spend exciting Sunday afternoons in Hampstead, having tea with their brother's girl friend and her sister. Apart from the family, Mary O'Farrell was the first actress Jack ever got to know.

With the war just ending, the Westminster O.T.C. was very active. For Jack the main consolation of wearing uniform to school was the freedom it gave him from the uncomfortable collars and the ridiculous top-hats. He went twice to O.T.C. summer camps. These were attended by battalions from public schools all over the country. The boys slept in round tents, nine to a tent, with bolsters and straw palliasses. Reveille was at six and the food was awful. In a pencil-written letter home, Jack described one characteristic 'stew' – 'i.e. boiling water, chunks of raw meat and potatoes with spotted fever' and in another he wrote 'you should see me eating jam and sardines (together) with the same knife'. There were drills, parades, lectures, route marches and often 'night-ops'.

In September 1919, a new Headmaster, the Rev Dr H.

Costley-White, took over the school. He kept a manuscript note-book in which he made comments about the boys, and his first note on Jack was 'doesn't concentrate and doesn't much like Classics. But must pass leaving certificate and wants to do mod. history after that.' His next comment is dated December 1919. 'Clever but slapdash and ill-regulated. Must pass School Certifi-cate. French and Maths bad.' The note for July 1920 is 'Good but Maths has probably spoilt his Certificate.'

Like most children, Jack went through an acutely religious phase at about the age of sixteen. Frank Gielgud had been brought up as a Catholic but never went to church now except for an occasional visit to Westminster Cathedral to listen to High Mass as if it were a concert at Queen's Hall. The children were not brought up to any particular religious convictions. At school Jack was registered as Church of England but, both at Hillside and at Westminster, he had always been disappointed by school prayers and sermons, much as he enjoyed hearing his own voice during hymn singing. Confirmation had been another disappoint-ment. But now he found himself going often to the Brompton Oratory to smell the incense, and in watching the ceremonies he enjoyed a strange feeling of exaltation. Religion, art and the theatre were all mixed up in these boyhood experiences of an intensity that almost overpowered him. In Westminster Abbey the figures on the tombstones fascinated him in almost the same way as waxworks, grottoes and aquariums. It was the peepshow element in all these that appealed to him so strongly. They were all theatrical, mysterious, and rather frightening.

While he was at Westminster he had longed for a great cere-mony to be performed, and when the Unknown Soldier was buried, it was like a great theatrical occasion in which the stars were all the famous figures of the day. The Westminster boys in their O.T.C. uniforms lined the path from the street to the door of the Abbey, holding their rifles reversed and their heads down, wishing they could look up at the procession of notables that passed so close to them.

It was when he was about sixteen that Jack suddenly made a definite decision to become an actor. His parents had arranged for him to specialize in History in order to sit for a scholarship to Oxford, where Lewis had done extremely well. After being second scholar of the year at Eton, he had won a Minor History Scholarship to Trinity, and though his undergraduate career had been interrupted by the war, he had been able to go back for a year after his demobilization in 1918, when he was awarded a Demyship at Magdalen. In 1920 Jack visited him there and fell violently in love with Oxford. He still has a vivid memory of the day he spent with Lewis, when they had lunch in New Buildings at Magdalen and fed the deer out of the windows. Then they visited the Haldanes in Woodstock Road and went on a river picnic with Aldous Huxley and Naomi Mitchinson, taking two big punts illuminated with Chinese lanterns and floating down the river to Magdalen just as it was getting dark. So next year, when Jack gave up the idea of an Oxford career, it was not without keen regret.

Meanwhile he was becoming rather vain about the potentialities of his appearance. He took to washing his long hair very frequently to make it fluffy. At the age of sixteen he was wearing light grey flannel trousers braced rather too high, black, soft-brimmed hats and sometimes even an eye-glass on a string, in imitation of his brother Lewis, who sometimes wore one.

It was not altogether easy to reconcile his parents to the idea of his becoming an actor. His mother knew that there was too much of the artist in him for him to be content to go into business but Frank very much wanted him to follow Lewis and Val to Oxford. Having conquered his own inclinations to become an artist, he was rather reluctant to let his son indulge his. With Jack's talent for drawing, it seemed he might have made a good architect. But he insisted that despite the private tuition his parents had arranged for him, his maths were still not good enough for him to cope with technical drawings and calculations.

Eventually they agreed to let him try his luck as an actor. Jack promised them that if he had not become successful by the time he was twenty-five, he would give up the stage and work to become an architect. Once again he had his own way.

3   Amateur Experience and Professional Training

In the Easter vacation of 1920 Jack went abroad for the first time, together with Frank, who, unlike his wife, enjoyed travelling and became far more relaxed and agreeable away from London. Since the war, his elderly parents had been living in Vevey, Switzerland, and Frank now took his sixteen-year-old son to visit them, staying in Paris on the way.

In Switzerland Jack enjoyed the mountains, but when he tried to sketch them he complained that the results were 'somewhat pudding-like'. He was delighted with his Catholic Polish grandparents and rather spoiled by his grandmother, who always wore a chatelaine with a silver bag on it. She took him to a confectioner's shop in Montreux, where he tucked into the rich cakes, and to see Francesca Bertini in a silent film.

Back in London, Jack began to lay plans for his future as an actor. Theatrically there had been nothing at Westminster to compare with the enterprising activities of Hillside, and the only success Jack scored there was in a recitation of John of Gaunt's dying speech at an end-of-term competition. But during the holidays he had several times taken part in amateur theatricals. He played Orlando in an open air production of *As You Like It* in the grounds of Battle Abbey, but he was very unlucky at the first performance. Interrupting the Duke's picnic in the forest with the line "Forbear and eat no more!" he brandished his sword as he strode across the lawn, only to trip over a log and fall flat on his face. And in the last act, pointing to the path where Rosalind should have appeared on his line "Ah, here comes my Ganymede", he saw no Rosalind. He repeated the line, more loudly, but in vain. From the other side of the lawn the prompter was trying to indicate that Rosalind had changed back into her girl's costume a scene too early.

In March and April 1921 he acted in two performances at the drama school which Rosina Filippi was running in Chelsea. A fine old actress who had played in many of Sir Herbert Beerbohm Tree's productions at Her Majesty's, she was still appearing occasionally in the West End. One of her students had been taken ill, and Jack took over from him as Mercutio in three scenes from *Romeo and Juliet*. The rehearsals went quite well, but he was rather put out at the performance when Miss Filippi sat down at a piano near the stage and played twiddly bits as an accompaniment to his Queen Mab speech.

She was disappointed with her own students' performances but apparently very pleased with Jack's. She wrote to his mother, saying how promising he was and offering him a run of small parts in some plays she was going to put on with her students and some professional help. The first of these clashed with the end of term, but he doubled the parts of an undergraduate and a young German officer in an adaptation of Rhoda Broughton's novel *Belinda*.

So in July, when he auditioned for a scholarship at the drama school which Lady Benson, Sir Frank's wife, had been running since 1919 off the Cromwell Road, he was not entirely a novice. When he arrived for his entrance audition, he found Lady Benson in a small office with the actress Helen Haye, whom he had admired on the stage a few weeks previously in Galsworthy's *The Skin Game*. For his audition piece, Jack recited 'Bredon Hill' from *The Shropshire Lad* by A. E. Housman. He had recently seen Henry Ainley declaiming it during a charity concert at the Grafton Gallery, dressed in an officer's uniform with breeches and spurs. Jack had no costume and he recited with what he thought was rather too much emotion. But a few days later he received a letter from Lady Benson, which told him that finding his performance 'natural and unstrained', Helen Haye had awarded him ten marks out of ten. He was entitled to a year's free tuition beginning in the autumn term.

Only four of the thirty students at the school were boys, so the slim girls had to be used in juvenile male parts and the fat girls in character parts. A girl played Bassanio to Jack's Antonio in scenes from *The Merchant of Venice*. He enjoyed the rehearsal classes but not the fencing, dancing or elocution, and it was a bad blow to his confidence when, only a few days after his arrival, Lady Benson burst out laughing in the middle of a scene. 'Good heavens! You walk exactly like a cat with rickets.' He had no trouble with his hands or arms, but he was in the habit of standing with his knees bent and walking more from the knees than the hips. From now on, of course, self-consciousness about his movement made him more awkward still. But he soon realized that he had a good memory, especially for Shakespeare, and that he could make himself weep by listening to his own cadences and modulations.

Hearing that drama students could walk on unpaid in crowd scenes at the Old Vic, he went along and got taken on without an audition. *Henry V* was in rehearsal, directed by Robert Atkins, who would shout to 'that boy in the brown suit' to take his hands out of his pockets as he stood, holding a spear, through endless repetitions of the same passage. Rehearsals were disappointingly unglamorous, held in a shabby old rehearsal room with a company of actors who had mostly spent their lives touring the provinces. To the seventeen-year-old boy they seemed rough and rather terrifying. He felt ill at ease amongst them and over-dressed, though nobody took much notice of him, except Austin Trevor, who was kind to him, and the women in the company, who seemed much more approachable than the men. He enjoyed watching Ernest Milton, whom he idolized, and Russell Thorndike. Jack was enormously impressed by his energy and versatility and by his feat of memory in learning Peer Gynt, Lear and Hamlet in rapid succession. To be working in the real theatre at last was very exciting, especially during dress rehearsals and first nights. The theatre was dirty and there was no dressing-room for the extras, who had to change in an upper box in the auditorium with only a curtain to hide them from the audience, which was local and working-class. But there was an atmosphere of liveliness and cheery goodwill.

On 7 November 1921 Jack made his first professional appearance as the Herald in *Henry V*. He had only one line to speak: "Here is the number of the slaughtered French." But he created such a bad impression that in *King Lear*, in *Peer Gynt* and in Halcott Glover's play, *Wat Tyler*, he walked on without being given a word to speak. In fact several of the actors in the company thought that someone ought to tell him he would be well advised to give up any hope of becoming an actor. But he did not at all mind the repetitiveness of the work, with only one line in one of the four plays. At least he was on the stage.

He got his first notice in a newspaper when he played the Reverend Pillenger in a production at Lady Benson's school of *Lady Huntsworth's Experiment*, a farce by R. C. Carton. He was not mentioned by name, but the critic reported 'The worthy parson, unctuously played by quite a beginner, drew much laughter from a critical audience.'

He did three terms at Lady Benson's, but though his grandmother wrote to congratulate him on his scholarship and later attended one of the school performances, and Great Uncle Fred toiled up the stairs to the top room in Gledhow Gardens to look at the designs he had painted for his model theatre, none of the other members of the Terry family had so far shown much interest in his budding career. Then one morning a letter arrived from his second cousin, Phyllis Neilson-Terry, Fred Terry's daughter, asking him to call at her Apollo Theatre office if he would like to go on tour with her, playing a very small part and understudying the lead in *The Wheel* by J. B. Fagan, a play she had recently staged quite successfully in London. Jack immediately accepted four pounds a week to play Lieutenant Manners as well as understudying and working as assistant stage manager. He would only have a few lines to speak at the end of the third act, and for the most part he would be busy prompting, giving cues and working the effects. But at least he had his first salaried job in the professional theatre.

4   The First Tour

The tour opened on 4 September 1922 in Bradford, which Jack found a very depressing town. 'No wonder Irving died here, poor man,' he wrote in a letter home, complaining that the locals were 'dull and heavy like the sheep whose wool they mangle'.

Compared with the Old Vic of 1921 the company seemed very professional, but for Jack it was a bit too much like going back to school, though it was exciting to see Phyllis Neilson-Terry every evening. The play was not very interesting and the assistant stage management side of the job was tedious, but Jack was pleased with his make-up and costume: 'I am assured I look quite the experienced militarist in my moustache.' He enjoyed the understudy rehearsals, in which he tried to copy the leading actor, Ion Swinley. The girl understudying Phyllis Neilson-Terry made no attempt to act, merely saying the lines and walking through the moves. But one day Phyllis Neilson-Terry herself came down to show him how to manage if ever he had to play the big love scene with her. Tall and statuesque, she had to bend her knees to be able to slip into his arms.

He felt very homesick in the Bradford digs. Uncomfortable in his bed – he wrote home asking to be sent a pillow – he was kept awake by a clock which struck every quarter outside his bedroom window. The landlady wore a large hat with feathers, which she kept on indoors. When she invited him for a drink in the kitchen to meet her other lodgers from the local music hall, he was ill at ease with them and it was no use pretending to be an experienced drinker. He was also taken on pub-crawls by some of the actors in the company. After mixing Guinness with gin and tonic, he turned green and fainted. But the others were kind and helpful, especially Ion Swinley.

As assistant stage manager, Jack had to superintend the dismantling of the set, its movement out of the old theatre and into the new one, where it had to be reassembled each Monday morning. The second touring date was Preston and the third Aberdeen, where Alexander Sarner, who played the Tibetan Lama, was suddenly called away by telegram because his father was seriously ill. His understudy, who normally played another quite important part, had to take his place. Jack was asleep in his digs when a message arrived that he would have to play Maclaren that evening. Apart from the lead, it was the biggest of four parts he was understudying and one he had only started rehearsing that morning.

He got through it without any trouble and wrote home at midnight 'Everyone seems to have been not too badly impressed. I only wish we were not too far off for you to come and see me but of course it is out of the question . . . anyway it has been quite a fairly thrilling experience.' Phyllis Neilson-Terry also wrote to his parents that he 'did *very well indeed* . . . His youth made the little bit where they think it's all finished quite pathetic and the funniest thing of all is to see the family gestures coming out again.'

A month later, when the play was at Oxford, she let him play the part again for one performance so that his parents could come to see it. He was very nervous, played badly and felt deeply ashamed all through the tea party she gave afterwards for his parents. This was the first of several experiences he had of doing something fairly successfully and then being unable to repeat it.

It was a long tour. Week after week the same routine of train journeys, new digs, cold provincial cities, and hours in the wings, following the prompt book as the all too familiar lines were spoken on stage.

Jack had shown some of his designs to Phyllis Neilson-Terry. When she praised them, he had thought she was merely being kind, but she surprised him one evening in Leeds by asking him to do some drawings for the music room and the dining room in a new production she was planning of a play by Temple Thurston called *A Roof and Four Walls*. With only a vague briefing about what she needed and with little hope that she could possibly intend to use what he did, Jack set to work, doing his utmost to avoid anything that she might call 'decadent'. After the tour ended, his mother helped him to construct two models, and after he had made some modifications which Phyllis Neilson-Terry suggested, he was thrilled that she finally accepted his designs. When the play later opened in London he was given a programme credit.

As the tour went on, an actor in the company suggested Jack should spend a year at the Academy of Dramatic Art (now RADA) where he had been trained himself. Jack decided to take his advice, knowing that he still had a great deal to learn and that he stood a good chance of winning a scholarship, as he had at Lady Benson's, so it would not cost his parents any money. He also knew he would probably be able to act in the professional theatre while still studying at the academy. (This would not be allowed today either by Equity or by the school.) While still on the tour he was already thinking about the interviews he would have to face with prospective employers. In a letter about his decision to buy a suit, hat and overcoat, he said 'I'm perfectly certain one creates twice the impression on managers if one's well dressed and it's well worth the extra two or three pounds between Bond Street and Selfridge.'

5   The Academy and Nigel Playfair

In December he passed the entrance test to the Academy and later won a scholarship. The school was much larger and better organized than Lady Benson's. Though Jack worked hard he did not always get the parts he wanted, but he began to find a basic facility and fluency. As he has written in *Early Stages*:

> I felt sure I had some sort of instinct for impersonation, but the imaginative part of my playing came too easily, and the technical side was non-existent. I strained every fibre in my efforts to appear violent or emotional, and only succeeded in forcing my voice and striking strange attitudes with my body. Rehearsing every day in a small room, with rows of girls sitting round on chairs staring at me, made me acutely self-conscious, and it was not until the performances at the end of the term that I was able to let myself go with any degree of confidence.

The actor Claude Rains was the most popular of his teachers, and Jack, greatly impressed, tried to imitate his style, to the point of becoming very mannered. His old friend Rosina Filippi, who was now teaching at the Academy too, wrote in his report 'He has inherited talent, an easy mentality and a sure sense of the stage. He needs physical culture and rougher and firmer movements, and a tightening up of all his limbs.'

At the end of his first term, his class was giving a performance of *The Admirable Crichton* in which he was playing Woolley, the silly ass, in the first two acts, and Crichton, the butler, in the last two. Nigel Playfair, who had made his name as an actor and director – becoming a theatre manager when he took over the Lyric Theatre Hammersmith in 1918 – was an old friend of Jack's mother, who persuaded him to come along to see the performance. Impressed by Jack, he immediately offered him the role of the Poet Butterfly in the English première of *The Insect Play* by the Brothers Capek, which he was about to produce at the Regent Theatre, which was opposite St Pancras Station. Claude Rains, Angela Baddeley and Nora Nicholson were in the cast and the costumes and sets were by a young designer Playfair had just discovered in Liverpool, Doris Zinkeisen. She dressed Jack in a white silk shirt, white flannels with a black stripe down the side, black pumps, a gold wig and a green laurel wreath. He also had a golden battledore and had to hit a shuttlecock across the stage, which was difficult as he was a very bad shot.

The play opens with the butterflies. In the original Czech version the scene is an erotic extravaganza, but by removing the improprieties from it, Playfair and Clifford Bax (who collaborated with him on the translation) made the play's opening very weak, contenting themselves with satirizing a twenties cocktail party. Rehearsals were quite exciting and at the dress rehearsal, while he was sitting behind Playfair in the stalls, Jack boldly whispered a suggestion to him, which, to his delight, Playfair accepted. But it was a difficult piece to perform. As Jack wrote to his grandmother, 'it is all so fantastic and unlike anything else, that even the old stagers in the cast seem to find the same difficulty in dealing with it'. Jack was mentioned in most of the papers, but the play only ran for six weeks, and on the last night Playfair sulked in his box with his back to the stage all through the first act.

All the same, he re-engaged Claude Rains, Doris Zinkeisen and most of the cast, including Jack, for his production of John

Drinkwater's new play, *Robert E. Lee*, which was to open at the Regent in June. *Abraham Lincoln*, Drinkwater's previous play, had been brought from Birmingham to the Lyric Hammersmith where it immediately became a big success. But *Robert E. Lee* turned out not to have the same appeal. Although the notices were good, business never picked up, and Playfair must have lost a lot of money by keeping it on for three months. Apart from understudying Claude Rains, Jack had only a small part as an orderly, marching about the stage behind Felix Aylmer, gazing through field glasses and trying not to count the empty seats. As the orderly he was very awkward and self-conscious about his movement, but when Claude Rains was ill and Jack took over from him for two matinees and an evening performance, he found that he seemed able to move the audience in the emotional scenes. Once again, he seemed to do much better when he was playing the part in front of an audience for the first time than when he had to repeat it.

All this time he was still working at the Academy. Claude Rains directed him in Tolstoy's *The Living Corpse* and in Hotspur's first scene from *Henry IV*. Jack played this in a diploma competition, winning a compliment from the judges. Sybil Thorndike rehearsed him in scenes from *Medea* and from John Masefield's *Pompey the Great*. Alfred Sutro worked with him on *The Walls of Jericho* and Rosina Filippi on the recorders scene from *Hamlet*. His French accent was good and Alice Gachet directed him in *Les Caprices de Marianne* and a scene from Rostand's *L'Aiglon*, though his vocabulary was poor and he never felt comfortable acting in French. With other teachers he rehearsed the first four acts of *Hamlet*, scenes from *The School for Scandal*, in which he played Sir Peter Teazle and Joseph Surface, and Sergius in *Arms and the Man*.

6   'Charley's Aunt', Oxford and Romeo

Charley in *Charley's Aunt* is a poor feed part, but it has often been played by young actors who have gone on to become extremely successful. When Jack ended his year at RADA, this was the role that was waiting for him in a Christmas season at the Comedy Theatre. He wanted to play Charley as a silly ass in horn-rimmed spectacles, but the revival was directed by the author's daughter, who informed him firmly that the play was a classic. Everything must be done as it had been done before.

They played twice nightly for six weeks and John found it very hard to keep a straight face, especially as the old actor who had played Mr Spettigue for many years took a perverse pleasure in making the young actors giggle and then reporting them to the stage manager, who in turn reported them to Amy Brandon-Thomas, who swept down in her chinchilla coat to reprimand them severely.

After Christmas, Jack went to meet J. B. Fagan, the author of *The Wheel* and now director of a small repertory company at the Oxford Playhouse. According to a friend, Fagan had said that Jack had given one of the best performances in *Robert E. Lee*, so he arrived full of confidence, and he was delighted when Fagan immediately offered him a contract.

When Jack arrived at Oxford, he found many of his Westminster contemporaries were still there as undergraduates, and one of them, Glen Byam Shaw, was now a member of Fagan's company. Tyrone Guthrie, whose mother had been Katie Gielgud's bridesmaid, was also in the company, together with Flora Robson, Veronica Turleigh, Richard Goolden, Reginald Denham and James Whale, whom Jack had met before in London, stage-managing for Playfair.

Of course Jack immediately found that working in a weekly repertory was very different from working at the Regent. The company rehearsed from 10.30 to 4.30 every day, which left very little time for learning lines. As the apron stage made it difficult for the prompter to help them, they would write their lines out and pin them about the stage. The theatre was difficult to play in, with rows of wooden chairs which creaked whenever anyone in the audience shifted his position, while outside, lorries, charabancs and buses rumbled incessantly past. The dressing-rooms were small and ill-equipped, with three actors sharing one wash-basin, and no hot water unless they boiled it for themselves. Reginald Denham and James Whale acted as associate producers, while Fagan and Whale took turns in designing the sets. The whole company would then help to paint and construct the scenery at the week-end.

The first production of the new season was *Captain Brass-bound's Conversion*. Jack was only one of the pirate crew but *The Times* reported that 'he showed both imagination and restraint in the small part of Johnson'. There was trouble, though, with one of the pieces of paper. Three pages of the final scene between Sir Howard and Lady Cicely were pinned to a table over which Raymond Massey, making a guest appearance as the American Captain, upset an entire bottle of ink. One night all the lights failed in the middle of the performance and the last two acts had to be played by candlelight, augmented by two motor lamps held aloft by Jack and another minor character, focusing them like follow-spots on the principals.

The second play, Congreve's *Love for Love*, was the biggest attraction of the season. Congreve's language shocked many of the theatre's elderly patrons, but it delighted the undergraduates, drawing many of them to the Playhouse for the first time. With Tyrone Guthrie as his servant, Jeremy, Jack played Valentine – his first big chance and his first big success. People who saw him remember how his talent blazed out. His style was undeveloped of course but he had great charm and great energy. The Terry blood in him was beginning to make itself felt. He made a huge impact on the undergraduate audience and undergraduate actors started to imitate him.

Performances often suffered from under-rehearsal, especially at the beginning of the week. When Jack played Young Marlow in *She Stoops to Conquer*, he was very nervous about his scenes with Reginald Denham, the producer, and with the stage manager and his assistant. All three were playing important parts, with very little time to study them.

The star of the Oxford University Dramatic Society (OUDS) in 1924 was Gyles Isham, who had just enjoyed a big amateur success as Hamlet, directed by Fagan. He now invited Jack to lunch in his Magdalen rooms, and talked about his plans to play Romeo at the RADA theatre in London during the vacation with an amateur cast and a rich young girl, who was in love with him, as Juliet. The next day Jack's face and neck began to swell, and the doctor diagnosed mumps. His mother promptly arrived at Oxford to take him home in a hired car with pillows in it for him to rest his enormous face. In a few weeks he was better, but just as the amateur *Romeo and Juliet* was about to go into rehearsal, Gyles Isham's face and neck began to swell. Jack helped him out by learning the part and rehearsing with the company until Isham had recovered, and then stayed on to play the part of Paris.

He was still in London on 3 April when a letter arrived from a forbidding, fur-coated Jewish agent who had a shabby office just off Leicester Square.

DEAR MR GIELGUD,

If you would like to play the finest lead among the plays by the late William Shakespeare, will you please call upon Mr. Peacock and Mr. Ayliff at the Regent Theatre on Friday at 2.30 p.m. Here is an opportunity to become a London Star in a night. Please confirm.

Yours very truly,

AKERMAN MAY.

Barry Jackson, who had used his own money to build the Birmingham Repertory Theatre, was putting on a London production of *Romeo and Juliet* at the Regent Theatre, to be directed by H. K. Ayliff and he was looking for a Romeo to play opposite Gwen Ffrangcon Davies, who had recently made a success as Juliet in Birmingham. After three auditions and agonizingly protracted suspense, the nineteen-year-old Gielgud was given the part.

Gwen Ffrangcon Davies had seen him as the Butterfly Poet and thought him weak and effeminate. But as soon as she met him and heard his voice, she said to herself 'That's all right.' She felt safe enough to tell him she had been quite horrified to hear he was going to be her Romeo. After this they got on together very well, and he took his father to see her in Rutland Boughton's opera, *The Immortal Hour*, in which she was giving a superb performance as a lost princess.

Partly because of her experience but mainly because of her sweetness and unselfconsciousness, she was extremely helpful to him in rehearsal.

She told me not to be frightened of our 'clinches', and when the moment came to embrace her passionately, I was amazed to find how naturally she slipped into my arms, sweeping her draperies in the most natural yet artful way so that they should not lose their line nor impede her movements, and arranging her head and arms in a position in which we could both speak and breathe in comfort, and extricate ourselves easily when the action demanded.

But a few days before the opening, he began to lose confidence. He was bitterly disappointed at the wig and costume he was given. The wig was coal-black and parted in the middle, the costume a low-necked doublet and white tights with soles attached to the feet instead of proper shoes. To get her costume finished, Gwen Ffrangcon Davies sat for hours working at it in the wardrobe, but at the dress rehearsal all the other costumes were still only half finished. They still smelt strongly of the gold paint that was stencilled on them and Jack's doublet was still full of pins which pricked him when he tried to kiss Juliet.

The actors' morale was lowered still further by a chaotic dress rehearsal. The auditorium was full of Barry Jackson's invited guests but Ayliff, knowing the production was not ready for an audience, succeeded in clearing them out of the theatre and then conducted the whole rehearsal with the safety curtain lowered, seating himself obtrusively in front of it to take notes. With his long austere face, his green tweed suit, brown boots and his toupet with a straight fringe, he was not a reassuring presence.

Gwen Ffrangcon Davies repeated her Birmingham success, but the *Morning Post* said Jack 'hardly gave the impression that he had swept Juliet off her feet' and four papers complained of effeminacy in his performance. Most wounding of all, Ivor Brown in *The New Age* pronounced 'Mr Gielgud from the waist downwards means absolutely nothing. He has the most meaningless legs imaginable.'

During a matinee, in the middle of the balcony scene, he suddenly felt very ill. Then everything went black and the audience saw Romeo crumple to the ground. The curtain was dropped and they applauded. After a few minutes he recovered and forced himself to go on, not only through the rest of the matinee but through the evening performance as well. But he had pneumonia and it was a fortnight before he was allowed to go on working. When his understudy was called to rehearse with Gwen Ffrangcon Davies, he went stone deaf from sheer terror. Ion Swinley, who had been her Romeo at Birmingham, took over for the first week of John's absence, and Ernest Milton for the second.

Before going back to Oxford, he made one more appearance in London, for a Sunday Club, the RADA Players, in John Van Druten's play, *The Return Half*, for which he got a good notice in *The Times*. Fagan celebrated his return by casting him as Marchbanks in Shaw's *Candida*. Harold Hobson, who saw this production, has since written 'What struck me in Gielgud was the electric, febrile energy of the man – the lithe, active, slim young man – as he sat perched on the arm of Candida's chair . . . I felt myself instantly in the presence of a great actor.' Next he was cast as Naisi, Deirdre's lover, in *Deirdre of the Sorrows*. But in this he was defeated by the Irish accent he needed to partner Veronica Turleigh, who was making beautiful use of her Irish lilt as Deirdre. His other parts in the next few weeks included Antonio in *The Cradle Song* by Gregorio and Maria Martinez Sierra, and Erhart in Ibsen's *John Gabriel Borkman*.

In December 1924 he was unexpectedly offered a part in a silent film *Who is the Man?* The part had been created by Sarah Bernhardt – in fact he had seen her play it – in *Daniel*, which was specially written for her by her godson, Louis Verneuil, after her leg was amputated, so that she could appear in only the last two acts on a divan, covered in rugs. In the film the character became considerably more mobile – a wild artist who took opium. Jack had to sculpt and go through a series of emotional tantrums, encouraged in the film studio by mood music on violin and piano.

Back at Oxford again, he had his first experience of Chekhov. Fagan allotted *The Cherry Orchard* more than the usual week's rehearsal and Jack was quick to see that as Trofimov he was facing different problems from any he had ever had. Taking his brother Val as a model for his make-up, he disguised himself with a thin-haired black wig, steel-rimmed glasses and a small beard. But he also found that his appearance provided a mask which had the effect of protecting him from his usual self-consciousness.

> For once I need not worry whether I was moving gracefully or looking handsome; I had not to declaim or die or express violent emotion in fine language. Instead I must try to create a character utterly different from myself, and behave as I imagine the creature would behave whose odd appearance I saw in my looking-glass.

Today every drama student learns that relaxation is basic to all successful acting and does exercises aimed to induce it. But Jack, with his highly emotional temperament, had not yet learnt at either of his drama schools how to control himself in a passionate scene. Playing for Claude Rains in *Robert E. Lee* he had found that it was his most intense moments which seemed to go best with the audience and ever since, both in drama school and in public, he had been playing on his own nerves, trying to whip himself up to a high emotional pitch, tightening instead of relaxing, driving himself almost hysterically towards actually feeling the passion he was trying to convey. But his Trofimov make-up released him in the same way that a mask can sometimes release an actor in a practice class.* Protected by the ugly hair-line of the wig, the steel-rimmed spectacles, the beard, the moustache and the clumsy eyebrows, he found a new freedom. It was as if he was no longer responsible for what he was doing. He was someone else. A real character, out of a novel, perhaps, rather than a play.

During rehearsals, Val, who was now out of work after several teaching jobs, came to visit John in Oxford. The brothers were together when Fagan was saying that he would have to find a replacement for the assistant stage manager, who had been going to understudy Jack and to walk on in the play, but was now going to leave the company at short notice. Half joking, Val said 'What about me?' After auditioning for Fagan and James Whale, he was given the job.

How the audience would respond to *The Cherry Orchard* was quite unpredictable. Jack wrote to his mother 'I fancy Oxford's verdict – if favourable – is likely to be "the best farce since Flubb"!' But when the first night came, he found he could shut the audience out from his consciousness in a way he never had before. With his keen eyesight, he was always liable to be distracted by recognizing faces as far back as the eighth row of the stalls and to come out of his part to study their reactions. In *The Cherry Orchard* he was conscious of no-one but the other characters around him on the stage.

The reviews were very favourable and Nigel Playfair offered to transfer the production to the Lyric Hammersmith as soon as the Oxford season was over. This was a very brave decision, for comparatively little time had gone by since the Stage Society had put on a production of the play in London only to find that the critics were bewildered and most of the audience walked out.

Before the transfer was arranged, Jack was suddenly asked whether he would understudy Noël Coward in *The Vortex*, as an actor was needed who could play the piano. *The Vortex* had been a sensational success at the tiny Everyman Theatre in Hampstead, where Jack had seen it with his parents. He found the end of Act Two 'with Noël sitting in profile to the audience, his white face lifted, chin jutting forward, head thrown back, playing that infuriating little tune over and over, louder and louder, till the

---

* I have described this in *Techniques of Acting*.

curtain fell . . . one of the most effective things I ever saw in a theatre'. But he had been less impressed when he met Coward at a Kensington cocktail party and thought him 'dreadfully precocious and rather too keen to show off on the piano'. He was four years older than Jack. Jack now had to audition at the piano for Coward, whose verdict was favourable. Fagan generously released Jack from Oxford and his career as a repertory actor was virtually over.

7   Understudying

He met Noël Coward again in the star dressing-room at the Royalty Theatre in Dean Street. The grease-paint was laid out tidily in little pots, there were large bottles of eau de Cologne on the washstand and a whole repertoire of dressing gowns in the wardrobe. Coward was charming, telling Jack what a relief it was to have someone reliable in the theatre and promising to help him in any way he could.

After weeks of sitting in the dressing-room with the other understudies, Jack's first chance to play Nicky Lancaster came when Coward wanted to see the opening of his new revue, *On with the Dance* in Manchester. Before leaving, he gave Jack two rehearsals with the principal actors. What he had learned from playing Trofimov had to be stored in his mind for the future; as Nicky Lancaster he was bound to play 'straight', using his own personality as well as he could. After watching Coward himself in the part so often, it was virtually impossible to avoid imitating his inflections, especially as they were exactly right for the part, which Coward had naturally tailored to fit his own personality. (All the best male parts in his plays are the ones he wrote for himself.) As in *Robert E. Lee*, when he was modelling himself on Claude Rains, Jack found that his most emotional moments were his best. In the rehearsals he was liable to be carried away by his own excitement and his best scene was the hysterical outburst against his mother, sweeping the glass off her dressing-table to throw himself into her arms. Jack went much too far,

and cut his hand with the bottles, but Coward and his leading
lady, Lilian Braithwaite, were obviously pleased at this im-
passioned sincerity.

When the great evening came, he was in a highly nervous
state and greatly disconcerted when the news was brought to
his dressing-room that several people had asked for their money
back because Noël Coward was not appearing. But the audience
responded to him well, once it had got over its disappointment.
After the performance Jack was summoned to Lilian Braithwaite's dressing-room to meet the actor George Arliss and his
wife, who had been in the audience. Afterwards Coward received
at least one letter saying how well his understudy had played.
This was from Violet Loraine, the revue actress who sang 'If
You Were the Only Girl in the World' with George Robey in
The Bing Boys during the 1914 war.

After this brief taste of glory, it was depressing to go back
to sitting in the understudies' room, but Jack could now afford
to be more sanguine about his professional future. He was not
yet twenty-one but he had come of age as an actor and there was
little danger that he would not achieve very much more than
the required degree of success by the time he was twenty-five.
It was at about this time that people began calling him John.
'Jack' no longer seemed to suit him, except at home among the
family.

Of course the surname had already presented a problem.
Should he change it for the theatre and call himself Terry or
Terry-Lewis, as his Aunt Mabel had done? John was oddly
obstinate about remaining Gielgud. As he said to a manager who
was trying to persuade him to change it, 'People won't be able
to spell it or pronounce it, but with any luck they'll remember it.'

8 The Theatrical Profession in the Twenties

All the great actors in the English tradition, from Burbage to
Irving, had built up their reputations mainly in Shakespeare,

but Gerald du Maurier, who since the end of the First World War had been the acknowledged leader of the profession, maintained his position till shortly before he died in 1934 by acting in sentimental plays like J. M. Barrie's and in light comedies and thrillers. When he was asked why he didn't try Richard III, his answer was that he would never want to embarrass his public.

Now that John's early career has become a theatrical history and not – as it was for him at the time – a matter of day-to-day living, the risks he took and the success he achieved emerge in a different perspective. So does the contribution he was to make in the next five years to the restoration of Shakespeare's popularity in the West End, though at the time, like any other actor, John must have been thinking primarily in terms of his own career.

Shakespeare and the classics were completely out of favour in the commercial theatre. It was in 1925 that the American actor John Barrymore scored an unexpected London success with his *Hamlet*, but this success probably derived partly from his popularity as a romantic film star.

The middle twenties were boom years. Such was the feeling of social euphoria that the middle-class playgoing public seemed to want a diet of soufflés – farces, light comedies, thrillers, revues and American musicals. Plenty of these were provided by writers now forgotten, and the leading actors appeared in a succession of trivial plays, many of them specially tailored for their personalities. Even the best emotional actresses of the period – Meggie Albanesi, Gladys Cooper, Madge Titheradge – were kept busy in light comedies and melodramas, never attempting the great classical parts. Marie Tempest, Yvonne Arnaud and Gertrude Lawrence devoted their careers almost entirely to comedy, as did du Maurier, Coward and Charles Hawtrey. Even Godfrey Tearle and Matheson Lang played very little Shakespeare. Tearle gave what was obviously a great performance as Othello in 1921 but no manager wanted to present him in Shakespeare again until 1932. Lang was an excellent Shakespearean actor but after touring in Shakespeare in South Africa and the Far East, playing Hotspur for Beerbohm Tree at His Majesty's, and starring in his own productions of *Romeo and Juliet* at the Lyceum and *The Merchant of Venice* at St James's, his only venture into Shakespeare in the twenties was his famous *Othello*, which he played only at matinees.

For the theatre historian, therefore, it is easy to say that the time was ripe for a new classical star to be born. Since 1894, when he founded the Elizabethan Stage Society, William Poel had concerned himself with the style in which Shakespeare's plays were originally produced, and in 1895 he did his first production on a reconstructed Elizabethan stage, but it took a very long time for his influence to filter into the theatre. Harley Granville Barker's productions of Shakespeare during his season at the Savoy in 1912–13 were very much ahead of their time. Barker introduced a swifter, more realistic approach in his revolutionary productions of *Twelfth Night*, *A Midsummer Night's Dream* and *The Winter's Tale*, which abolished the footlights for the first time. Barker used a small, built-out forestage, a stylized semi-permanent set, stylized costumes and very few cuts. But his career as a producer was interrupted first by the 1914–18 war and then by a second marriage which led to his retirement. Although he had a very good company led by his wife, Lillah McCarthy, and Henry Ainley, who played Malvolio and Leontes, his season at the Savoy did not produce any new star to embody the new influences in a way that would capture the imagination of the public. It was in this sense that there was a vacuum waiting to be filled, though it was not one which could have been visible at the time.

J. B. Fagan had achieved some success with a Shakespeare season on a small scale at the Court Theatre but many of the non-Shakespearean plays – Elizabethan and Jacobean, Restoration and eighteenth-century – would have been ignored, just as they were in the nineteenth century, but for societies like The Stage Society, the Phoenix Society and the Fellowship of Players. These periodically staged experimental productions usually on a Sunday evening and the following Monday afternoon in a West End theatre where another play was running. The actors were only paid a couple of guineas, and they would be involved in several weeks of rehearsals, but whereas today the actors working in West End theatres may well be busy during the day, filming or televising, there was nothing else for them to do in the daytime in the twenties, and such is the boredom of a long run, especially in a bad play, that most West End actors were quite glad to spend the day rehearsing a classic or a non-commercial modern play in the hope of attracting attention from the managers or critics. Edith Evans, Isabel Jeans, Robert Farquharson, Ernest Thesiger and Esmé Percy all widened their experience and improved their reputations by working for the

Sunday societies, as did many of the new directors like Theodore Komisarjevsky and Edith Craig. But for the Stage Society, R. C. Sherriff's war play, *Journey's End*, would never have arrived in the West End. Laurence Olivier scored one of his first big successes in the Sunday night production, but he was not available to appear in the subsequent commercial run.

John was now approached by the Phoenix Society to play in Thomas Otway's tragedy *The Orphan, or The Unhappy Marriage* in May 1925. Castalio was one of Betterton's old parts and, in playing it, John found that the fact of working in costume helped him (as his Trofimov make-up had helped him) to overcome his self-consciousness about his movement. Desmond MacCarthy's review predicted that 'Mr Gielgud with his charming voice and pleasing vivacity is sure to make his mark quickly.'

During the Monday matinee he noticed two shadowy ladies whispering together in the stage box and he heard one of them say quite loudly 'Now I know how he must have looked as Romeo.' The line was spoken in a stage whisper, but he recognized the voice from the Christmas parties at Gledhow Gardens. It was Ellen Terry's.

9   Chekhov and Komisarjevsky

On 25 May 1925 *The Cherry Orchard* opened at the Lyric Hammersmith. The advance booking was unpromising and even on the first night the theatre was not full. The performance went well but the audience seemed uncertain how it was expected to take the play. When John spoke Trofimov's line, "All these clever people are so stupid," a woman in the stalls shouted back 'That's very true.'

The morning papers were mixed in their reactions and feeling sure the play could not run for long, Playfair rapidly made arrangements for a revival of *The Beggar's Opera*. But James Agate came to the rescue with an enthusiastic broadcast and a notice in the *Sunday Times*, which saluted *The Cherry Orchard* as 'an imperishable masterpiece and the best play in London', while another critic, Basil Macdonald Hastings, called it the worst. When Playfair exploited their disagreement by printing Agate's and Hastings's notices side by side on the same poster and in the newspaper advertisements, business gradually improved. Although a few people walked out at each performance, the general verdict was favourable. Unfortunately *The Beggar's Opera* was already in rehearsal, so there was no question of running on at the Lyric, but Playfair and Fagan transferred the production to the Royalty Theatre in Dean Street (now demolished).

Meanwhile *The Vortex* had moved from the Royalty to the Little Theatre and John was asked to play in it for three weeks after Noël Coward left for a holiday before going to America with the play. Lilian Braithwaite, who was also to be in the American production, generously gave up her holiday to stay on in the London production so as to give John his chance. The performances went well and John was conscious of entering into an easy relationship with the audience.

After the success of *The Cherry Orchard*, Philip Ridgeway (an impresario from Blackpool) conceived the idea of a Chekhov season in the tiny theatre across Barnes Bridge, where his production of *Tess of the D'Urbervilles* was running very successfully with Gwen Ffrangcon Davies and Ion Swinley. He planned to follow it with *The Seagull*, but the Hardy play went on doing such good business that he finally opened *The Seagull* at the Little Theatre in the Adelphi with John as Konstantin and the twenty-two-year-old Valerie Taylor as Nina. The director was A. E. Filmer.

It was a self-consciously 'Russian' production, and John obviously had to give much more of a 'straight' juvenile performance than he had as Trofimov. He was embarrassed when his entrance in Act Two with the dead seagull was greeted with laughter, but he, Valerie Taylor and the production generally were praised by the critics.

John's friends, though, were more critical about his acting. They told him that his mannerisms were becoming more pronounced, his walk no better and his diction affected, with closed vowel sounds. 'Wirds, wirds, wirds.' He seemed to have a good sense of pace, could time pauses and build successfully to an emotional climax. But he still found it difficult, once he had achieved an effect, to repeat it with equal success at every performance. And he could not resist showing off when he thought he was playing well.

His next experience of playing in Shakespeare was in a series of matinees presented by Robert Courtneidge (Cicely's father) with a handsome provincial star called Henry Baynton. He played Hamlet in a string of pearls and took a curtain call at the end of *Lear* in a straight make-up and a dressing-gown. For prestige reasons, Courtneidge presented him in London for a week or so each year. Normally his Ferdinand in *The Tempest* had been Eric Portman, whom he had discovered in Huddersfield, but this year they had quarrelled and John was offered the part in London. Rosaline Courtneidge (Cicely's sister) was the Miranda. John was asked to strip to the waist in the log scene. 'Eric Portman always does,' Baynton said. Not wanting to own up to the acne spots on his back, John had to think very quickly of another reason for refusing: 'I couldn't possibly have got sunburnt in two hours after the shipwreck. Even on an enchanted island.'

At this crucial point in his development, he met Theodore Komisarjevsky, the Russian director who was to exert such a strong influence on him over the next ten years. The son of an operatic tenor and a Russian princess, and the brother of the famous actress Vera Komisarjevskaya, he had succeeded Meyerhold as artistic director of her theatre in St Petersburg. After she died in 1910, he ran a theatre in Moscow, where he was made director of the Imperial and State Theatres. In 1919, at the age of thirty-seven, after working in Paris, Switzerland and New York, he had come to England to produce opera for Sir Thomas Beecham. He directed several plays in London and became friendly with Arnold Bennett, one of whose plays he directed, and with Fagan, for whom he designed costumes at the Court. When directing, he nearly always designed his own sets and costumes, arranged the music and lit his productions very skilfully. An architect as well, he later decorated the Phoenix Theatre when it was built in 1930, and several suburban cinemas.

He was a near-genius, phenomenally versatile and violently moody, dynamic and charming, but liable to bouts of depression, when he would sulk in silence for hours on end. He was a born rebel and in each country where he worked, he soon became resentful of the prevailing conditions. A man of great sensitivity, he was also capable of being extremely insensitive, and ruthless.

He found the production of *The Seagull* 'very funny' and not in the least like Russia. When Philip Ridgeway (in a rare moment of inspiration) engaged him to direct *Three Sisters, Ivanov, Uncle Vanya* and *The Cherry Orchard*, Komisarjevsky invited John to play Baron Tuzenbach, but the only other member of *The Seagull* cast to be re-engaged was Margaret Swallow, who had played Masha. Rehearsals started in a Bloomsbury flat where Komisarjevsky was staying with actor friends. After several days spent reading the play round a table, the cast arrived one morning to find elaborate chalk marks on the floor. Careful use of the restricted space was a valuable preparation for the tiny stage at Barnes.

Komisarjevsky laid great stress on finding the right rhythm for every scene and every speech. He was fond of interrupting the actors during rehearsals by shouting 'Pause' in the middle of their lines. He made a number of cuts and alterations to the text, which tended to make it more romantic. He dressed it picturesquely, but twenty years earlier than Chekhov intended, making the sisters wear the bustles and chignons of the eighties.

Tuzenbach is a character part which John should have been allowed to approach in the same way as Trofimov. Both characters are shy, sensitive and ugly. But Komisarjevsky was convinced that Tuzenbach, if played as Chekhov had written him, would not appeal to an English audience. He cut out all reference to his ugliness, making John play the part in a romantic juvenile make-up with side-whiskers and a smart uniform. He was rather baffled by the changes in the text but he did not like to say so. He was greatly impressed by Komisarjevsky and of course he fancied himself as a handsome *jeune premier*.

Visually Komisarjevsky's exploitation of the small stage was ingenious. In the first and fourth acts the interior of the room was shown through large open windows which spread right across the front of the stage, with the big luncheon table angled off into the wings. A clothes-line in one downstage corner and the shadow of a tree in the other created the impression of a garden outside the house. For the second and third acts the windows were removed and the same back walls re-angled and hung with different lamps and pictures, producing a cosy indoor atmosphere. At the first dress rehearsal, when the actors first saw the scenery, they burst into spontaneous applause.

The press was enthusiastic. Far from resenting the liberties

Komisarjevsky had taken with Chekhov's play, Ivor Brown rhapsodized in the *Saturday Review* about 'a marriage of true minds' between author and producer.

The production ran for eight weeks, playing twice daily to good audiences. The actors all received £10 a week, which was paid out by a good looking young man called Hugh Beaumont, Philip Ridgeway's business and box office manager, who was later to become a close friend of John's, and Managing Director of H. M. Tennent, the management which has presented almost every play in which John appeared from the forties onwards.

Instead of continuing with the Chekhov season, Ridgeway followed *Three Sisters* with a play of Andreyev's called *Katerina*, and Komisarjevsky surprised John by casting him in a middle-aged character part, Katerina's hysterically jealous husband. Without any justification, he is so persistently suspicious of her that his compulsive persecution goads her to the point of becoming a nymphomaniac.

All the productions at Barnes were done on a very small budget and there was so little money to spend on *Katerina* that the sets had to be made in the theatre, which did not even have a workshop. The carpenter, who was also property master and electrician, worked on them for a week and then confessed himself unable to cope. Komisarjevsky and the stage manager, Keith Moss, had to take over the work themselves. The set was not ready in time for the dress rehearsal and it was still unfinished on the first night. Keith Moss collapsed from exhaustion just before the performance and the curtain went up forty minutes late with Komisarjevsky prompting himself and improvising the set for the next act during each interval. Some of the flats were missing, others were dripping wet, and not all the ceiling pieces fitted. The pianist, whose repertoire was soon exhausted, had to go on playing the same pieces again and again to fill the long intervals.

The curtain goes up on a darkened room in the middle of an off-stage quarrel. Muffled at first, the voices get louder and louder till, after nearly a minute, two revolver shots ring out, the door opens and Katerina rushes on pursued by her husband Georg, who fires at her again, missing her. The cartoon of John by Hazelden in *Punch* was captioned 'Oh how I miss my wife.'

John received some high praise but he was still far too self-conscious. James Agate wrote:

Mr Gielgud is becoming one of our most admirable actors; there is

39

mind behind everything he does. Only he must avoid the snag of portentousness, of being intense about nothing in particular. Twice in this play he has to make an entry upstairs from below stage. The first time is an occasion of great solemnity, but on the second he is merely paying a friendly call, to do which it is unnecessary to put on the manner of one rising from the grave.

10 'The Constant Nymph'

By now, John was being invited to a great many parties, including luncheons in Lord Lathom's Mayfair flat, where the guests often included Marie Tempest, Gladys Cooper and Mrs Patrick Campbell. At other houses John met Max Beerbohm and Somerset Maugham. Lady Colefax used to invite all the celebrities she could muster: she is reputed to have invited Shaw and H. G. Wells to the same luncheon party by telling each of them (quite untruthfully) that the other had said he wanted to meet him.

Social life on this level made John more impatient than ever to become a star in the London theatre. His opportunity materialized in July as a result of another Sunday night appearance – with Cathleen Nesbitt at the Royal Court in a play called *Confession*. After the final curtain he was told that Basil Dean was waiting outside the theatre to see him. Of all the theatre managers of the day, it was Dean who put on the most interesting plays. John dressed as quickly as he could and hurried out to find Dean waiting in the street under a lamp-post. Murmuring that he had liked John's performance, he pushed a script into his hand and disappeared into the darkness. When John read it late that night, he was incredulous at his good luck. It was *The Constant Nymph*, Margaret Kennedy's best-selling novel of the year before, adapted by the authoress herself in collaboration with Dean.

What followed was bitterly disappointing, though at the same time it provided a turning point in John's career. He arrived early for his appointment with Dean and waiting impatiently for his name to be called, he watched other actors being shown in to the office, wondering what was going on behind the green baize door. He only found out much later that Dean had also approached Ivor Novello about the part, although Margaret Kennedy insisted she would rather have John. It was nearly lunchtime before he was called in. By now most of his confidence had drained away and when Dean started to discuss dates and salary, John asked whether he was quite sure he really wanted him for the part. Dean assured him he would receive a contract as soon as the play had been passed by the Lord Chamberlain. Rehearsals would begin in a few weeks. A letter of confirmation followed, saying that after the most careful consideration Dean had decided to give John the opportunity of playing the part of Lewis Dodd, the composer-hero.

Elated, he went off into the country for a fortnight's holiday and arriving back in London he invited an actress friend from his Academy days, Fabia Drake, to lunch at the Ivy to celebrate his good luck. On his way in, he nodded to Noël Coward, who was at a table by the door. As they were leaving, Coward beckoned him over to his table. 'I think I ought to tell you before Dean does. I am going to play Lewis Dodd for the first month of the run.' John just managed to say that he thought Noël would be very good in the part.

In the afternoon he was summoned to Dean's office again. Would he understudy at a salary of £10 a week, which would go up to £20 when he took over the part? The £20 would go up to £25 if the play were a great success. Despite the written offer he had received, John knew it was better not to quarrel with Dean or Coward. He agreed to understudy but insisted on £15 a week. Looking rather relieved, Dean told him 'You are taking this very well.' Dean and Edna Best, the leading lady, had both been extremely keen to have Coward create the part, even though he could only play it for a month before he went to New York with his play *This Was a Man*.

Dean began rehearsals by reading the play to the cast. His reading lasted two hours and forty-five minutes without breaks and without 'putting in the expression'. The rehearsals which followed were tempestuous. Dean was a sound technician but a despot. He was a stickler about inflections and rehearsed in detail with unflagging energy, forcing his actors to the limits of their endurance.

Coward argued incessantly with him and with Margaret

Kennedy and Edna Best. Each time he threatened to give up the part, John's hopes soared. One afternoon, when it seemed that the quarrel had gone too far to be patched, Dean asked John whether he knew his lines. He stayed up very late studying them, only to find in the morning that the others were all friends again.

When the first night came, John was too dispirited to watch. He went to see Cochran's *Blackbirds* at the London Pavilion but when he came back during the interval to the stage door of the New, he heard that the first night audience was spellbound. The curtain did not come down until half past eleven, but the actors knew they had a big success on their hands. In the morning, the press was unanimously favourable.

The next few weeks were very uncomfortable for John, being part of the show without yet having a part to play. But instead of going on for a full month, Coward sent for him in the third week. He had been overworking for some time before Dean's strenuous rehearsals began and was now beginning to feel terribly ill. He gave his last performance on the Wednesday evening and John gave his first at the Thursday matinee. He had had a few under-study rehearsals but only one with Dean and the principals, and one with Coward. Nevertheless his first performances went well and Coward's departure did no apparent harm at the box office. But John was slipped into the cast without any of the publicity Dean had promised him. It was several days before he was even given newspaper billing, and Coward's photographs stayed outside the theatre all through the year's run.

John was not happy with the rest of the cast. They naturally resented Coward's abrupt departure, and Dean was in America directing Coward's new play. Most of the others had worked together before; John was a stranger to the West End and after his appearances in Chekhov and with the Sunday night societies, he was considered to be a highbrow. Edna Best did not like him and few of the company talked to him off stage. John, who was later to become such a harmonious influence in any company he was working in, was in no position to act as peacemaker. He was also afraid that, as in *The Vortex*, his performance was too closely modelled on Coward's.

It was twelve weeks before Dean came back to watch a performance. 'Very nice for an understudy,' he told John. 'You know we want more than that.' He called a rehearsal for the next day, when he reduced Edna Best to tears and John to a state of nervous distraction. 'You work much too hard and let the audience see it,' Dean said. 'And you don't think, you don't use your mind on the stage. You're so busy projecting, forcing your emotion.' Once he had got over his disappointment, John realized this was true.

The atmosphere of unease continued, but John was now sufficiently well off to take a flat of his own. For some while he had been growing restive in his parents' house. When he had borrowed a flat in Mecklenburgh Square from an actor-friend, George Howe, during the run of *Robert E. Lee*, he had felt pleasantly independent, and now, hearing that Frank Vosper was about to move out of his flat in Seven Dials, near the Cambridge Theatre, he arranged to take over the remainder of the lease. The flat was on the fourth floor, with no lift, but John had taken a fancy to it.

> There was no proper kitchen, and the bathroom, with a rather erratic geyser, was down a very draughty flight of stairs. But otherwise the place was charming. The sitting-room walls had been covered with brown hessian by Vosper, and there was a ceiling in one of the bed-rooms painted by an artist friend of his (under the influence, I imagine, of Braque), with large nude figures sprawling about. This I thought very modern and original.

John asked John Perry to share the flat with him. Perry was a not very successful actor, who afterwards became, with Hugh Beaumont, a director of H. M. Tennent. During the run of *The Constant Nymph* he tried to persuade John to save money but could not prevent him from going out on Saturday mornings to buy records (Bach, Beethoven and Mozart, with a leavening of dance tunes), books and small pictures. He also bought a baby grand piano on the instalment system. An electric gramophone now replaced the old portable he had had at home and he began to spend more on his clothes. John Perry remembers meeting him at Hyde Park Corner one morning during the General Strike (May 1926). John turned up in a large grey trilby hat and pearl grey flannel trousers (known then as Oxford Bags) so wide you could hardly see the narrow patent leather shoes underneath.

His brother Val was now walking on as a policeman in Edgar Wallace's thriller *The Ringer*, which was filling Wyndham's Theatre, while John was still at the New Theatre on the other side of St Martin's Court in *The Constant Nymph*. The cast of *The Ringer* included Leslie Faber and Naomi Jacob, the writer, who used to give parties in her Marylebone flat. Here John met Leslie Faber. They had worked together briefly in two Sunday night productions, one of which Faber directed. John had always admired him very much as a character actor, especially in *Jane Clegg*, St John Ervine's play, in which he played Sybil Thorndike's drunken husband. One afternoon Faber called in after a matinee of *The Constant Nymph* to congratulate John on his performance and during the evening he sent his dresser across the court with a long letter of praise.

At this time John was enjoying his leisure much more than his work at the New Theatre. The atmosphere there had improved, but he was playing nine performances a week. He had six quick costume changes and was scarcely ever off the stage except when he was making them. Eventually the strain became too great. He broke out in a skin rash on his face, which forced him to stay away for ten days. Returning to a slightly friendlier atmosphere, he was surprised when Edna Best asked him (during a scene in which they had to make conversation) why he was not coming on the provincial tour with them. The answer was that he had not been asked. The next day, when he was, he demanded £35 a week and second-star billing, expecting to be refused. But another actor, who had been tried out for the part, had turned out to be unsatisfactory, so John got his way.

The tour opened in Manchester. For the first act they had a new set, which seemed very small and cramped, and the first night was disturbed first by a fire engine, which drowned the love scene, then by a big laugh in the death scene when the gas lit itself with a click before John had even struck the match.

He had bought himself a car, a snub-nosed Morris. John Perry taught him to drive it and he enjoyed the journeys from one provincial town to another. As usual, he was reading a lot of books – novels, short stories, biographies. With newspapers and magazines, he has always ignored the political, economic and sporting pages, spending his time on arts pages, gossip columns, crime reports and crossword puzzles. On tour, as always, he enjoyed going for long walks, seeing the local sights and visiting art galleries and museums.

The tour lasted for just over four months, until the end of 1927. Altogether he had been in the play for over fourteen months.

11   A Taste of New York

It was thanks to Leslie Faber that John now had his first chance of going to America. Faber had the leading part in the Broadway production of Alfred Neumann's *The Patriot*. Quite late in the rehearsals, the actor playing the Tsarevich had to be replaced, and on Faber's recommendation, the role was offered to John only forty-eight hours before he had to sail.

He immediately liked New York. It was a fine day as the boat drew in to the harbour and the skyline was much as he had pictured it, except that in the clear air the outlines of the buildings were so surprisingly distinct. He was met at the docks by a tall, distinguished-looking Negro from the Gilbert Miller office. They drove straight to the theatre where the play was already being dress-rehearsed. There were magnificent sets by Norman Bel Geddes, mounted on revolving trucks. The staff of technicians, secretaries and stage management was bigger than John had ever seen in England, but there was an atmosphere of pandemonium, with Gilbert Miller and Norman Bel Geddes shouting to each other from different parts of the theatre.

John was pleased with his costume – a blue cloak with an ermine cape, a black coat with silver and red facings, white breeches and high boots. He had a good wig, powdered brown hair with long side pieces curling below his ears. But though it was a fairly small part, it was alarming to be making his New York debut after only two rehearsals – all the more so since Miller nagged at him about his voice, movement and pace. He was particularly anxious to give of his best because he was acting with Faber, with Madge Titheradge, whom he had always idolized, and with Lyn Harding – a famous Bill Sikes in *Oliver Twist* with Tree as Fagin. He was now playing the mad Emperor, Paul the First.

The play was a failure. Many of the first night audience walked out, the critics were unimpressed and it closed after only eleven performances. It had cost about 40,000 dollars to mount, but the loss was partly covered by the sale of the film rights for 30,000. Emil Jannings was to appear in Lyn Harding's part.

45

John got favourable reactions from some of the critics, including the eccentric Alexander Woollcott, who wielded an extremely powerful influence in New York. Sidney Howard (who wrote *The Silver Cord*) said he liked John best of anyone in the play and so did Constance Collier, who thought she might be able to use him in a revival of *Our Betters* with Ina Claire. There was also talk of a wonderful part in a play about splitting the atom by Maurice Browne and Robert Nichols. John was interviewed by various managements, who promised to give him work if he stayed on. But he could not afford to go on living there without working. Much as he had been enjoying the parties and the plays he had managed to see, he decided to come straight back to London.

12   Back to the West End

1928 was the centenary of Ibsen's birth, so a series of special matinees of *Ghosts* was arranged, first at Wyndham's and then at the Arts, with Mrs Patrick Campbell as Mrs Alving and John as Oswald. Working with her was an extraordinary experience. John had met her before at parties. When she was acting in Brighton, a lunch party had been given for her at the Metropole and though Marion Terry had always been one of her great rivals, she admired Ellen and obviously liked John for his unusual sensitivity. There were very few people she really liked. She was a great snob and capable of being very cruel. Rehearsing *Ghosts*, she took a dislike to the actor who was playing Pastor Manders. She referred to him as 'that dreadful old man with sweat dropping down to his stomach' and in the long scene where Manders is liable to become the dominant character, she focused the audience's attention on herself by hanging a complete set of curtains.

But she had an intimate knowledge of every part in the play and a picturesque way of coaching John. 'Keep still. Gaze at me. Now you must speak in a Channel-steamer voice. Empty your voice of meaning and speak as if you were going to be sick. Pinero once told me this and I have never forgotten it.'

Though unreliable, talkative, unpunctual and inaccurate throughout rehearsals, she was suddenly word-perfect and in full control of the part at the dress rehearsal. But her enthusiasm seemed to peter out at the public performances, which were played to small, unenthusiastic audiences, who must have been as distracted as the actors were by the noise of pneumatic drills in the Charing Cross Road. Mrs Pat would turn upstage to tell John in her best party voice 'The Marquis and Marchioness of Empty are in front again.' And in the pause which preceded the key line she had carefully taught him how to say – 'The disease I suffer from is seated here' – she turned her back to the audience again and remarked in her famous bell-like tones 'I'm so hungry!' She also told him off for letting himself get carried away and shedding real tears, 'You silly boy. Now you've got a dirty face.' But they enjoyed having lunch together – he took her to the Escargot Restaurant in Soho, where she taught him to eat snails.

Some of the notices were good. J. T. Grein wrote 'Mrs Patrick Campbell's Mrs Alving and Mr John Gielgud's Oswald will be as memorable as the play itself.' But he may have been prejudiced, as it was he who had organized the matinees. James Agate was highly critical of Mrs Campbell – 'the Lord Mayor's Coach with nothing inside it', he said, but he thought John's Oswald 'extremely fine'.

John's next two engagements were something of a disaster. First he starred in a farce called *Holding Out the Apple*. Described in the programme as 'a comedy with a catch in it', it was written by a lady who had almost certainly put up the money to get it staged. The play depended mainly on prolonged comic confusion, and the dialogue was full of innuendos and veiled allusions to pregnancy and illegal operations. The production came to London but only played for a few weeks to audiences consisting almost entirely of people who had received complimentary tickets.

In August John was in an American thriller called *The Skull*, playing a detective who turned out to be the villain. The action was set in a haunted church, with trap doors, bats, tolling bells, ghostly hands at the organ, a coffin which fell in when a door was opened, and an international criminal who wore a mask, hooted like an owl when about to commit a murder, and left a grinning skull on the scene of the crime, 'as if in mocking derision', as one of the characters put it.

Next John was asked by James Whale to appear in a double bill – two Spanish plays – *Fortunato* and *The Lady from Alfaqueque*

47

by the Quintero Brothers, which Anmer Hall was to present at the Court Theatre. Whale was directing and designing both plays, as well as playing Fortunato, and John had good parts in both.

The plays had been translated by Harley Granville Barker and his second wife, Helen. Like his first wife, Lillah McCarthy, Barker had created many Shavian roles, including Marchbanks in *Candida* and Dubedat in *The Doctor's Dilemma*. He had also written several plays, including *The Voysey Inheritance*, *Waste* and *The Madras House*, and together with John Vedrenne, he had managed the Royal Court Theatre, where, with a semi-permanent company, he staged brilliant productions of Yeats, Euripides, Ibsen, Maeterlinck and Galsworthy, as well as directing the premiéres of several of Shaw's plays. After his revolutionary productions of Shakespeare at the Savoy Theatre, he went on working as a director until the 1914 war. But in 1918, after being divorced by Lillah MacCarthy, he married a rich divorcee, Helen Huntington, who did not want him to have any working connection with the theatre. She also put an end to his long friendship with Shaw. With her he retired, first to a manor house in Devonshire and later to Paris, where he lectured at the Sorbonne and collaborated with her in translating plays from the Spanish. He also wrote his famous *Prefaces to Shakespeare*, thinking he could have a more permanent influence on the theatre from outside.

The Barkers paid only fleeting visits to James Whale's rehearsals of the Quintero plays:

> Barker was certainly a revelation. He rehearsed us for about two hours, changed nearly every move and arrangement of the stage, acted, criticized, advised, in an easy flow of practical efficiency, never stopping for a moment. We all sat spellbound, trying to drink in his words of wisdom and at the same time to remember all the hints he was giving us, none of which we had time to write down or memorize. Everything he said was obviously and irrefutably right. Even when he announced that James [Whale] could not possibly play Fortunato and that O. B. Clarence must be engaged, everyone gasped but nobody ventured to disagree. Finally we came to my last and best scene in *Alfaqueque* . . . Barker showed me exactly how to play this scene – the business, the timing, everything which would make it effective in performance. I implored him to wait a moment and let me rehearse it two or three times running, but he looked at his watch, signed to Mrs Barker, who was concealed somewhere in the dress-circle, bade us all good morning, and disappeared through the front of the house to his luncheon engagement at the Ritz.

But not everyone in the company was as impressed as John was by Barker. Margaret Webster, who was playing a small part, remembers the 'long, long waits while he went into a private huddle with the director. After this he would deliver to the company a pontifical – and fascinating – lecture on the history of the drama, on psychology, on Spanish literature, habits and domestic architecture. After this he would disappear completely for a week. When he came again – the company by this time was brimful of Spanish lore – nothing Spanish would be mentioned at all. But he would take one tiny section of the play and go over it again and again and again, leaving other major sequences completely untouched.'*

This is what Granville Barker later wrote in a letter about John's performance in the two plays:

> He struck me as having the real thing in him. A trifle too much finesse perhaps. A little apt to let his sword blade turn just before he made the stroke; he was in fact not quite crude enough for his youth.

1928 was a bad year for John. His last West End appearance in a verse play was in a mediocre poetic melodrama which only ran for a week. In *Out of the Sea* by the American writer Don Marquis, the heroine and villain were reincarnations of Isolde and King Mark. John was a young American poet, who played Wagner on the piano.

1929 began with two Russian plays. In the revival of *The Seagull* at the Arts Theatre Club, again directed by A. E. Filmer with Valerie Taylor again playing Nina, John repeated his performance as Konstantin. The production was far too much a repetition of the earlier one to satisfy John. 'Criticize', he begged Filmer, 'we ought to make it better this time.' 'Nonsense,' was the reply. 'You always want to gild the lily.'

At the Little, in *Red Dust* (by V. M. Kirchov and A. V. Ouspensky) he had a good part as an idealistic student and a stage fight with Ion Swinley, who taught him how to pull his punches and break chairs without doing either of them any harm. But the play only had a very short run.

When Reginald Berkeley's play about Florence Nightingale, *The Lady with the Lamp*, was transferred from the Arts to the Garrick Theatre, Leslie Banks, who had to leave the cast, suggested that John should take over from him. Oddly enough John

* Margaret Webster, *The Same Only Different*, Gollancz, 1969.

49

had originally been offered another part in the play but had been too busy to accept.

Edith Evans was playing Florence and Gwen Ffrangcon Davies was Lady Herbert. After seeing them acting together as the Serpent and Eve in *Back to Methuselah* at the Court, John had written Gwen a five-page fan letter. *The Lady with the Lamp* gave him his first opportunity to work with Edith Evans. As yet he had little opportunity of getting to know her but he did ask her advice on a key decision he had to make.

13   The Old Vic

In 1914 Lilian Baylis had taken over the management of the Old Vic from her aunt, Emma Cons, who had been running it since 1880 as a temperance music hall called 'The Royal Victoria Hall and Coffee Tavern'. Lilian Baylis had been trained as a musician and during her aunt's regime had introduced films and opera into the programme, while still giving variety shows four nights a week. She started the Shakespeare seasons rather reluctantly when she took over in 1914. 'I found it so difficult to really get clean pictures that I turned in despair to Shakespeare.' But whatever her motives for turning to him, she was indefatigable once she had committed herself. She knew nothing about the theatre but, like Joan of Arc, she was a zealot to whom people did not say no. Matheson Lang donated the scenery, costumes and props from his Shakespeare tour in the Far East and sat on her advisory committee, and Rosina Filippi helped her to get her Shakespeare season under way. By 1923, her producer, Robert Atkins, had put on all thirty-seven of Shakespeare's plays. He had to work on a tiny budget with a minimum of scenery, but he presented the plays with few cuts. And in spite of having to offer meagre salaries, he attracted fine actors like Sybil and Russell Thorndike, Ernest Milton, Hay Petrie, Edith Evans, Balliol Holloway and Ion Swinley to play in the Waterloo Road to an unfashionable audience of Shakespeare enthusiasts, students and local residents, who could buy tickets in the stalls for only five shillings or in the gallery for sixpence.

In 1929, Lilian Baylis appointed a new director, Harcourt Williams, a forty-nine-year-old actor who had been on the stage for more than thirty years. After receiving an excellent training – as so many actors did in the absence of drama schools – in Benson's company, touring Shakespeare in the provinces, he had been greatly influenced by Martin-Harvey and by Ellen Terry, who coached him when he was in her company and thought him one of the best young actors of his time. A vegetarian, mild, vague and benign, simple and dedicated, he wore sandals, ate Bemax and lived in a cottage in the country with an outside lavatory and a well, which he used for keeping his cheeses cool in hot weather.

He had not been at all impressed by John in *The Insect Play* or in *Robert E. Lee*, but in *Ghosts* and *The Lady with the Lamp* he found that 'artistically he had grown out of all knowledge'. So one day when John was lunching in the restaurant of the Arts Theatre, Harcourt Williams came across the room to ask whether he would consider joining the Old Vic as a leading actor in the new company he was forming.

The offer sounded tempting. West End managers seemed to be interested in John only for highly-strung romantic parts and latterly in very mediocre plays. There were plenty such parts in the twenties (nervous tension being very much in vogue) and he could no doubt have gone on, at least for the time being, to make a career for himself doing little else, although he had had to work for a few weeks in 1929 as Leslie Howard's understudy in *Berkeley Square*. If he had decided to stay on in the fashionable West End, his whole career might have been different. He might never have either discovered or developed his potential as a classical actor. Fortunately a healthy instinct was at work, deriving partly perhaps from his Terry heritage. Right from the beginning he had had a strong feeling for Shakespeare. At Lady Benson's it was Shakespeare he enjoyed more than anything else and when he was staying with George Howe, who was playing Puck at Stratford-on-Avon soon after leaving the Academy, John longed to be invited into the company. Of course he wanted to do everything possible to make himself into as good an actor as he was capable of becoming. He was acutely aware of needing experience in a variety of character parts in a variety of plays. As Trofimov, he had caught sight of a potentiality in himself which he knew he was unlikely to develop in the commercial theatre. Earning a meagre salary at the Old Vic, he would obviously have to live more modestly and he did not give Harcourt Williams an immediate answer, but asked several friends for their advice.

Four years earlier, Edith Evans had herself faced a very similar problem, and after one of the matinees of *The Lady with the Lamp* John knocked at her dressing-room door to ask her advice. Normally she liked to sleep between the two performances, but she talked to John at length about her experiences at the Vic and her reasons for going there. She had been working as an apprentice in a hat-shop when William Poel happened to see her in an amateur production in Streatham Town Hall. He cast her as Cressida in an amateur production of *Troilus and Cressida*. After touring with Ellen Terry, she had a big personal success in Sutro's *The Laughing Lady*, but turned down the opportunity of creating the role of the Duchess in Maugham's *Our Betters* because she was determined not to go on being type-cast in 'silly society parts'. Instead she went to work for Barry Jackson in Birmingham, where Nigel Playfair saw her as the Serpent in *Back to Methuselah*. She was brilliant as Millamant in *The Way of the World* at the Lyric Hammersmith and later as Mrs Sullen in *The Beaux' Stratagem*, but when she played Helena in Basil Dean's Drury Lane production of *A Midsummer Night's Dream*, she was dissatisfied with her Shakespearean technique and decided to devote a year to improving it in the Waterloo Road.

Knowing that his own experience, varied though it was, was far less varied than hers had been when she had to make her decision, John went to meet Lilian Baylis.

> There was a faint smell of size from the painting dock, and of steak and tomatoes from the purlieus of the office, where Lilian's lunch was being cooked. I was ushered in through the glass door, and found Lilian sitting behind her big roll-topped desk, surrounded by vases of flowers, photographs, two dogs and numerous cups of tea. I had on my best suit, and tried to look rather arrogant, as I always do when money has to be discussed. 'How nice to see you, dear,' said Lilian. 'Of course, we'd love to have you here, your dear aunt, you know – but of course we can't afford stars.' By the end of the interview I was begging her to let me join the company. We both evaded the question of salary as long as possible.

Negotiations were rather protracted. Obviously it was essential to have a good leading lady and John made it a condition that Martita Hunt should join the company too. She had not done much classical work but she had played Mrs Helsted with Madge Titheradge in *The Doll's House*. She and John had become very friendly since *Holding Out the Apple* – together with Hermione Baddeley they had shared digs in Southport and made a lot of jokes at the expense of the play. Martita Hunt now agreed to come to the Vic, and Harcourt Williams persuaded Lilian Baylis to agree to a higher salary for John than had originally been discussed. She signed the contract and Harcourt Williams took the counterpart to John's dressing-room at the Garrick.

A few days later, when he was in the country, Harcourt Williams received a telegram to say that Martita Hunt had refused the contract. The salary in it was ten shillings less than the one he had mentioned to her. But eventually he got both contracts agreed. John was to open as Romeo and to play Richard II and Antonio in *The Merchant of Venice*, but Lilian Baylis would promise nothing beyond that. 'I expect you'd like to play Hamlet, wouldn't you dear? But of course Gyles Isham is coming to us too, and we shall have to see.'

The company rehearsed at the top of the theatre in a big room with a bad echo and iron girders which reminded John of the dormitory at Hillside. There were about two dozen Old Vic students who were allowed to watch rehearsals, rustling the pages of the printed texts in their laps. There was no canteen, and the smell of the steaks that Lilian Baylis cooked for herself could filter into the rehearsal room, making the actors long for their lunch break. John's mother became very popular when she began to appear discreetly at dress rehearsals with thermos flasks of coffee, packets of sandwiches and a tin of Bemax for Harcourt Williams.

More intellectual and less formidable than Robert Atkins, Williams was an ardent disciple of Poel, Gordon Craig and Granville Barker. At his first rehearsal he told the actors to read Barker's Prefaces to Shakespeare and later read to them himself from the proofs of the second volume of Prefaces, which was about to be published. He planned four of his productions very much on the lines Barker had laid down – *Romeo and Juliet, Antony and Cleopatra, King Lear* and *The Merchant of Venice*.

Of course, as always at the Vic, he was severely handicapped by the shortage of money. Apart from John and Martita Hunt, his leading actors included Donald Wolfit, Adele Dixon, Leslie French and Gyles Isham, but while it was hard enough to get leading actors as good as these for £10 a week, which was all Lilian Baylis could afford to pay, it was impossible to get good actors for five or six pounds a week to support them in the minor parts.

Only £20 could be spent on the set and costumes of any one production – and even this was an improvement on what had been budgeted during the Robert Atkins regime. Much of the scenery was painted by actors and apprentices, the prop department was run by semi-amateurs, and rostrums and sets of steps often had to be painted to serve both in an opera and a play. The cloaks and wigs were recognizably operatic, and Margaret Webster, who was also in the company, was once given a whole uncut roll of cloth by the wardrobe master, who told her to pin herself into it without cutting it because it would be needed later for the opera.

Sometimes actors would hire their own costumes, but for the most part they had continually to wear what was provided by the ramshackle wardrobe – doublets and robes that had already been seen again and again by the faithful Old Vic regulars in the audience. Some of the costumes still dated from Matheson Lang's Far East tour. Crowns were improvised, jewellery was bought from Woolworths and it was very hard to sustain an illusion realistically from a rickety throne against a background of one of Benson's old drop-cloths.

Still, the very inadequacies of the costumes and scenery made it more necessary than ever to concentrate on Shakespeare's lines. John's combination of energy and enthusiasm, his voice and his vivacity, his appearance and the swiftness of his thought-processes made his performances outstanding. He launched himself on the tide of the verse, held energetically to his course and after some preliminary skirmishing, won over the Vic audience to accept him totally.

Harcourt Williams was violently opposed to the old-fashioned style of Shakespearean acting and the traditional pieces of stage business which had been so overworked. Because of the Prologue's reference to 'the two hours traffic of our stage', he maintained that *Romeo and Juliet* could be played without cuts in about two hours, and from the first rehearsal onwards he timed each scene with a stop-watch. His main aim was 'to restore the pace to Shakespeare's plays, not only in the speaking of the verse but in the movement of the scenes'.

This is how Eric Phillips, an actor in the company, remembered Harcourt Williams at the first rehearsal of the season. 'He was wearing a white shirt, open at the neck, with sleeves rolled back above the elbows and a pair of old flannel trousers. His untidy hair literally stood on end and his eyes shone with

John's mother, Kate Terry Gielgud, in 1953 at the age of 84

John in 1907

John and Eleanor in fancy dress (1912)

Frank Gielgud with Lewis in uniform and *(L. to R.)* John, Eleanor and Val. (1915)

(L. to R.)
Lewis, Val and
John (1909)

John *(third
from the R.)*
as Mark Antony
in the Hillside
production of
Julius Caesar

A schoolboy letter with four reversible drawings. Turn Edward VI and Victoria upside down to find caricatures of Val and John

'Chimneys'—an ink drawing done by John in 1919

The first Hamlet.
At the Old Vic (1930)
(Pollard Crowther)

As Hamlet,
1934
*(Yvonne
Gregory)*

As Hamlet, 1936
(*T. H. Fordham*)

As Hamlet, 1939 (*Howard Coster*)

As Hamlet, 1944
(*The Rank
Organization*)

As King Lear, 1940 *(Radio Times Hulton Picture Library)*

As King Lear, 1950 *(Angus McBean)*

As Romeo with
Peggy Ashcroft
as Juliet (1935)

Laurence
Olivier as
Romeo, Edith
Evans as the
Nurse and John
as Mercutio in
*Romeo and
Juliet* (1935)

The first Richard II.
At the
Old Vic (1929)
(E. T.
Williamson)

As Richard II (1937)
(Central
Office of In-
formation)

As Prospero in *The Tempest* (1940) *(Gordon Anthony)*

As Angelo in *Measure for Measure* (1950) *(Angus McBean)*

John with Noël Coward in Dublin during the pre-London tour of *Nude with Violin* (1956) *(Radio Times Hulton Picture Library)*

A recent photograph

As Leontes in *The Winter's Tale* (1951)
(Norman Parkinson and Conde Nast Publications Ltd.)

fanatical enthusiasm . . . By contrast, the rest of the company
were very well groomed. John Gielgud, the leading man, wore
a red carnation in his buttonhole and so did Gyles Isham. Martita
Hunt, chic and soignée, floated round in a flowered silk frock . . .
Lilian Baylis made a speech welcoming the new members of the
company and then the rehearsal began. A young actor strolled
across the floor in a somewhat leisurely manner and spoke the
first line . . . "Gregory, o'my word, we'll not carry coals!" Harcourt Williams raised his hands and beat on the table with a
clenched fist. "No," he roared. "Not like that! This is Italy –
the hot passionate south. You are a tempestuous Latin character.
You must convey that to the audience the moment the curtain
rises. And ladies and gentlemen, please – all of you – right
through this play I want pace – pace – pace." '

He achieved such pace on the opening night of *Romeo and
Juliet* that one reviewer wrote 'England won another world's
speed record on Saturday night, when, at the Old Vic, Shakespearean blank verse was spoken faster than ever before.' But the
critics had made the same complaint when Barker opened his
1912 season at the Savoy with *The Winter's Tale*. In any case,
the pace at the Old Vic was slightly modified and the company
was never again accused of gabbling.

Adele Dixon was Juliet, Martita Hunt played the Nurse,
Donald Wolfit Tybalt and Gyles Isham Mercutio. Williams was
unsatisfied with John's Romeo. He later called it 'the least
interesting performance of his two years at the Old Vic . . . He
never touched the last scenes. He failed to bring off the distracted
boy, jolted by disaster into full manhood; the ecstasy, too, of the
last moments transcending death escaped him.'

Williams preferred John's performance in *The Merchant of
Venice*, which opened a month later. 'He was far less solemn
than most Antonios and never dreary. One felt that this merchant
had the right to carry the title of the play.' But Antonio is an
unrewarding part and John already had his eye on Shylock, which
was played by Brember Wills, who was a fine character actor
but recoiled with such antipathy from the notion of hatred
that he was unable to realize Shakespeare's Jew convincingly.
After seeing the production, Barker wrote to Williams that the
company needed, above all 'to let the verse seem to be carrying
them along, not they to be carrying it, and not, some of them, to
be so damned explanatory.'

Lilian Baylis was unlike any other theatre manager. She

behaved more like a landlady, shuffling down the corridors in a shabby fur coat, followed by a companion and two yapping dogs. During the performances she would write letters in her box, with the curtains closed to keep the light from spilling into the auditorium. But whenever there was an unexpected silence on the stage or an unexpected reaction from the audience, she would peer out to see what was going on.

A devoutly religious woman who would regularly go into retreat, she was liable to ask actors to kneel down and pray to God for their success and for more money for the Vic. On Sundays she would sometimes persuade members of the company to play at a leper colony in Essex. But she was shrewd enough to know which actors could be coaxed and which were best left alone. John was neither asked to kneel nor to play to the lepers. Once he heard her say 'I've got the Almighty in my pocket.'

The actors had to work extremely hard, even though they only gave nine performances a fortnight, as the theatre was also being used for opera and ballet. On average each play was rehearsed for three weeks and only performed about thirteen times. *The Merchant of Venice* was followed by Molière's *Le Malade Imaginaire*, with John playing Cléante in the evenings and rehearsing his first Richard II during the day. He had seen Leslie Faber and Ernest Milton as Richard and found them both highly effective, but he did not know the play well when rehearsals began, and it must have given him a very strange feeling to know that he would actually be wearing the costume Ernest Milton had worn, a long black velvet robe with great fake ermine sleeves hanging to the floor. It was now that he began to feel he was on the verge of discovering himself in Shakespeare.

Richard II gave him a better opportunity than any previous part to find out how much he could do with his voice. He may still have been using it too much like a musical instrument, treating the lines too much like a score, over-emphasizing the beat. He may have indulged excessively in elegiac self-pity and he was liable to become shrill and hysterical at the climaxes, but (as we can still judge from a recording he made about a year later of a speech from Act Three Scene Three) his voice was superbly effective, and there were thrilling modulations, which seemed to rise directly out of a change of pulse in the character's flow of thought and feeling. Obviously, with only three weeks to rehearse, it was impossible to think out what he was doing as carefully as he did when he repeated the role nine years later, but in giving comparatively free play to his instinct and in exploiting his own personality for the first time in a part which temperamentally suited him so well, John was moving and exciting, and the production was the first real success of the season. In some ways the performance must have been more gripping than John's Richard II of 1938, less subtle but more spontaneous. To take just one specific example of a different reading of a line: in 1938 he introduced into "Dear earth I do salute thee with my hand" an undercurrent of suspicion. In 1929 he played it with sheer unsophisticated pleasure.

Eric Phillips remembers him 'sniffing an orange stuck with cloves or striding petulantly about the stage with a riding whip . . . The turn of his head, the curve of his body, the movements of his hands each told a story of their own and were beautiful to watch. Again I picture Gielgud, robed in black velvet with a high collar and broad flowing sleeves lined with white ermine. A red wig, parted in the middle, was brushed back so that the ears were partially visible. The face was pale and the hands – those powerfully aesthetic hands – were almost white and adorned with immense rings. Under the curves of pencilled eyebrows the eyes were set back a little by means of a faint flush of rouge. The mouth was scarlet and its downward curves were accentuated by a wispy red moustache which curved downwards too, like little lines of insubstantial red smoke.'

And this is his description of John's exit from the deposition scene. 'The lords drew their swords in fealty to the new king. There was a faint roll of drums from the orchestra which merged into a slow and mocking march. Gielgud tottered down the steps and moved slowly towards the exit, dragging his feet behind him and tilting his chin upwards in a last exhibition of majesty.'

At the final curtain, the audience could hardly contain its enthusiasm. People rose to their feet, clapping, and cheering, stamping and shouting. Ivor Brown called the performance 'exquisite' and Harcourt Williams was later to write 'His playing of the Abdication Scene will live in my mind as one of the great things I have witnessed in the theatre.'

In his book *William Shakespeare*, John Masefield argues that *A Midsummer Night's Dream* must have been written 'for performance at the festivities of a noble wedding, during which perhaps several couples were married'. This gave Harcourt Williams the idea of dressing his production of it in Jacobean clothes. Some of the actors disliked the idea but John came out strongly in support of it and, together, he and Harcourt Williams carried the day. There were farthingales and high wired collars for the ladies and folk-songs instead of Mendelssohn. Lilian Baylis was overheard saying 'Well I suppose I'm old-fashioned but I do like my fairies to be gauzy.' But for John the production was a very pleasant experience. Oberon is not physically a taxing role like Richard II or like most leading Shakespearean parts. The verse is beautiful to speak and John was rightly becoming confident that he knew how to speak it.

> It gave me a wonderful sense of power to feel that I was beginning to control the lovely language which at rehearsals moved me so much that tears would spring to my eyes.

But in performance he held the tears back.

Meanwhile he was beginning to think less in terms of his own performance than of the production as a whole, and Harcourt Williams encouraged him to take a hand in the direction. 'Do help me with this scene.' 'Do suggest something.' Martita Hunt, John and sometimes Leslie French as well would have a picnic lunch with Williams in Martita Hunt's dressing-room, while the others ate in the bar. The unfortunate consequence of this was that the rest of the company, understandably, felt excluded from the inner circle, but it gave John a chance to bombard Williams with ideas. According to Williams, none of John's suggestions were ever made for the sake of glorifying his own part. 'John's influence in the company was always electric. He sparked with ideas and would beget ideas in other people which would spark back again.' He would often ask John to take other actors aside and rehearse them. John also had a lot of scenic ideas which he sketched out for Williams, who accepted many of them. Two and a half years were to go by before John did a production of his own, but his career as a director obviously had its roots in this experience with Harcourt Williams and the Old Vic.

After Christmas, *Richard II* was revived for a fortnight, followed by *Julius Caesar*. John's performance as Mark Antony was praised by the critics and by Robert Donat who wrote a letter to *The Times* saying it was 'superbly done'. According to Gordon Crosse* John's best moments were the sharp bark of laughter with which he greeted Cassius's offer of a share in the

---

* *Fifty Years of Shakespearean Playgoing.* Privately printed, 1940.

spoils, and another more derisive laugh when Cassius reminded Brutus whose fault it was that Antony was still alive.

After not being very interested in Orlando (*As You Like It*) and then amusing himself as the Emperor in *Androcles and the Lion*, peering through a large fake emerald, John was surprised and excited when Harcourt Williams suggested he should play Macbeth. He could hardly believe that it was within his range, but he agreed to try. He wanted to base his performance on the impression he had formed of Irving's Macbeth from Ellen Terry's descriptions of it and from the drawings by Bernard Partridge he found among the Lyceum souvenir programmes his mother had given him. Like Irving in the drawing, he would make his first entrance with his sheathed sword on his shoulder, but he could not decide how to get rid of it – until it struck him during a rehearsal that he could let it fall in his surprise at being hailed by the Witches as King. According to Williams he 'achieved the appearance of age and weight in a surprising manner. He chose heavy cloaks from the wardrobes and wisely rehearsed in them . . . He has certainly inherited Ellen Terry's skill in his ability to make a cloak act.' But John now says that the photographs of the production make him look more like a Wagnerian hero than a Scottish chieftain.

The other actors in the company, who had been pleased but not altogether surprised at the degree of success he had achieved as Richard II, were equally pleased but very surprised when he made such a success of Macbeth. The part had seemed so far outside his natural range.

During the first interval of one of the matinees, James Agate bustled into John's dressing-room. 'I have never seen the murder scene better done, so I have come to congratulate you now. At the end of the performance I shall probably have changed my mind for you can't possibly play the rest of it.' This monumental piece of tactlessness naturally made John intensely self-conscious during the second half of the play, but in his *Sunday Times* review Agate admitted to being quite carried away. 'For the first time in my experience Macbeth retained his hold upon the play until the end.' Ivor Brown said that John's acting had 'ripened into a rich masculinity', and one of the papers advised its readers 'See *Macbeth* at the Old Vic and be able to tell your children that you saw the great John Gielgud in his prime.' He was now twenty-six.

John had thought of both Richard II and Macbeth as character parts, but when he heard that he was going to play Hamlet after all (with Gyles Isham as Horatio) the question he asked himself was 'How could I seem great enough, simple enough to say those hackneyed, wonderful lines as if I was thinking of them for the first time? How could I avoid acting certain passages in the manner of other actors I had seen, how could I put into the part my own personal feelings – many of which fitted the feelings of Hamlet – and yet lift them to a high classical style worthy of the character?' The answer, he found, was by over-coming his fear of showing his own personality to the audience. Ezra Pound once said 'I believe in technique as the test of a man's sincerity.' John was just at the point of mastering the technique which made openness and sincerity possible for him. Komisarjevsky had taught him something of the importance of acting from the inside outwards and now Martita Hunt was being a splendidly constructive critic. She helped him to find the confidence to display more of his own personality including the less attractive traits.

Of course it was much easier to arrive at a clear conception than to execute it. All through rehearsals he was very uneasy. He could neither lose himself in the part nor find himself in it. Fortunately he knew the play extremely well. Since boyhood he had known much of it by heart and he now found it compara-tively easy to memorize his lines. He had seen at least a dozen actors in the part and had worked on scenes from the play both at Lady Benson's school and at RADA. From Ellen Terry's description in her autobiography, he had a clear idea of how Irving must have played the part. He particularly loved her account of his first scene with Horatio – a half-abstracted greet-ing, blazing into realization on "Saw! Who?" after Horatio's line about the dead King, "My lord, I think I saw him yesternight." This gave John a clear indication of how that whole scene ought to be played. But at the same time he was nervous of merely giving an anthology of other actors' Hamlets. And suddenly, when the moment came and he was actually in front of an audience, he had the strong feeling that there was no way of playing the part but his.

For preparing it he had less time than ever. While he had been playing Macbeth, he had been rehearsing the lead in Pirandello's one-act play *The Man with a Flower in his Mouth*, which is almost a monologue. It opened on 18 April. Five days later he had to appear as Oberon, Antonio and Richard II in scenes from the plays, and as Mr Hughes, the young actor who appears as Lady Macbeth in Maurice Baring's one-act play *A Re-hearsal*. (All this was for a Shakespeare's Birthday Festival.) Then on 28 April 1929, at 6.30, he had to open in *Hamlet* without cuts.

Today when we are so used to seeing young Hamlets, it is easy to forget that all through the nineteenth century and up to the 1920s actors had scarcely ever been entrusted with the part until they had spent half their career building up a reputation. Forbes-Robertson had been forty-four, Irving thirty-seven, Barrymore forty and none of the major performances that are remembered were by an actor under the age of thirty-five. According to the text, Hamlet is meant to be thirty at the time of the graveyard scene, though Shakespeare (never a realist about the passage of time) may have thought of him as younger at the beginning of the play, where there is more stress on his being a student at Wittenburg.

Youthfulness, voice and appearance – these were John's main advantages, allied to a natural nobility of bearing and the quick-silver speed at which his mind seemed to work. This made it more feasible for him than for most actors to give the impression that his thoughts were pulsing quickly enough to give birth to Hamlet's words, to suggest that each line of Shakespeare's verse had formed itself spontaneously in his mind. At the age of twenty-six, with a physical strength to match his mental agility, he was just beginning to master the art of conveying physical and verbal excitement simultaneously to the audience. Once he had conquered the fear of allowing his own vulnerable personality to shine through the performance, he was able to embody the Hamlet that he saw so clearly in his imagination. His voice could vary in pitch and tone with an astonishing speed and subtlety, combining sensitivity with a vigorous attack and momentum which seemed to derive entirely from the emotion of the situation, not at all from the metre of the verse, though, far from being ignored, the rhythm helped him to shape the emotional curves. In his *Richard II* recording there is an over-consciousness of the verse beat which produces a certain deliberateness in speech pattern and insufficient variation of tempo. But in the records John made at the same time of two of Hamlet's soliloquies, there is no such rigidity. Genuinely excited both by Shakespeare's lines and the emotional echo that he could simultaneously hear inside himself, John had suddenly learned the knack of riding the poetry, whipping himself and the audience into the same gallop-ing excitement.

But this was only possible because of his natural affinity with Hamlet's disposition. In an unscripted talk John gave on the radio over twenty-five years later, he emphasized Hamlet's loneliness, his longing for communication with other people. The only real contacts he makes are very brief – with the Player King and the Gravedigger. Horatio's friendship is taken very much for granted – as friendship between two men so often is in Shakespeare – but it has little effect on his isolation. In *Richard II* audiences had been captivated by John's verse speaking; now they were caught up in Hamlet's mind and in Hamlet's situation, in the intensity of his love for his dead father, and his horror at the rottenness that surrounded him. By revealing so much of himself John disappeared almost completely into the part.

The production must have been the best of the season. Donald Wolfit and Martita Hunt made an excellent King and Queen, and both parts emerged much more clearly than usual because Williams was using an uncut text. This also gave John more periods of rest between his big scenes. Williams dressed the play in Elizabethan costume because he felt that its spirit was best expressed in terms of the immediate values of Shakespeare's time. The performance lasted for four and a half hours but it was a huge success.

John's press was the best he had yet had. Ivor Brown reported 'This performance puts him beyond the range of the arriving actors; he is in the first rank.' J. T. Grein, who was old enough to have seen Irving and Forbes-Robertson as Hamlet, called it 'a great performance', remarking in particular on 'the profound study that he bestowed, not merely on the soliloquies, but on almost every line of the text, some of which shone in a new light in the illumination of his reading . . . He saw in almost every line a deeper meaning.'

He also won the approval of his own family. Marion Terry, who had already been to see her great-nephew as Oberon and as Macbeth, wrote to her brother Fred urging him to see it. 'I was in the *uncomfortable* stalls for *Hamlet* for just *five* hours and didn't *want* to move (though I'd have liked to do so but couldn't, the place was crammed) . . . it's *very young*, very thoughtful (without dragging it with long pauses and mouthing) graceful without effort and every word distinct and of course he looks charming – I told him I was proud of my nephew, he replied he "was proud of knowing he had some of the Terry blood in him, and hoped to go on doing better." '

The production formed a turning point in the fortunes of the Old Vic. Following the enthusiastic reviews, there was so much talk all over London about John's Hamlet that for the first time since Shakespeare had been played at the Vic, West End theatre-goers went in droves across the river. And for the first time, Lilian Baylis was invited to transfer an Old Vic production to the West End.

Maurice Browne was an American, an actor and writer as well as a theatrical manager. Earlier in the year he had presented Paul Robeson in *Othello* at the Savoy, playing Iago himself with Peggy Ashcroft as Desdemona and Ralph Richardson as Roderigo. Despite his beautiful singing voice, Robeson had no ear for blank verse, and Peggy Ashcroft's lively and moving performance could do nothing to save the production from failure. But Browne was making a fortune out of *Journey's End*, which had been running since January 1929.

For the transfer of *Hamlet* he secured the Queen's Theatre, but arrangements had to be made very hurriedly and no-one realized that the rake of the stage was much steeper than at the Old Vic. On the first night, when John entered for the graveyard scene, he noticed that the First Gravedigger seemed worried, and soon he realized that the skull was missing. He had to make a rapid choice between acting as if he were cradling a skull in his hands or cutting all the references to Yorick—about thirty lines. Deciding to cut, he spoke the line "But soft! but soft! aside, here comes the King" more loudly than usual. As he moved to the side of the stage, leaving it clear for the funeral procession to enter, he saw some very surprised faces in the wings, but the actors hurried into their positions and, after a brief pause, the mourners made their entrance. The stage manager had seen the skull rolling out of the Gravedigger's reach but all he could do was send an assistant to the theatre next door, where Alexander Moissi was just about to open in a production of *Hamlet* in German. But by the time the assistant stage manager got back with a borrowed skull, the scene was over.

There were twenty curtain calls and the influential James Agate, who did more than any other critic to make John into a star, reported 'This actor is young, thoughtful, clever, sensitive; his performance is subtle, brilliant, vigorous, imaginative, tender and full of the right kind of ironic humour. It has elegance of body and elevation of mind, it is conceived in the key of poetry and executed with beautiful diction. I have no hesitation in saying that it is the high water mark of English Shakespearean acting in our time.'

The transfer of *Hamlet* to the West End brought John the biggest fan mail he had yet had. Many people wrote to say it was the best Hamlet they had ever seen and the closest to their idea of what Shakespeare's intentions must have been. John was touched to hear from his old French teacher at RADA, Alice Gachet. 'I have seen many Hamlets and you alone have absolutely satisfied every craving and longing in this part.'

The young Diana Wynyard wrote that it was 'the most completely satisfying and lovely acting that I have ever seen'. Sybil Thorndike found herself unable to go to bed without starting a letter to him at 1.30 in the morning. 'I never *hoped* to see Hamlet played as in one's dreams . . . tonight it was Hamlet Complete. When you spoke your final word I said to myself what I said when I read the first chapter of *Moby Dick*. "This is too good to be true" . . . I've had an evening of being swept right off my feet into another life – far more real than the life I live in, and moved, moved beyond words.'

He also received two letters from his parents. Frank Gielgud wrote:

> You gave me and many others great pleasure and satisfaction last night, but I think there were moments of too rapid rhetoric in your violent outbursts when (to me) the words did not come over. I am sure you were getting tired towards the end, and had to some extent lost the self control over your powers which pleases me so much in your acting.
>
> At the beginning of your 'the readiness is all' speech before the duel, I would like you to touch your breast when referring to the aching heart within. Every time I have heard you I wanted that gesture, and these little points can only be mentioned in quiet moments and not after an exciting evening!
>
> Your mother was quietly resting when I left this morning, and her joy at your success last night was very moving.
>
> Much love dear boy and husband your strength with plenty of rest and proper food.
>
> Your critical old
> Father.

Two days later, his mother wrote herself.

> I feel that I've told you so little of the delight you have given me throughout all these Shakespeare plays. At the rehearsals I've felt I was there to look out for possible flaws – and in the few minutes available

I spoke of details – when you come I've such joy in your presence – when you are gone I think of all I meant to say and hate myself for being so inarticulate – I always am when I'm most *grateful* and I can't tell you what joy it gives me to have you give up your spare time and forsake your many friends, to come along here and let me share your interests, to weigh the pros and cons of the future, to be ever my dear sympathetic loving son as well [as] the brilliant artist. I love your enthusiasm for the fine things in your art, your exquisite sense of rhythm and proportion, your grasp of character, your 'readings' and that great gift of translating them to the audience – not by niggling details (so easily mere tricks) but with breadth and true imagination – and you are always advancing – even in the lesser parts there was some fresh difficulty overcome – if only in keeping in your due relation to the play. You can dominate but I have never seen you step out of the canvas to distort the picture – only to fill it – You do not demand the centre of the stage in and out of season – but can hold your audience spellbound by a whisper, and their eyes with a gesture. When I see *Hamlet* again I'll probably find scenes and speeches to praise individually – now it is the 'wholeness' of your conception, the dignity, the variety in its constancy, the beauty and breadth and simplicity of the delivery of your lines – the power and the restraint of it all that fills my heart with wonder and with admiration. Hamlet is many men in one – so too is John Gielgud – you understand – and you make us understand – and give us joy and delight past expression – and to no one more than your devoted Mother.

K.T.G.

This is *not* one of the letters you have to answer!!

The London public that summer had three *Hamlets* to choose from. Apart from Moissi's German production, Henry Ainley's was still running at the Haymarket, but all three productions were doing bad business. At the Queen's, the gallery was always full, but the more expensive seats were mostly empty in spite of the general enthusiasm. But one friend of John's told him she had been too impressed to move during his death scene, although a pipe had burst during the performance, and water was creeping along the floor from one side of her stall and a mouse from the other.

A long run seemed unlikely and when Nigel Playfair offered John the part of John Worthing in a stylized black and white production of *The Importance of Being Earnest* at the Hammersmith Lyric, he accepted at once. He had already played the part in an amateur production and he knew the play almost by heart. It was the kind of comedy part he had always fancied and an ideal contrast to Hamlet. His aunt, Mabel Terry Lewis was to be Lady Bracknell with Jean Cadell as Miss Prism. But after he had signed the contract with Playfair, business suddenly improved at the Queen's and Browne was angry at being unable to continue the run.

As John Worthing, John won an immediate success. With his slim, straight back, his meticulous elegance and his air of nobility which he can tilt into a lordly languor, he has all the qualities for Wilde's mannered comedy. Adjusting the angle of his hat with arrogant affectation, shooting a cuff as if he were playing an ace, dabbing fastidiously at his crocodile tears with an immaculate black-edged handkerchief from his breast pocket, John was the perfect incarnation of John Worthing. As in *Hamlet*, he conveyed the impression of being quite capable of inventing for himself the perfect lines the author had given him, and in *Earnest* he exploited again his characteristic combination of seriousness and sincerity which had served him so well. But this time there was a subtle exaggeration of the basic qualities and a delicately measured self-consciousness which produced the ideal quotient of comic affectation. James Agate went on for years stubbornly insisting that John was a tragic actor who should never attempt comedy. 'We are invited to watch a serious actor pretending to be serious, which is nothing.' But for Charles Morgan, who wrote a newspaper article headed 'Notes on the Acting of Comedy', John Gielgud and Mabel Terry Lewis 'stand out as models for the true interpretation of Wilde.'

John had already decided to go back to the Old Vic for a second season. After his successes as Hamlet and John Worthing, he might well have had a much more rewarding season in Shaftesbury Avenue than in 1928–9, but he resisted the temptations of bigger money, a more comfortable dressing-room and star billing.

At the end of his first season at the Vic, a newspaper interviewer had asked him what was the most important lesson he had learned. His answer was 'the value of teamwork'. He had also freed himself from any fear of imitating Noël Coward. Certainly he had learnt a good deal from Coward, and from his experience of playing in *The Vortex* and *The Constant Nymph* he acquired a lightness of touch which he imported deftly even into the most serious scenes of *Hamlet*, just as he used a Hamlet-like seriousness to good effect in Wilde. But at last he was able to digest the influence of other actors without imitating them. In *Richard II* and *Hamlet* he had at last found his real self, and *The Importance* matured his natural stylishness. Already he was developing organically as an artist — he was able to enrich himself at each new phase with what he had gained from the previous phase.

When he agreed to go back to the Vic, Lilian Baylis raised his salary and Harcourt Williams consulted him about the new company. At first he was uncertain whether Ralph Richardson ought to be engaged but, for his part, Richardson says he 'sprang at the opportunity' of going there 'because Johnny Gielgud was a kind of miracle'. Besides, if Richardson were a success, he would stay on as leading man when John left at the end of the season.

At first Richardson was very disappointed in John. 'I found his clothes extravagant, I found his conversation flippant. He was the New Young Man of his time and I didn't like him.' The first play they did together was *Henry IV Part I*, with John as Hotspur and Richardson as Prince Hal. As an actor he admired John. 'He was so brilliant, he shone, he was so handsome and his voice was so splendid.' They played well together and their scene in the last act was particularly exciting, though they were both terrified of injuring each other in their final sword fight, which they had not had time to rehearse properly. Richardson used to count the strokes aloud, regardless of the audience.

In the second play, *The Tempest*, he was fully won over by John, who was 'magnificent' as Prospero, costumed like an Indian magician in white robes and a turban. As Caliban, Richardson had great difficulties in rehearsal. 'I couldn't find my feet very well and after a rehearsal, John said to me one day "Would you care to run over your scene with me?" So I thought to myself "Not much." So rather grudgingly I said "Oh yes, all right." So we ran it through, just the two of us in the theatre with the director and Johnny said "Well you know Ralph, I think that when you come on, you might do this or you might do that, you might do this" — he gave me, as he usually does, about three or four suggestions. I thought to myself "My God, so I might, I might do one of those." And he talked about Sycorax my mother . . . he gave me about two hundred ideas as he usually does, twenty-five of which I eagerly seized on, and when I went away, I thought "This chap, you know, I don't like him very much but by God he knows something about this here play." He helped me so much that I looked at him afterwards in quite a different way. And then out of that we formed a friendship. We used to go out to lunch together. I was always rather amazed at him —

a kind of brilliant sort of butterfly, while I was a very gloomy sort of boy.'

As he had once done before with Leslie Faber, John was able to instil a taste for music in his new friend. Ralph had a gramophone but only one record, *Tea for Two*. John lent him records – Beethoven, Scarlatti and Bach. 'Johnny taught me the moment when I learned to hear music.'

John's Prospero won the full approval of Fred Terry, who on 17 February 1931 wrote to his niece:

> My dearest Katie,
>
> Yes I had a really wonderful time. John gives a fine performance – his movements were those of a man of fifty, tired and worn – this is in itself (to me) a great accomplishment – I know the difficulties and – tho' I watched for it I never saw him 'break'. His voice, and delivery, are beautiful. Only one 'question' I'd like to ask him . . . Is he right to be as 'angry' with Ariel as he is with 'the Monster'?

The letter goes on to complain bitterly about Ariel's near-nakedness. 'Nakedness I think (on the stage) is reducing an artist to the level of the slave market . . . No I like my Beast on the stage cooked. *En chemise* not *au naturel*. Potatoes alright – even they are better baked in their jackets.'

There were three more productions before Christmas – George Coleman's *The Jealous Wife* with John playing 'with an exquisite levity' as Lord Trinket, a revival of *Richard II* and *Antony and Cleopatra* with John as a juvenile Antony in Elizabethan costume with a padded doublet.

In the New Year, Lilian Baylis opened Sadler's Wells, dividing the repertoire between the two theatres. The first production was *Twelfth Night* (with John as a stiff and tragic Malvolio and Richardson made up like the Laughing Cavalier as Sir Toby) in a triangular set based on an idea of John's. There was a gala first night with speeches from mayors and aldermen and also from the last great actors of the Victorian Theatre, Dame Madge Kendal and Sir Johnston Forbes-Robertson. Lilian Baylis wore her academic robes as Master of Arts and her cross as a Companion of Honour. In response to the ovation she received, she started to speak, holding a huge basket of fruit in her right hand. First an apple, then a pear thudded onto the stage. John could not help laughing and the audience followed suit. It was a hilarious end to a solemn evening.

After *Twelfth Night*, Harcourt Williams revived *Richard II*, and John's performance won him a letter from Naomi Jacob which must have delighted him. 'Only once before have I seen it played so that I got great pleasure out of it. Some years ago Leslie Faber (God rest him) played it at a Sunday show. I saw him and for the first time listened and watched Richard, feeling that at last he was real, possible, pathetic and very beautiful. Last night, I saw it all again. I came out of Sadler's Wells having cried so much that I dared scarcely face the lights . . . I am paying you the greatest possible tribute when I say that so often you reminded me of Leslie. Your voice has so much colour – as his had, your movements are so "right" and so easy – as his were. I remember his once saying to me, of you, "That young man will go a very long way. He's got arrogance. And he isn't afraid to use and show it!" '

Having introduced Shaw into the Old Vic repertoire with *Androcles and the Lion*, Harcourt Williams now cast John as Sergius to Richardson's Bluntschli in *Arms and the Man*. Shaw himself came along to the first rehearsal. He arrived a quarter of an hour early and read through the play in his rich brogue with the company sitting around him in a circle. He characterized each role and half way through the first act he threw back his head to roar with laughter. 'You must forgive me. I haven't read this play for a long time and you know it's really very funny.'

He came back later to see a dress rehearsal.

> We could not distinguish him in the darkness of the stalls, but we saw the light of his pocket-lamp bobbing up and down as he made his notes. He assembled the company in the first interval, produced his written comments, and reduced everybody to a state of disquiet. Then he departed. Unfortunately I was not able to gather from him any hints about my own performance, as Sergius does not appear until the second act.

But Richardson did get a few words from the great man. He had worked hard at Bluntschli's first entrance, which is made after escaping from the enemy and scaling up a drainpipe to climb in through a window. Very politely Shaw asked Richardson to eliminate all the breathless gasps and pauses he was putting in to indicate exhaustion. 'You've got to go from line to line, quickly and swiftly, never stop the flow of the lines . . . Always reserve the acting for underneath the spoken word.' It was the same advice he had given to Ellen Terry in his letters about her performance as Imogen in *Cymbeline* at the Lyceum in 1897.

After Sergius, John gave his first performances in two parts he was later to make very much his own – Benedick in *Much Ado about Nothing* and King Lear. For an actor of twenty-seven, Lear was a much more difficult old man than Prospero, but given the choice between Lear and a revival of *Hamlet* for the final role of his two seasons, John felt bound to accept the greater challenge.

In his student days of walking on at the Old Vic ten years previously, he had helped to hold Gloucester's chair while the old man's eyes were put out, and he had seen a production by Komisarjevsky at the OUDS with golden trumpets and an impressive flight of steps. He made up his mind to avoid the image of a doddering old man and to emphasize Lear's physical strength. He based his make-up on a seventeenth-century print of Anger, which was as virile, he thought, as a Michelangelo drawing. At the same time he managed to suggest old age by giving the impression that his head was too heavy for his body. His stance was totally different from the erect carriage to which the audience was accustomed.

In his own judgement:

> I was wholly inadequate in the storm scenes, having neither the voice nor the physique for them. Lear has to *be* the storm, but I could do no more than shout against the thundersheet. The only scene I thought I did at all well was the one with the Fool, when Lear leaves Goneril to go to Regan: 'O, let me not be mad, not mad, sweet heaven – '

But in this period when *King Lear* was widely held to be unactable, he had demonstrated that, as he said in his curtain speech, it was 'a play that shrieks aloud to be acted'.

The critics were kinder to him than he was to himself, though they had their reservations. The consensus was that if John was not yet a good Lear, at least he might become one. Peter Fleming (who had himself acted in Komisarjevsky's OUDS production) wrote in the *Spectator* 'I have never seen a better bit of acting than Mr Gielgud's "Oh fool I shall go mad". He says the words in a voice become suddenly flat and toneless, quickened only with a chilling objective interest in their no longer contestable truth.' But he regretted that the imminence of collapse never terrified: 'it had the deliberate threat of distant gunfire rather than the unpredictable menace of a volcano.'

If the performance was not wholly a success, it certainly did nothing to curb the rapid growth of John's popularity. The *Evening Post* correspondent reported to New York 'There is a young actor in this town named John Gielgud who has taken the place the way John Barrymore took New York when he was known as "Jack" and was knocking the flappers out of their seats. His pictures sell like mad among the earnest young students who flock to his performances.'

And so his two seasons at the Old Vic were over. Harcourt Williams's parting present was a glove which Ellen Terry had once given him. Irving had worn it as Benedick. 'Apart from all else,' he wrote in the accompanying letter, 'your enthusiasm and "theatre etiquette" have been a shining example and of untold service to me. I know from these foundations that stand beneath your power as an actor that you will grow and expand until you shatter that theatre falsely termed commercial (all good theatres must function commercially to be effective) and create one – either of brain or brick, I don't care which! – that we shall be proud of.'

14   Back to the Commercial Theatre

John went back to the West End in Edward Knoblock's adaptation of J. B. Priestley's popular novel *The Good Companions*. It was not at all easy to adapt his style to the Priestley dialogue.

The scenes were very short and sketchy, and there was hardly any development of character. Jollifant in the play was a 'type' – a very ordinary juvenile who had to carry off a few slight love scenes and a couple of effective comedy situations with the aid of a pipe, under-graduate clothes, and the catchword 'absolutely' . . . The sets were enormous, the orchestra vast, and the stage as wide as a desert. I had learned from playing Shakespeare not to be afraid of acting broadly, and the size of the theatre did not dismay me as much as I had feared at first, but the manner and pace had to be very different from anything I had ever done before. I had to try and catch the audience's interest with the first word, and sweep my little scenes along to a climax in a few short minutes. However though the robes and the large effects that troop with majesty had not come with me from the Old Vic, my followers had. On that exciting first night at His Majesty's, when my performance of

Inigo might have been smothered under the reputation of Priestley's book, Knoblock's adaptation, and the immediate success of Edward Chapman and Frank Pettingell, at least a hundred of my staunch friends had crossed the river to greet me. My reception when I first appeared was out of all proportion.

As the young schoolmaster, Inigo Jollifant, he had to play some of Richard Addinsell's music at the piano. Since he plays only by ear, he had great difficulty in learning it, even with the composer to tutor him. He had previously had the same trouble with Eugene Goossens's more difficult music in *The Constant Nymph*, when he had been coached by Noël Coward's devoted arranger and accompanist, Elsie April. But in *The Vortex* – as later in *Musical Chairs* – he was able to strum as he pleased in the keys he could manage. He was amused, years afterwards, to find that Coward's piano playing was almost as limited as his own. They sat down at two pianos in Coward's home in Switzerland, trying to harmonize together in tunes they both knew, but as each could only manage his pet keys, they had little success.

In one scene in *The Good Companions* an old actor persistently upstaged him, in spite of John's polite protests. Lunching with Fred Terry, John asked what he should do. 'Walk in front of him while he's speaking, my boy. He'll have to come down level with you then, otherwise the audience won't be able to see him.' This turned out to be excellent advice.

The Good Companions was a huge success and it gave John nearly a year in the West End, his first long run since *The Constant Nymph*, but this time his salary, dressing-room and billing were all encouraging. It was no longer a surprise when he heard people in the streets saying 'That's John Gielgud.' And suppers at the Savoy were no longer a luxury. He often went there with Martita Hunt, who was acting just up the street at the Lyric in *Autumn Crocus*.

In January and February 1932 he directed his first production – *Romeo and Juliet* for the OUDS in the old theatre at Oxford. He managed to persuade Edith Evans and Peggy Ashcroft to lead the undergraduate cast as the Nurse and Juliet. The Romeo was Christopher Hassall and of the other undergraduates in the cast, George Devine, the President of the OUDS (Mercutio), William Devlin (Tybalt) and Hugh Hunt (Friar Laurence) went on to lead successful lives in the professional theatre. So did Terence Rattigan, who had a single line to speak as one of the musicians who came to awaken Juliet for her wedding, and he tried to say it with a different inflection each night.

As costume designers John used three girls he had met when they were art students. Margaret and Sophia Harris and Elizabeth Montgomery had sent him some studies of himself, drawn during performances at the Old Vic. He bought some to give to his mother and friends and helped the girls, who assumed the collective name of Motley, to arrange an exhibition of their work. They shared John's enthusiasm for Craig and for Lovat Fraser, who had designed *The Beggar's Opera* for Playfair, and it was through John that they later met Michel St Denis, who invited them to work in his London Theatre Studio and at the Old Vic School, where they developed ideas many of which had been born during their previous work with John. Sophia, who was afterwards to marry George Devine, met him at Oxford during rehearsals of *Romeo and Juliet*.

Apart from the superficiality of so many of the plays he had worked in, one of the points which had most depressed John before his two seasons at the Vic was the feeling that he was chosen at random, that none of the managers particularly cared whether he accepted the part they were offering him or whether they used some other personable juvenile. But now he was in a very different position. Playwrights had started sending him their scripts and in fact it was two plays which reached him in this way that were to dominate the next phase of his career. Both plays were by unknown authors, *The Discontents* by Ronald Mackenzie and *Richard of Bordeaux* by Gordon Daviot, who turned out to be a woman who also wrote thrillers under her other pen-name, Josephine Tey.

In the letter accompanying *The Discontents*, Mackenzie reminded John that they had been schoolboys together at Hillside. Feeling very enthusiastic about the script, John invited him to lunch at the old Gourmets Restaurant in Lisle Street. Unfortunately Mackenzie turned out to be a vegetarian and every bit as shy as John himself. Five managements had already turned the play down but John took it to Bronson Albery, a leading theatrical manager and theatre-owner, who had just signed him up for a three-play contract. Albery immediately offered two special try-out performances at the Arts Theatre in November 1931. John suggested Komisarjevsky as director and Frank Vosper as Old Schindler, the father of the consumptive hero. Young Schindler was by far the best modern part that had come John's way.

Apart from giving him yet another chance to play the piano on stage, there was a Hamlet-like bitterness in the character and a Chekhovian quality in the writing, so John was once again able to draw simultaneously on several different areas of his past experience. It was a relief to have a meaty emotional part after the long spell of frustration as Inigo.

Mackenzie had written an exterior scene in the second act, when an oil well caught fire, but Komisarjevsky persuaded him to set the whole action in a claustrophobic interior, which he designed himself. Everyone thought 'The Discontents' a depressing title and after endless disagreement John suggested *Musical Chairs*.

The play's Chekhovian quality pleased the critics and they nearly all praised the cast, which included Jessica Tandy, Jack Livesey and Carol Goodner. The production was soon transferred to Albery's Criterion Theatre but by this time Komisarjevsky was busy with another West End play and it was left to John to take many of the rehearsals. The dress rehearsal was disastrous, with cues and effects continually going wrong. There was thunder in the wrong place and a noise of hammering backstage. The actors were all on edge and pessimistic about the play's chances.

There is an old superstition that a bad dress rehearsal means a good first night, and this first night went extremely well. Everyone felt very happy about it and John afterwards had a big supper party at the Savoy. In the morning Agate hailed the play as 'a little masterpiece ... marvellously well acted'. He singled out John 'who played with every nerve in his body and his brain'.

Musical Chairs was to provide John with another long run in the West End, from 1 April to 31 December 1932, but because it was a much better acting part than Inigo Jollifant it was more difficult to sustain – to repeat the same words with the same inflections, the same moves and the same gestures night after night and twice on matinee days. At some performances, knowing he was becoming mechanical, John would recite passages of Shakespeare in his dressing room to keep himself mentally alert. Playing a consumptive, he began to feel neurotic and even lost weight. A friend of Ralph Richardson's told him 'I went to see your friend Mr Gielgud the other night. Is he really as thin as that?'

It was unfortunate that John's eyesight was so good. One

night he noticed Artur Rubinstein sitting in the second row of the stalls, which made him feel very uncomfortable when he sat down to the piano. Another night he caught sight of Noël Coward, which made him overact out of nervousness and play for laughs, looking in the direction of Coward's seat each time he had a good line. Towards the end of the first act he suddenly saw it was empty. When Coward found out that John had noticed his absence, he wrote to explain. 'I thought you were overacting badly and using voice tones and elaborate emotional effects, and as I seriously think you are a grand actor it upset me very much.' He also complained that Frank Vosper had a wig with such a bad join that it looked like a yachting cap.

The second play, *Richard of Bordeaux*, was to make John into a big stage star. The script was rather discursive and over-elaborate in the first version he read but he was quick to realize that he could to some extent base his performance on what he had learnt from playing Richard II. It was only later that Gordon Daviot told him she had written her play with him in mind after seeing his Richard II.

Anne of Bohemia would be an ideal part for Gwen Ffrangcon Davies. He wanted Komisarjevsky to direct but he was abroad when Bronson Albery offered the Arts Theatre for two consecutive Sunday-night try-out performances while *Musical Chairs* was still running, so John asked Harcourt Williams to co-direct it with him.

The audience was enthusiastic and the press fairly favourable, though few of the top-line critics came. John knew that parts of the script were weak and, rather influenced by Ronald Mackenzie's negative reaction, he did not try to persuade Albery to transfer it to the West End.

In the summer, John was given a fortnight's holiday from *Musical Chairs*. He went to the South of France and, on his way back to England, stayed for a night in Chartres to see the Cathedral. In the lounge of his hotel he picked up an English newspaper and read that Ronald Mackenzie had been killed in a driving accident. He had used his royalties from the play to take his first holiday for eight years. He had been driving in France near Beauvais when a tyre-burst overturned the car, killing him instantly.

While *Musical Chairs* was nearing the end of its run, John was still full of energy and longing to direct another play. The opportunity soon came. His first professional production in which he did not appear himself was Rodney Ackland's *Strange Orchestra*, a play about paying guests in a Bloomsbury flat. At John's suggestion, the leading part was offered to Mrs Patrick Campbell. When she accepted provisionally, he was surprised, delighted and rather nervous, knowing how difficult she could be. At the first rehearsal she pretended not to understand the script. 'Who are all these extraordinary characters? Where do they live? Does Gladys Cooper know them?' She also tried to change the play's title. 'Oh Mr Ackland, I hope you don't mind. Herbert Griffith rang up to ask me what the play was called and I told him it was *Jazz*.' Fortunately there had already been a play called *Jazz*.

One of the parts had to be recast and when John, after great trouble, succeeded in getting David Hutcheson for it, Mrs Pat greeted him 'Oh how do you do? I hope you'll stay. We've had four already.'

Every afternoon she went to sit with her pekinese, which had been locked up in quarantine since she had been caught trying to smuggle it back from America with her. 'I brought it in twice – once as a false bust and once as hip-disease.' But this time she had put it in a hat-box and it had barked on the way through customs.

She argued incessantly with John. 'Oh Mr Gielgud, why are you cutting all the author's best lines?' And she quarrelled with Rodney Ackland. During one rehearsal row he threw his hat on to the stage and stormed out – only to have to come back to fetch the hat. Each time Mrs Campbell threatened to leave, John's spirits sank. She was rehearsing brilliantly and her presence in the play seemed virtually a guarantee of success. Eventually she did leave, and John engaged Laura Cowie, who was too beautiful and distinguished to be ideal for the blowzy, slatternly Mrs Lyndon. But thanks to a first night accident she got off to a very good start. When the curtain went up, she was spreading jam on a slice of toast. Her hand was trembling with nerves, and some of the jam fell on her stocking. She scraped it off and put it straight back on the toast, which put the audience into the right mood.

Later in 1932 John was engaged to play his old part of Inigo in the film of *The Good Companions*, with Jessie Matthews. Since *Who is the Man?* he had played in two other films, *Insult* (1932) and *The Clue of the New Pin*, an Edgar Wallace thriller. As Inigo Jollifant he had made a success in the theatre which ought to be easy to repeat on the screen and he was hoping the part might be developed more fully. But his good looks were not really those of the romantic juvenile type of the contemporary cinema. The popular Jessie Matthews was usually favoured by the camera in their scenes together and when the film was shown at the old Gaumont Cinema in the Haymarket, John's name was not even on the marquee, though he was still starring across the street in *Musical Chairs*. Jessie Matthews was helpful and sweet. Her main memory of working with him on the film is that whenever he was missing he was always to be found 'with his nose in a book'. He gave a stylish, charming, energetic performance, producing a pleasant singing voice for one of the musical numbers.

His first professional production of a Shakespeare play was *The Merchant of Venice*, which opened on 12 December at the Old Vic with Peggy Ashcroft as Portia, Malcolm Keen as Shylock and Harcourt Williams as the Prince of Arragon. Unfortunately the film of *The Good Companions* overshot its schedule, which meant that Harcourt Williams had to take many of the early rehearsals for him. This was almost certainly the first production at the Vic for which costumes were specially designed. John insisted on this and took no fee for directing, so that all the available money could be spent on the production.

In fact, very little was ever spent on costumes or scenery at the Vic. Shylock's robe was made out of dishcloth which cost three-pence farthing a yard, while other costumes were made from mosquito-netting, bath towelling, painted linen and black tailor's canvas. Some of the ideas John and the Motleys devised for the costumes were derived from their memories of the Russian ballet. As Morocco, for instance, Anthony Quayle wore a huge fez and a long white towelling robe with bobbles all down the front and carried a large cardboard scimitar.

In his programme note for the play John wrote:

> The entire pictorial and musical side of the production is frankly decorative and unrealistic. I believe this treatment to be a good one, preserving the fantasy of the Portia story, and throwing into strong relief the realism of the character of Shylock.

One member of the audience to welcome the result was Tyrone Guthrie: 'Here, for the first time in my limited experience, was a Shakespeare comedy which was not heavily and boringly trying to be funny but was instead elegant and witty, light as a feather and so gaily sophisticated that beside it Maugham and Coward seemed like two Nonconformist pastors from the Midlands.'

The critic of *Punch* called it the best *Merchant of Venice* he had seen and several other critics compared it favourably with Komisarjevsky's recent production at Stratford-on-Avon. Ivor Brown wrote that it confirmed the overthrow of the Bensonian tradition. There was a huge ovation at the first night, but in his curtain speech John made one of his public gaffes. He thanked Harcourt Williams for doing all the donkey-work on the production.

John had already formed what was to become a life-long habit of taking on two and sometimes three jobs at the same time. Apart from playing eight performances a week, during the nine-month run of *Musical Chairs*, he appeared in two films, directed and played in the two Sunday night performances of *Richard of Bordeaux*, and directed *The Merchant of Venice* and *Strange Orchestra*. In 1933, during the West End run of *Richard of Bordeaux*, he would have liked to do matinees of *Richard II* as well, to provide audiences with a fascinating double focus on the same character. But the other actors in the company were not at all enthusiastic about the idea. Francis Lister's response was typical. 'Good God, you do like work.'

15 'Richard of Bordeaux'

Bronson Albery now proposed a full scale production of *Richard of Bordeaux* at the New. At first John was not at all keen on the idea, but once he started working on the script, his enthusiasm for the play revived and Gordon Daviot was gratifyingly responsive to his suggestions for rewriting. Even so, more changes had to be made when rehearsals started. In modernizing the characters, the dialogue made it difficult to give them the necessary stature and there was an uncertain balance between melodrama, comedy and pathos. Scenes like the banishment of Mowbray and Bolingbroke were dangerously close to Shakespeare, but by the way he spoke them, John was sometimes able to make prosaic lines sound like poetry – 'I was thinking that even if the heavens fell, you would still be there.'

John had wanted the Motleys to do the costumes and now they had persuaded him to let them design the scenery too – a decision he never regretted. For them, it was the turning point of their career, as they soon realized when society ladies started ringing up to ask whether they could make medieval evening dresses for them.

Besides Gwen Ffrangcon Davies and Francis Lister, John had Donald Wolfit, Henry Mollison and Richard Ainley in his cast, none of whom had been in the try-out at the Arts. Altogether he had an admirable company. Frederick Lloyd, Ben Webster and Eric Stanley were all experienced old stagers who contributed weight and style, wearing their costumes with fine authority, and who seemed remarkably willing to take directions from a young man of twenty-eight. At least this seemed remarkable then – it would not be today. But Wolfit and Mollison, much younger men, were both very difficult to direct. Mollison disagreed completely with John's interpretation of Bolingbroke, bluntly refusing to play the part as John was directing it. At one point it was so hard to compromise that John asked Albery to get rid of him – only to arrive at rehearsal the next morning to find Mollison standing defiantly on the stage with John's letter to Albery in his hand. Fortunately both actors were so well cast that their performances turned out effectively, though they never liked the play and rather resented its success. Wolfit, who had never got on with John at the Old Vic, remained hostile all through his life.

On the day of the dress rehearsal, John made a last minute decision to cut a tableau of the burning of Sheen Palace, realizing just in time that he had been trying to imitate the Edwardian style of Tree's productions at His Majesty's (which he had read about but never seen). But once again a bad dress rehearsal was followed by a good first night.

The audience received the play with what W. A. Darlington called 'a glorious full-throated roar such as the West End seldom hears in these sophisticated days'. The critics were generally enthusiastic, especially about John's performance. Words like 'great' and 'brilliant' were showered on him, and one critic marvelled that 'with apparent effortlessness he can hold a February audience so that there is not a cough in a theatre full to the brim'. Desmond MacCarthy wrote 'the range of his emotional scope and the intelligence with which he conceived his part put him right at the top of his profession'.

The box office did not immediately profit from the good press.

The takings on the second night were only £77 but the turning point came at the matinee on Thursday. Bookings in the morning were so slack that the box office manager let his assistant go out to lunch. Just after one o'clock, telephone calls came in one after another and soon there was a long queue. The curtain had been due to go up at 2.30 but it was 3.15 before the audience was all seated.

From then on there were queues every day outside the New. John could see them from the window of his flat further up St Martin's Lane, and when he walked home after matinees he would invariably be followed by fans and autograph hunters. Strangers rang at his front door, letters and presents arrived by every post, giggling schoolgirls telephoned him because their friends had dared them to. Some people came to see the play as many as forty times and John went on being mobbed throughout the long run and the successful tour which followed it. On the last night at Golders Green the police had to be called in to protect him and Gwen Ffrangcon Davies from the crowd at the stage door.

Alfred Lunt and Lynne Fontanne, who were appearing at the Lyric, came to a matinee. 'You are a very strange and very beautiful actor,' Lynne Fontanne wrote. 'I adored your feet, too, they were the youngest feet I have ever seen, in the first act, with that complete lack of direction that a new born colt has.' This was a compliment which John, after his long struggle to achieve a natural-looking stage gait, especially cherished.

During the scene at Eltham Palace, he had to become hysterical, shouting at the Duke of Gloucester and stabbing at a table with his dagger. Being too short of breath to shout from his diaphragm, he found he was hurting his throat at each performance. He asked Elsie Fogerty, the famous voice teacher and Head of the Central School, to tell him where he was going wrong. After watching a performance, she seated him in a chair and told him to relax very slowly, concentrating on each part of his head and body in turn. 'Imagine your head is a two pound pot of marmalade. Now slacken every muscle, every limb, by slow degrees.' She also set him a few simple voice exercises. All this was nothing like the elaborate therapy he had expected from her, but a few days later his voice came back and he had no more trouble.

As soon as the play's success was established, Albery increased John's salary to £100 a week, the highest it had ever been. Had he been better at planning ahead, he would have asked to buy a share of the play and secured a first refusal of the American rights so that he could have appeared in the part on Broadway. As it was, within four weeks of the London opening, Albery had sold the American rights to Dennis King, an English actor who lived and worked in the U.S. Gordon Daviot sent John a present of £200 but this was little consolation. Not only had he lost his chance of taking the play to New York but he was also to lose three of his leading actors to America. Instead of giving them run-of-the-play contracts, Albery had only signed them up for three months, and Dennis King had no compunction about taking them away. In fact, after watching John's performance several nights in succession, he even sent a message round asking for a list of his pauses. But the play was a failure in New York.

Meanwhile, John settled down to enjoy his success. At first it was very exciting, arriving in the dressing room each day to find about thirty letters waiting for him, and dancing and dining out each night. But soon the grinding routine of the long run set in and his enthusiasm ebbed away. The costumes which had delighted him soon lost their glamour. The soles of his shoes got dirty and the colours faded as the clothes were continually cleaned. Matinee days became more and more of a strain. Repeating the performance twice in one day, it was impossible to avoid faking effects that he had previously produced by a genuine expenditure of emotional energy. Still the discipline and experience stood him in good stead and the play never lost its large following of fans, who came to see it again and again. In his curtain speech after the final performance of the long London run, John made another of his public gaffes. 'What a wonderful audience you've been. Some of you have come again and again in spite of the changes in the cast.'

John was not yet thirty but he had reached a very strong position in the theatre. It was not only that he was popular, with enormous box office appeal – he had provided himself with a solid enough background of experience to ensure that he would not be edged out of the limelight as soon as the fashion changed. At the Old Vic he had played even more parts than he had at the Oxford Playhouse, proving his versatility. In the careers of younger actors like Paul Scofield, Alec Guinness, Vanessa Redgrave, Albert Finney, Richard Burton and Peter O'Toole, there have been apexes in the growth of their popularity comparable to the point John had reached with *Richard of Bordeaux*. There have been periods when any one of these actors could have attracted large audiences in almost any play. But Olivier is the only actor since John who has created the same kind of legend and constructed his career with the same kind of care, consistency and, of course, luck.

16   Somerset Maugham and Emlyn Williams

While *Richard of Bordeaux* was still running, John directed two more productions, *Sheppey* by Somerset Maugham and *Spring 1600* by Emlyn Williams. He found it difficult to resolve the three acts of *Sheppey* into the same style. The first struck him as Pineroesque, the second as Shavian and the third as a fantasy.* Maugham, who was living in France, did not arrive until the end of the second week's rehearsal, when he was helpful, but only over points of detail. It was impossible to tell what he felt about the production as a whole. The only clue John got was at a luncheon party in Claridge's after the play had opened. At the end of the meal Maugham drew John into the cloakroom and pressed a book into his hands. It was the published script of *Sheppey*, dedicated to him.

Emlyn Williams was an Oxford undergraduate when John first met him. Fagan had discovered him, staging his first play *Full Moon* and giving him a part in it. As soon as John read his new play, which was called *Spring 1600*, he liked it very much and (since Albery was not interested) decided to present it himself, together with his friend Richard Clowes, whose father offered to find the backing. It turned out to be a very expensive production. There were elaborate sets designed by the Motleys. John engaged a large orchestra, madrigal singers and a mass of extras. Isabel Jeans, who played Lady Coperario, had a Negro attendant and a monkey which she carried on her shoulder until it bit her. £4000 had been spent before the curtain went up.

---

* A friend of Maugham's later told John that Maugham had planned out, years in advance, a schedule of what he was going to write. It may be that *Sheppey* – like *The Circle*, which was written in 1913 but not produced till 1921 – was partly written, put aside, and finished after the original flow of inspiration had dried up.

Emlyn Williams responded amiably enough to most of John's suggestions for cutting and rewriting. The only moment of strain came at a rehearsal when John did not know he was in the theatre. Directing with a megaphone from the dress circle, he announced 'The last act is thin. We must try to make the best of it.' 'I think we all know the last act is thin, John,' a quiet voice said at his elbow, 'but you needn't announce the fact to the whole cast. You might wait for the critics to do that.'

It was only at the dress rehearsal, when Frank Vosper advised him to cut twenty minutes out of the first act, that John realized he had not timed the play properly. But there had been so many changes already he did not want to give the cast new cuts at the last minute. Hoping for the best, he hurried away to perform in *Richard of Bordeaux*. *Spring 1600* ran for three and a half hours.

The press was by no means hostile. But the general feeling was that the story was not strong enough, and despite the cuts that Emlyn Williams (after telephoning John for his permission) quickly arranged, the play ran for only a few weeks.

Richard of Bordeaux, which had opened at the New on 2 February 1933, now ended its London run on 24 March 1934, followed by an eight-week provincial tour.

John could look forward to appearing in modern clothes again in another play which Ronald Mackenzie had finished just before his death – *The Maitlands*. But John had agreed in the meanwhile to direct Gordon Daviot's new play, *Queen of Scots*, which she had written for Gwen Ffrangcon Davies. Ralph Richardson was cast to play Bothwell, but after only one rehearsal he seemed to shy at the big love scenes with Gwen Ffrangcon Davies and withdrew from the production, to be replaced almost immediately by Laurence Olivier, who was now twenty-seven. He had scored big successes in *Beau Geste* and *Private Lives*, but John had never worked with him before.

John created a highly effective ending for the second act by dropping the curtain on the murder scene earlier than Gordon Daviot had planned it. Glen Byam Shaw as Darnley was lying ill in a big four-poster, while George Howe, as his servant, sat on the other side of the candle-lit bedroom, reading from the Bible. John ended the act as Bothwell's hired assassins appeared at the door with spears and lanterns.

Ronald Mackenzie had never shown *The Maitlands* to John, but he had discussed the play at some length with Komisarjevsky, whom he wanted to direct it. Now, a few months after the fatal car smash, Albery started planning a production and Komisarjev-sky sent a script to John, who liked the play but was uncertain whether to play the schoolmaster or his actor brother. The actor struck him as the better part but Komisarjevsky wanted him to play the schoolmaster, which seemed an effective contrast to Richard of Bordeaux. But it turned out to be very unwise to follow Richard of Bordeaux with a part so much less glamorous and so much further away from the image the public had now formed of him. And it was ironic that Komisarjevsky, who had insisted on glamorizing his Baron Tuzenbach in *Three Sisters*, should want to make him dry and unattractive in *The Maitlands*.

The play opened on a very hot night. There had been huge queues all day for pit and gallery tickets. When the curtain went up, John had a paper crown on his head. He was being fitted for a Neptune carnival costume and wearing a shabby sports coat, flannel trousers and a moustache. There was a tremendous burst of applause, followed immediately by an uproar in the gallery. The only word that was clearly audible was 'Idiots'. As soon as the dialogue began, the gallery quietened down and there were no more interruptions. But at the end, after several curtain calls, when John stepped forward to speak about Ronald Mackenzie, a voice from the gallery yelled 'Rubbish'.

The press was fairly respectful but most of the critics thought the play inferior to *Musical Chairs*, and Agate accused John of repeating 'the vein of elegant umbrage at this crude world'. He ambiguously suggested John was 'much too fine and romantic an actor to be happy away from rhetoric and robes', adding that 'if this fine player must be modern it should only be in a Russian blouse. All that goes with the bowler hat defeats him.' Most of the other critics disagreed and Ivor Brown reported that he had 'all his poignant quality with a new muscularity of attack to suit the energy of the writing'.

As *The Maitlands* was nearing the end of its four-month run, Albery offered to present John in his own production of *Hamlet* at the New in November 1934. Here was a magnificent opportunity for him to design a new framework for his own performance without having to economize as Harcourt Williams had done at the Vic. He would have four weeks to rehearse but there was very little time before rehearsals began. Fortunately, ever since *Richard of Bordeaux*, he had been having discussions with the Motleys about how *Hamlet* ought to be designed. He disliked both the late Elizabethan and the early Gothic solutions to the problem, but he had been very impressed by the Dürer note which Fagan had introduced into his OUDS production. 'Rich furs and velvets, plumed helmets and elaborately decorated armour, heavy surcoats and square-toed shoes for the men, sweeping skirts and tightly laced bodices for the women, all this suggested admirably the atmosphere of sensuality and crime and supernatural happenings, played out against a background of cold Northern skies and chilly dawns and the tramp of armies on the march.'

The Motleys showed John some of Cranach's work and quickly produced some promising costume designs. The clothes were made not of expensive materials but of scenery canvas, beautifully stencilled and ornamented with trimmings of fur and velvet, with necklaces and chains of painted rubber, solid-looking but actually quite light to wear. 'Oh it did look *rich*,' Jessica Tandy, the Ophelia, later said, 'Frank Vosper and Laura Cowie as Claudius and Gertrude, looked like two sleek evil cats.' But the whole production cost only £1000. The intention was to run it for only six weeks. It ran for six months.

The permanent set was conceived under the influence of Craig and partly inspired by the set Komisarjevsky had used for *Lear* in his Oxford production of 1925. John had been very impressed by his gold cyclorama and his use of rostrums and steps. For *Hamlet* the Motleys designed a bluish-white cyclorama which could be masked for the interior scenes by festooned canvas curtains, painted with bold stencilled patterns and draped in different ways for different scenes. The stage was filled by a large rostrum which provided various levels, connected by steps and inclines, rather like an impressionistic battleship. This provided an excellent base for variations of grouping and silhouettes but made it hard to suggest that the actors going up and down the stairs were on their way anywhere.

In this, his first Shakespearean production as an actor-director, John did what he was to go on doing in all his productions – engage the best available actors for the supporting parts. There ought, of course to be nothing extraordinary about this, but in fact, with the honourable exception of Tree, many of the star actor-managers had been careful to employ only actors they could rely on to offer little competition to their own performances.

Apart from Jessica Tandy, Frank Vosper and Laura Cowie, John's cast included Jack Hawkins as Horatio, Glen Byam Shaw as Laertes and George Howe as Polonius. John had seen Alec Guinness, who was now twenty, as a drama student, and after trying, unsuccessfully, first to get Bronson Albery to give him a job as an understudy and then to persuade the almost penniless Guinness to accept a loan of £20, John gave him his first chance as Osric. But in the early rehearsals Guinness seemed ineffective, and after ten days John said 'It's no good. Go away for a week and get someone to teach you how to act.' Guinness was utterly miserable. Uncertain whether he had been sacked, he went away and came back at the end of a week. He has no memory of anything he did to improve his performance, but on his return John seemed delighted with it.

His grouping for the Council Chamber scene was based on the drawing Craig had done for the Stanislavsky production in 1910, with Hamlet placed in the foreground by a dark pillar, separated from the courtiers by a shadow which slants across the front of the stage. The King's and Queen's heads formed the apex of a brilliantly lit group in the centre. John ranged his courtiers in a semi-circle around the thrones, hiding Hamlet from the King until Laertes's exit created a space through which Claudius suddenly became aware of Hamlet's menacing figure. Then, as he began to speak, courtiers turned towards him and as Gertrude approached him, the audience's attention was focused on Hamlet's side of the stage.

Anxious to slip "To be or not to be" as smoothly as possible into its context, John walked about as he spoke it, doing his best to get under way before the audience realized that this was the passage that most of them knew by heart.

Not wanting to wear a sword in the Play Scene (because it would have encumbered his movement) but needing to kill Polonius in the scene which immediately follows, John invented a piece of business. In the Play Scene the sword was carried in front of the King, and at the beginning of his prayer scene, although Claudius had taken off his robe and crown, he kept the sword on the floor beside him, as if nervous of being alone without it. Hamlet then picked it up and, standing behind him, made as if to stab him there and then. After deciding not to, it seemed quite natural for Hamlet to go on to his mother's closet still holding the sword in his hand. Then, as the King rose from his knees, he found the sword missing, and the scene faded out on the look of alarm on his face.

John staged the final scene with the Queen and Laertes dying on the thrones, which were set downstage, one on each side. The King died upstage centre on a higher level. The final sequence between Hamlet and Horatio was played on the steps. Fortinbras entered above them with his soldiers, who dipped their banners at the final curtain. In the final scene it is always hard to make the extras' reactions to the foreground action realistic without being distracting. John solved the problem by having the soldiers hold the courtiers back with their halberds.

The most unconventional point about the production was its lack of solemnity. Unlike *Richard II*, *Hamlet* has many moments of comic relief and both in his direction and in his performance, John emphasized the humour wherever he could, even in the graveyard scene. Directing the production, he realized that his experience of comedy was relevant to the task in hand and he had the taste to know just how far he ought to draw on it.

It struck him that as the children of an old father, Ophelia and Laertes should both be decadent and rather shallow. This he thought would help to explain the oddities in their behaviour — Ophelia's instability and Laertes's inconsistency in allowing himself to be manipulated so easily by the King, after such a sturdy display of independence on his rebellious return from France. It was also an innovation to make him wear black on this entrance in mourning for his dead father. Traditionally none of the characters ever wore black except Hamlet. Ellen Terry had wanted to play Ophelia's mad scene in mourning, but Irving had carefully discouraged her.

It was a marathon task to direct at the same time as playing Hamlet. John could not help keeping his eye on his cast while he was acting and often gave them notes afterwards. Glen Byam Shaw was nervous that John would let his attention wander during the duel and that he would go down in history as the actor who put out John Gielgud's eye. Meanwhile John, who was never a good fencer and had to rehearse the fight before each performance, was equally nervous about wounding Glen.

The advance bookings for the production exceeded £1000 – a record then for a non-musical play. The first night audience applauded when the lights went up on the court scene and there was a tempest of cheering at the final curtain. Several critics complained of near-inaudibility, but they also noted John's exhaustion.

In any case it was a historic occasion. J. C. Trewin has called it 'the key Shakespearean revival of its period'. But the critics were not unanimous. For Agate it was 'Everest half scaled' and several reviewers said that the performance lacked passion and depth of emotion. Raymond Mortimer thought 'he makes Hamlet too purely the intellectual'. One reviewer complained of the costumes. 'Hamlet attended the funeral in a sort of burnous of white fur which suited Mr Gielgud but not the scene.'

As usual though, the reviews are only an approximate guide to what actually happened on stage and to the atmosphere in the auditorium on the first night. Few actors are then at their best, and for one who has directed the production besides playing the lead – as John has so often done – exhaustion and a dozen distractions are inevitable. Had the critics come to a later performance of *Hamlet*, their reviews would probably have been more favourable. In any case the verdict of the public was overwhelmingly affirmative. The production ran till 30 March 1935 – 155 performances, a record beaten only by Henry Irving.

18   'The Old Ladies' and 'Noah'

When he was in his twenties, Rodney Ackland had read Hugh Walpole's novel, *The Old Ladies*, which struck him as a good story for a film. Impulsively he sat down to adapt it and, on completing a screenplay, wrote to Walpole asking whether he would be interested to see it. Walpole invited him to tea and advised him to rewrite it for the stage, making no attempt to sell the film rights until the play had been produced.

As soon as the stage version was finished, Ackland brought it to John, who knew and liked the novel. In fact he had already thought of adapting it for the stage himself and had even met Walpole, asking whether he would collaborate on a script. But Walpole had been too busy on another book.

John liked Ackland's script very much but Albery thought the idea commercially unpromising, and so did Horace Watson, the manager of the Haymarket. In the end John decided to put the play on himself in partnership with Richard Clowes, whose father again provided the backing. When they managed to secure Edith Evans, Jean Cadell and Mary Jerrold for the three old ladies, they started rehearsals at once, without having found a theatre. Edith Evans was unhappy about this arrangement. 'I'm awfully sorry John but I can't understand this part until I know which theatre we're going to open in.'

Her relationship with Walpole had been strained from the moment he had explained to her how something happened in the book. 'Oh is it from a book?' she asked. And at one early rehearsal, when both Hugh Walpole and Rodney Ackland were in the theatre, she called out 'Oh Mr Author . . .' Both men stood up, which confused her, and she made matters worse by suggesting 'Oh, shall I call you the author and you the authoress?'

It was difficult to find a suitable theatre. The rehearsal period had finally to be extended from three and a half weeks to six, but this turned out to be an advantage, and John found that of all the plays he had directed it was in this one that he came closest to realizing his intentions. Since three rooms, a hall and a stairway all had to be visible, his first idea was to use a set built straight on to the audience, with two open floors, like a doll's house. But one day, in a rehearsal on the *Hamlet* set at the New, when Edith Evans was sitting in a rocking chair on the highest part of the rostrum while Mary Jerrold was making cups of imaginary tea on a lower level, it occurred to him that this slight differentiation of level was sufficient to suggest that the old ladies were in different rooms. In the lunch break he rushed over to the Motleys' studio on the other side of the road and sketched his idea for them. By the morning a new set had been designed. The training John had unintentionally given himself with his toy theatre was paying rich dividends.

The advantages were twofold: as the sinister, gipsy-like old woman who has designs on the spinster's amber, Edith Evans could dominate the action far more effectively than she could have done if she had had to play all her important scenes near the top of the proscenium opening; she was also able to create a far greater initial impact than she could have done if she had been visible in her room upstairs all through the opening scene, in which she had no part. Instead, the wall which concealed this room was flown out in the blackout.

Ideally the play needed a smaller theatre than the New, but it was here, three days after *Hamlet* closed, that *The Old Ladies* opened. W. A. Darlington's notice paid high tribute to John's direction. 'Not for years in any theatre have I felt the thrill of sheer horror as I felt it last night . . . And not for months have I heard any first night audience cheer as last night's did . . . The certainty with which John Gielgud has timed his effects – the terrifying pause, for example, before Mrs Payne (Edith Evans) moves to enter Miss Beringer's bedroom and frighten her till her poor heart stops.' John had created this pause by making Edith Evans appear on stage earlier than she does in the script.

The first week's box office takings were promising, but though it had seemed a good idea to run the play during the celebrations for George V's Jubilee, and though the streets were full of people, few of them bought tickets for *The Old Ladies*. In a smaller theatre it might have survived, but the overheads at the New were too high. The production moved to the St Martin's but lasted there only for a few weeks.

About this time John received several offers from Hollywood to make a film of *Hamlet*. Had he accepted, his career might have taken a different turn. It might have been he, and not Olivier, who brought Shakespeare successfully to the screen. But he had never been happy in a film studio, and he believed it impossible to make a satisfactory film out of a Shakespeare play. In the next two or three years he saw several Shakespeare films – or at least the beginnings of several. He walked out after ten minutes of *Romeo and Juliet* with Leslie Howard* and Norma Shearer, and he was unable to sit through Max Reinhardt's film of *A Midsummer Night's Dream*, which provoked him to write an indignant letter to Peggy Ashcroft about 'the cuts and the

* He had been approached to play Romeo in it himself but had not been free to accept.

squandering of idiotic money and the whole damn thing . . . it's really like having an operation to see anything you really love, like this superb play, butchered in such an unspeakable way'.

It was in 1935 that John first worked with a director who was to exert almost as much influence as Komisarjevsky on his development as an actor. Michel St Denis was the nephew of Jacques Copeau, the great French director who had founded the company at the Vieux Colombier, where his actors included Louis Jouvet and Charles Dullin. St Denis had first worked as assistant to his uncle and in 1931, seven years after the company had moved from Paris to Burgundy, he took over the direction of it and reorganized it as the 'Compagnie des Quinze'. It was only to survive for three years, but in 1931 the company visited London with productions by St Denis of *Noë* and *Le Viol de Lucrèce* by their resident dramatist, André Obey.

The ensemble playing impressed John enormously and when he read some months later that the original Noah, Pierre Fresnay, an actor of about his own age, was playing the part in English in New York, he was very eager to read the translation. Eventually a script arrived, but it was disappointing – full of American colloquialisms like 'Hey you floozies'. But the part of Noah was extremely attractive and the play imaginative, original and an ideal contrast to *Hamlet*. Albery, who had presented the French production, was keen for the play to be seen in English, and St Denis was keen to direct it again.

Time was short, so instead of having the play retranslated, Albery, St Denis and John decided to use the American version, adapting it as they went along. John contributed most of the rewriting: Michel St Denis could not yet speak much English. John suggested the curtain might go up on him humming the Sailor's Hornpipe but for the rest, he put his performance entirely into the hands of St Denis, who had also played the part himself during the latter half of the French company's London run, taking over from Auguste Bovério, who created the part in France.

John wore the same costume the French actors had worn— enormously wide velveteen trousers, sabots and a fur cap. In fact Noah was dressed like a stage version of a French peasant. The play opened in a heatwave and it was an extremely strenuous part, which involved climbing through trap-doors, balancing on a ladder, miming the storm, all in thick padding and heavy clothes, which were invariably sweat-soaked by the end of the performance.

Marjorie Fielding played Mrs Noah, Marius Goring was Japheth, Alec Guinness was the Wolf and George Devine the Bear. John managed to disguise himself so well that his voice and movements were hardly recognizable. As for his appearance, E. A. Baughan wrote 'For the first time since he has become a star, John Gielgud made an appearance without any applause. Who was the old man working on the Ark while he sang "Life on the ocean wave!!" His red face (strangely suggestive of the rubicund W. C. Fields) peered out of a mass of grey hair. That could not be John Gielgud. But it was.' His front teeth were blacked out with ink, the wide beard and the bushy eyebrows broadened his face, while the mesh of wrinkles combined with long grey hair hanging from the bald wig and the red complexion to transport him fifty years away from Hamlet. But the heavy wig did no good to his own hair, which had already been growing thin during *Musical Chairs*.

Ivor Brown called his Noah 'a prodigious mixture of Lear, Job, Tolstoy and the Old Man of the Sea plagued with a Load of Mischief'. He praised John for avoiding sentimentality, while Agate blamed him for divesting himself of 'Gielgudry' and allowing himself to be clay in the hands of a director who would not let him contribute anything of his own, having made his mind up that all Noahs must be the same.

Accustomed to a much longer rehearsal period than he now had, St Denis had tried to teach his English actors a new technique of stylization, combining mimed and rhythmic movements with naturalistic comedy and realistic emotion. So much of John's performance was *taught* to him by St Denis that it was several weeks before he felt any real freedom inside the role, but it was good to know that he was successful in concealing his own personality, and sometimes he had the feeling of achieving some of the quality he was aiming at. He felt most at home in the scene in which he was lying on deck with the animals, waiting for the wind to come. Of course he lacked the weight that was really needed for the part, but he used something of the technique he had used as Lear at the Vic, and he developed his physical capacity through making different experiments with the part during the ten weeks of the run. At the final performance St Denis said 'At last you are beginning to find the way to play the first act.'

19 Romeo and Olivier, Hitchcock and Komisarjevsky

John had spent most of the summer of 1935 collaborating with Terence Rattigan on a dramatization of *A Tale of Two Cities*. John planned most of the scenario while Rattigan wrote the dialogue. They showed the first two acts to Albery, who promised them that if the third act was equally good he would put the play on in the autumn. They made a great effort to finish it within a week and the Motleys began working on preliminary designs. Albery immediately started casting it, and though no contracts were signed, he made verbal agreements with Fay Compton (for Lucy Manette) Martita Hunt (for Miss Pross) and Mary Clare (for Mme Defarge). John was to double the roles of Sydney Carton and the wicked Marquis St Evrémonde. But then a letter arrived from Sir John Martin-Harvey, who was now almost seventy, demanding that the project be abandoned. He was planning, he said, to play Sidney Carton again himself in another farewell tour of his version of the novel, *The Only Way*. Surely John could not want to take the bread out of an old man's mouth? After consulting Agate and several other drama critics who, surprisingly, all took the view that Martin-Harvey was in the right, John and Albery reluctantly abandoned the whole scheme.

But they were not long at a loss for an alternative. Edith Evans and Peggy Ashcroft were both available: why not revive *Romeo and Juliet* with them as the Nurse and Juliet again, while John alternated the roles of Romeo and Mercutio with another star, preferably Robert Donat? Albery was very enthusiastic about the idea but Donat turned out to be planning a production of *Romeo and Juliet* himself. He was willing to abandon his production, but not to appear in John's.

John now suggested Laurence Olivier. By a maddening coincidence, he too turned out to have plans for a production of his own with his wife Jill Esmond as Juliet, but he agreed to abandon the idea in order to appear with John.

John had already committed himself to start filming with Hitchcock in *The Secret Agent* during the last two weeks in

October, so *Romeo and Juliet* had to be launched by then, leaving only three weeks for rehearsal. At first there were serious problems over the decor. Working very intensively, the Motleys produced three projects for a permanent set within three days, but none of them quite satisfied John. He was in a corner of their studio, distractedly looking over the discarded designs for *A Tale of Two Cities* when a solution occurred to him. The scenes for the Dickens play had been planned to alternate between the two sides of the stage, with some intermediate episodes played on an upper stage reached by a central stairway. This gave him the idea that Juliet's balcony could be built in the centre of the stage and remain there throughout the action, with the upper level concealed by curtains or shutters for the street scenes and the ball. For the scenes in Juliet's bedroom, the balcony could be shown again, together with the interior of the room. Developing the idea he had used in *The Old Ladies*, John asked for the whole of the room's interior to be visible on the platform, together with the balcony outside the windows. With changes of lighting, the action could shift between the balcony, the room within, the below-stairs area where household preparations for the marriage were going on, and the Friar's cell, which remained in position on the far side of the stage, hidden when necessary by a curtain.

John never designed sets for his own productions as Komisarjevsky did, but he worked so very closely with the Motleys that he could collaborate with them at every stage of their work, from the moment they all agreed on a conception. Their set now offered the flexibility of movement he had wanted for *Hamlet*. In that the curtain had to be dropped for each scene-change or the stage-hands would have been seen operating the revolve, but *Romeo and Juliet* had continuous action.

It opened on 17 October 1935 with Laurence Olivier as Romeo and John as Mercutio. He also played the Chorus, wearing a gold mask. Peggy Ashcroft found herself very much in sympathy with Olivier's performance, but it was too modern for the critics. Agate complained that Mr Olivier's Romeo 'showed himself very much in love but rather butchered the poetry', and John was perhaps too gentlemanly as Mercutio. He built his performance around the Queen Mab speech, and certainly that whole scene went extremely well, after getting off to a splendid start when Romeo, Mercutio and Benvolio swept on to the stage in white cloaks, carrying lighted torches. But as

Mercutio, John set fire to his shoes. With a flaming torch in his hand he made such an extravagant gesture that the wadding soaked in methylated spirit fell out and went on burning on the stage-cloth. Bravely he stamped on it, and when his shoe caught fire he stamped on one foot with the other, getting a round of applause from the audience. At subsequent performances, the scene was less spectacular. The L.C.C. banned the torches, alleging fire danger.

Two weeks later, John started work on *The Secret Agent*, which was based not on the Conrad novel but on *Ashenden*, Somerset Maugham's book of short stories. Hitchcock had originally tempted John by describing the part as another Hamlet, only in modern dress — an agent who cannot reconcile himself to the necessity of killing. But, disappointingly, as Hitchcock moved further and further away from Maugham's stories, developing his own ideas, John's part became progressively smaller. Besides Madeleine Carroll, who had just had a big success in *The Thirty-Nine Steps*, Hitchcock engaged Peter Lorre and Robert Young. In the end, the interest was divided between the four of them, with John's part turning out to be rather less effective than the others.

Hitchcock amused himself by playing incessant practical jokes on his actors, but John detested the waiting about and the lack of continuity inevitable in filming. Each sequence had to be split into fragments and each fragment repeated innumerable times. As he told a newspaperman, it was very different from acting in his own productions, in which he could make all his own decisions. 'Alfred Hitchcock has often made me feel like a jelly and I have been nearly sick with nervousness.' Hitchcock too gave interviews to the press about working with John. 'His stage experience is no use to him here. I've had to make him rub out everything and start blank. I've had to rely purely on his intelligence.'

Peter Lorre was addicted to morphine. After withdrawing to his dressing-room to give himself a fix, he would be missing when he was needed on the set and eventually be found hiding in the studio's attics. He was amusing and friendly but a formidable scene-stealer. John would obediently try to keep to the marks on the floor and speak his lines exactly as they were written. So did Lorre in the rehearsals, but as soon as the cameras started rolling, he would improvise new lines and edge himself into positions where the camera would favour him.

95

Much of the work was very uncomfortable. John had to sit for hours in a cramped set representing a railway carriage, while a machine blew vapour across the window before each take. There was a train smash in the film for which he had to lie during several days of filming under a mass of iron girders and rubbish, and he also had to sit for hours in front of a blank screen while Lake Como was unrolled behind him in back projection.

He was still filming every day of the week at the end of November, when he had to replace Laurence Olivier as Romeo, while Olivier took over as Mercutio. The idea of exchanging parts was attractive to the audience, and it was interesting to discover that two totally different performances in each part could fit equally well into the same production. Harley Granville Barker later described it in a letter as 'by far the best bit of Shakespeare I'd seen in years'. But in the scenes they shared, John and Olivier knew each other's lines too well and had to be very careful not to go wrong when the cues came.

Much as Peggy Ashcroft had liked Olivier's less musical approach to the verse and his more realistic approach to the love relationship with Juliet, she found that John as Romeo seemed to carry the audience along with him. He too was full of admiration for the naturalness of her Juliet. Without being at all balletic or self-conscious, she moved with spontaneous impetuosity and charm.

After Hamlet, John found Romeo a far less satisfying part than he had expected. Nor was he pleased with his own performance. *Romeo and Juliet* ran on at the New till the end of March, with John playing Romeo now all the time. It was the longest run of the play on record.

In his review Agate complained 'This Romeo never warms up to Juliet until she is cold.' But in a broadcast he awarded the palm to John. 'If Romeo were just a lovesick gumph, occasionally falling into a deeper trance in which he speaks unaccountable poetry, then Olivier is your Romeo. But if it is a question of playing Shakespeare's analytical and critical lover, then Gielgud's the man.' Herbert Farjeon was representative of the critical consensus: 'Mr Olivier was about twenty times as much in love with Juliet as Mr Gielgud is, but Mr Gielgud speaks most of the poetry far better than Mr Olivier.'

The rivalry between the two actors, which was to last through their careers, was launched in fine style. In an interview with Kenneth Tynan, Olivier has said of John:

> I've never thought of myself as quite the same actor as he is, not the same sort of actor. I've always thought that we were the reverses of the same coin, perhaps. I've seen, as if you had a coin, the top half John, all spiritual, all spirituality, all beauty, all abstract things; and myself as all earth, blood, humanity; if you like, the baser part of humanity without that beauty. I've never been so interested in that side, though naturally I've had to develop something of it in order to be an actor at all. But I've always felt that John missed the lower half and that made me go for the other. I suppose I must have sensed a sort of possible rivalry between us, that might last all our lives, I don't know. But whatever it was, when I was playing Romeo I was carrying a torch, I was trying to sell realism in Shakespeare. I believed in it with my whole soul and I believed that Johnny was not doing that enough. I thought that he was paying attention – to the exclusion of the earth – to all music, all lyricism, and I was for the other side of the coin. I dived for that.

To him it seemed that John was going through a phase of over-adjusting to what was expected of him, over-conscious of his beautiful voice and his lyrical gift, at the expense of reality. 'It made me rebellious.* It made me think that Shakespeare was now being handled in a certain way, and because of the extremely strong influence that any man of John's power and gifts would have on a company, all the company would be going that way. So when I entered this company I rather cut across it, thinking in my innocence that they'd say "Ah, this is the real one, because the other's not quite right." But of course it never works like that. I think John rather leant towards my sort of naturalism, but it didn't alter his own convictions. All it did was that I saw him going a little further into the expected field of florid elocutory renditions. By that time he had almost settled for almost singing it, which I didn't like.' Nevertheless, the influence that John exerted on Olivier was not entirely negative. He told me in the same interview that he would never have gone to the Old Vic in 1937 if John had not gone there first. But for John he might never have become a classical actor at all, but after an experiment in management with Ralph Richardson, he might have gone on devoting himself to modern plays by writers like J. B. Priestley.

The last production in John's three-play contract with Albery was *The Seagull* which was to open on 20 May 1936, directed, at John's suggestion, by Komisarjevsky. This was the first full

---

* I am no longer quoting from the Tynan interview but from one Sir Laurence gave me.

scale West End production of a Chekhov play. Edith Evans was Arkadina, Peggy Ashcroft Nina, Stephen Haggard Konstantin. Alec Guinness had only a few lines as a workman in the first act. Komisarjevsky provided a new translation of his own.

He had a very ambivalent attitude towards the commercial theatre. He never asked high fees for directing, but he designed a wilfully expensive set for the first two acts, demanding that the leaves on the trees should be made of silk, and he opened the first rehearsal with a most unflattering talk about the state of the English theatre and the behaviour of West End actors. Later it came to John's ears that Komisarjevsky had said 'Of course John Gielgud and Edith Evans are so successful now that they only want to play themselves.' This was unfair. At thirty-two, John could still have played Konstantin, as he had before, and the people who came to the play specially to see him would have been much happier to find him in the younger, more romantic part. But John, rightly concerned to go on widening his range, preferred to play Trigorin.

Although he had already suffered, as Baron Tuzenbach, from Komisarjevsky's interference with Chekhov's characterization, he was not expecting to be asked to romanticize Trigorin. When Stanislavsky had played the part at the Moscow Art Theatre, Chekhov complained that instead of making Trigorin handsome and elegant, he ought to have worn torn shoes and check trousers. Knowing this, John felt puzzled and unhappy when Komisarjevsky insisted on making Trigorin dress and behave like a fashionable gigolo. He may have been trying to cover what he imagined was a weakness in the play, but it is more likely that he was yielding to what he thought the West End public would want from John – that Komisarjevsky himself was being 'commercial'. But John put himself entirely in Komisarjevsky's hands and in his first night curtain speech he paid generous tribute to the 'inspired direction' which had made the cast love the play as much as Komisarjevsky did himself.

The critics were not altogether convinced by the new-style Trigorin. Agate was sure that 'nobody who could look and listen to Nina as this actor did in the third act would have behaved towards her as he does towards the end of the play'. Ivor Brown was uneasy at the excessive charm and at the failure to highlight Trigorin's insincerity, but he was sentimentally willing to forgive: 'He softens the edges of the part and rightly for Trigorin has looked into his own heart and found but the dough and sustenance of comfort.'* In any case it was certainly good for John to be playing Chekhov again at this stage of his development. As he has said himself, 'With the Shakespeare parts I learned how to project a performance and with the Chekhov parts I learned how not to project it.'

The production was a big success, but John, who had agreed to play Hamlet in New York, could only stay in it for six weeks. Before he left he had a letter from Marie Tempest. 'You are a grand artist, my dear, and with your taste *and* sanity, will go very far. I still remember your poor dear face with Edith on her knees to you. Lovely!'

20 'Hamlet' on Broadway

For two years the American impresario Guthrie McClintic, husband of the actress Katharine Cornell, had been offering a New York production of *Hamlet*, but John had demurred because he knew Leslie Howard was also planning to play the part in America. But after seeing John's Hamlet in Edinburgh McClintic made him a definite offer for the autumn, assuring him that Howard's plans had now been abandoned. McClintic, who wanted to direct the new production himself, said he could 'present' John's performance to better advantage than he had in his own production.

After *The Seagull*, John went on holiday to the South of France, where he rented an old farmhouse with a vine-covered verandah and a swimming pool. McClintic arrived with his designer Jo Mielziner for a conference about the *Hamlet* decor. John stipulated that he would like his costume to be much the same as it had been in London – breeches and a sixteenth-century Spanish collar rather than the tunic and tights of an

---

* After he read the notices, Komisarjevsky defended himself in a letter to John, pointing out that each of the three fine Russian actors he had seen as Trigorin had been dressed elegantly – Dalmatov at the Imperial Stage, Stanislavski at the Moscow Arts and Bravich at his sister's theatre.

earlier period, as worn by Barrymore and other previous Hamlets. Mielziner was thinking of basing the costume designs on Van Dyck. But John felt that Van Dyck was too domesticated and mild, with his silks and satins, and that Rembrandt might have been a better source, with his chiaroscuro of dramatic light and his men in armour with helmets, fur caps and cloaks. But the Americans did not seem to appreciate the distinction.

John was much happier about Mielziner's proposals for the set – variations of level and two big towers which would be re-angled, to produce different pictorial effects. The play scene was to be done with a semi-circle of braziers in front, the players with their backs to the auditorium and the King and Queen on a platform above in the centre, the lights showing up their faces and casting shadows on to a big arras behind them with glimpses of the night sky through a high doorway.

Apart from John and Harry Andrews, who had been brought to New York as a possible Fortinbras and ended up as Horatio – a promotion which only earned him an extra ten dollars a week – the only other English actor was to be Malcolm Keen, who would play the King, as he had in the London production with Barrymore, and speak the part of the Ghost, which would be represented on stage by a masked figure. Glen Byam Shaw, the London Laertes, was to have played the part again, but to John's disappointment, this plan fell through. When the time came to leave England, John was nervous about the whole project and sorry to be leaving London, though the pangs of departure were alleviated by a party given for him by Peggy Ashcroft, who was now married to Komisarjevsky.

He sailed to New York on the *Normandie*, trying not to think about the play. Approaching the harbour, he rushed to the upper deck to see the view which had impressed him so much eight years ago. This time he had rather too long to look at it, as the boat took nearly six hours to dock. McClintic, who was on the quay to meet him, drove him to his house on the East River. Katharine Cornell was away and John was given her room. It was a very hot evening and they had dinner in the garden, watching the lights on the boats that passed beyond the garden wall. After dinner Judith Anderson, who was playing the Queen, arrived straight from the hairdresser with her hair dyed and elaborately styled for the part. John stared at it. 'Why not wear a wig?' he asked. 'It looks better and it's so much less trouble.'

The first readings were held in the bar of the Martin Beck

Theatre. Pressmen were allowed in, and McClintic posed for the photographers, perching on a chair with his hat tilted on the back of his head. He was very nervous and made a lot of jokes. Lilian Gish, the Ophelia, and Judith Anderson both wore enormous hats and bent low over their scripts, hiding their faces. John, though he had not looked at a script for two years, found he knew every word of his part. But he had to endure two more weeks of readings and to try not to show off in front of the new company.

The Council Chamber scene was very different from John's London staging of it. The courtiers left Hamlet alone with the King and Queen as soon as the King began to address him. This seemed to John a pity: Hamlet's ironic formality and Claudius's measured paternalism have a greater edge when a group of obsequious courtiers is listening. It also deprived Hamlet of the emphasis on his loneliness as the courtiers leave the stage before his first soliloquy. But naturally he tried to behave tactfully about all McClintic's direction.

Generally the costumes were over-elaborate and the stage pictures unnecessarily sumptuous, but this did not prevent John from giving a brilliant, highly charged performance, full of original detail and mercurial changes of mood and voice. In the Council Chamber scene he was morose and abstracted, weighed down with a grief he communicated to the audience at once on the simple line "Ay madam, it is common". But he held himself firmly in check until he was left alone for the first soliloquy, in which he revealed the full depth of his misery and disgust. At Horatio's entrance he leapt to his feet with a cry, giving the audience a sudden glimpse of Hamlet as he must have been before his father's death.

One of his best moments was at the end of the Ghost scene, when Horatio, seeing Hamlet shivering with cold and nervous exhaustion, took off his cloak to wrap it round him. Hamlet started towards the exit, then suddenly noticing that Horatio was now without a cloak, stepped back and threw his arm and cloak together round Horatio's shoulders as they left the stage together.

Another swift change of mood came immediately after the note of defiance he struck at the end of the Closet Scene. As the Queen goes out, 'his braggadocio drops from him like the false mask that it is. He sways against the wall, his head and shoulders sink. For a moment he looks after her and then, with repressed anguish, the one word, "Mother" – the cry of a child left in the dark.'*

At first John rebelled against McClintic's suggestion that he should play the death scene standing up, but he soon came to like the idea, realizing how impressive it looked to command the audience with his full height for the last words spoken before his death and to sink to the ground after "the rest is silence" with Horatio catching him as he fell.

The play was to open in Toronto on Wednesday 30 September 1936. But on Monday the set was still not ready, so on Tuesday there were two complete dress rehearsals. John had the last scene completely rearranged as he wanted it and several other major alterations that he suggested were accepted although there were only six days before the New York opening at the old Empire Theatre in Times Square.

After the week in Toronto, the company travelled to Rochester for two performances in a huge theatre which had a wide orchestra pit with a big Wurlitzer organ in the middle of it. John caught a heavy cold and was unable to sleep on the long journey to New York. There was a dress rehearsal but he did not go to it. He went to bed for the day in a fever of anxiety that his voice might fail before the opening.

On Thursday he felt restless all day. He went to a cinema for an hour or two of the afternoon and at six in the evening he went to the theatre, to find a mass of good luck telegrams in his dressing-room, most of them from American actors and actresses he did not even know. It was the first fashionable opening of the season and John tried not to listen when McClintic came in with the news that the theatre was packed with celebrities. Lilian Gish came in with a Hawaiian 'lei' of white carnations, hanging it round his neck for luck.

He found his way to his position in the darkness between the first and second scenes and when the lights came up there was such a roar of applause that he was almost too moved to speak his first lines. At the final curtain, the ovation was overwhelming, with a lot of cheering, which was unusual in New York. John had three or four curtain calls alone, with the cast applauding him from the wings, and the first person to congratulate him in his dressing-room was Noël Coward. But in the morning the *New York Times* was surprisingly cool and the *Herald Tribune*

* Rosamond Gilder, *John Gielgud's Hamlet*. Methuen, 1937. This was one of the first books ever to be devoted to a single performance.

disappointing, though most of the other critics were more favourable. John Mason Brown saluted 'a sensitive clear-cut face which is so moulded that it can amplify every passing thought that takes possession of his mind and which is the equal of his voice in flexibility'. There was cheering again on the second night and at subsequent performances. It was the first time this had happened in New York since Alla Nazimova had appeared the previous year in *Ghosts*.

Leslie Howard had decided to stage his production after all, and only ten days later it opened in Boston, scheduled to arrive in New York within four weeks. But there were changes in the cast. Gertrude Elliott, the widow of Sir Johnston Forbes-Robertson, who was rehearsing as the Queen, withdrew from the production and an actress who had once played the part with Raymond Massey was rushed in to replace her. The rest of Howard's cast was mostly English, which was embarrassing for John, with his mainly American cast, and he was afraid that his own run might not last for more than ten or twelve weeks. He could hardly hope to compete with Barrymore's New York record of 101 performances.

Meanwhile Maxwell Anderson had sent him a verse play about Rudolf of Austria called *Masque of Kings*, but John was more interested in doing another play by Emlyn Williams, who was in New York at the time. John was also considering the possibility of following *Hamlet* with a limited New York season of *Richard II*, which he could perhaps bring back to London afterwards. He would have liked America to see his own production of a Shakespeare tragedy and *Richard* had not been produced in New York for a long time.

One night he received a note from Mrs Patrick Campbell. 'I am in front tonight. Give me the beauty I long for.' Afterwards she advised him not to walk about during "To be or not to be" because the movement distracted from the words. He took her advice and when she saw it again afterwards she was most enthusiastic. 'It was wonderful last night. With "To be or not to be" you performed a miracle — I felt I had never heard it before ... I knew you were tired — the two ladies with me exclaimed often "How marvellous he is" and one lady with tears said "I never saw Hamlet look as though he knew he were going to die — I hope he won't die — is he strong?"' Mrs Pat was less kind about the Closet Scene. 'Why do you sit on the bed?' she asked Judith Anderson. 'Only housemaids sit on the bed.' And talking to McClintic about the Ghost, who wore a large mask, 'Why does the Ghost have mumps?'

Writing to his mother about Mrs Pat, John said 'She looks well but is very sad – has been alone in a cottage up at Arrowhead, above Hollywood, for six months, till her heart was affected by the height, and she had fainting fits. She was told to come down and rest, and stays in bed here a great deal – is writing another bad book – no maid or companion but the eternal pekinese – but she is grand and majestic as ever. Woollcott wrote she is like a sinking ship firing on her rescuers.'

It was only after Leslie Howard's *Hamlet* had opened that John's became a real success. People must have been waiting for the critics to make up their minds for them which production they ought to see. Leslie Howard had taken ten curtain calls and made a speech, but the morning press was hostile. John Mason Brown said that Howard's production was better, but 'unlike Mr Gielgud's, his performance can scarcely be described as an interpretation – Mr Gielgud's Prince may be lacking in consistency, it may introduce us to several new Hamlets before the evening is over, but it is almost unfailingly brilliant in its scene rendering and in its delivery of individual speeches. Mr Howard's Prince is consistent in only one thing – its avoidance of what lies behind the lines.' One reviewer announced that John could drop the GIEL: his Hamlet would simply be known as the GUD Hamlet.

Alexander Woollcott, who had given up his influential radio show two years before, broke his silence to go on the air in support of John, whom he classed with Barrymore and Forbes-Robertson – 'a great play so beautifully done' that he wanted 'to ring the church bells and arrange with the Mayor for dancing in the streets'. John's telephone rang incessantly. A member of the company told him that Leslie Howard was said to be 'more an antique Romeo than a Dane'. John's Wednesday matinee was sold out, with 62 people standing, and the week's takings were up by 3000 dollars.

The Leslie Howard *Hamlet* did poor business at the box office but he tried to turn it into a success, making a speech every night and advertising in the papers. A Ladies' Club tried to arrange a dinner for the two Hamlets to meet, but John declined, though he and Howard exchanged courteous telegrams. There were rumours that each actor, wearing dark glasses, had been to a matinee of the other's performance, but John never went to Howard's and no-one seemed to know for certain whether Howard had been to his.

Now that the production had settled down, John had a certain amount of time for parties, concerts, exhibitions and nightclubs. He enjoyed seeing the Lunts, Helen Hayes, Ruth Gordon, Katharine Cornell, Burgess Meredith, Thornton Wilder, Woollcott and Noël Coward. Hearing that a lawsuit on his behalf against Gaumont British had been favourably settled out of court for £700, he spent three hundred dollars on a Dufy watercolour of Versailles with the statue of Louis XIV on horseback.

Despite the pre-Christmas slump business kept up very well and the *Hamlet* production was moved to a larger theatre, the St James's, where McClintic hoped for at least three weeks good business with a short tour to follow. The St James's was on a main street, and on New Year's Eve *Hamlet* was played to an accompaniment of hooters and penny whistles. But it was a record week at the box office, which took just on twenty thousand dollars.

Mrs Pat gave John what he afterwards described as one of the most impressive experiences of his life. A friend of hers, the playwright Edward Sheldon, had suffered for fourteen years from a petrifying paralysis, which had also blinded him. Earlier he had been a close friend of John Barrymore and had written several plays including *Romance*, a phenomenally successful melodrama about a clergyman's love affair with an Italian opera singer. Sheldon was then in love with Doris Keane, who created the part of the singer. But now, lying on a bed like a catafalque, with his head bent right back and a black bandage across his eyes, he received endless visits from theatre people in a cheerful penthouse room, surrounded by flowers, books and photographs. He had all the newspapers read aloud to him and he was astonishingly well informed about everything, especially the theatre. Neatly shaved and wearing a jacket, collar and tie, but with his hands hidden under the counterpane, he could talk to strangers as if he had known them all his life. 'He seems quite removed in some marvellous way from everything but the mind,' John wrote, 'like some extraordinary human oracle.'

Alexander Woollcott gave a dinner for John, Ruth Gordon, Lilian Gish and Thornton Wilder. John described the writer as 'a funny little nervous man like a dentist turned professor – shy at first and then suddenly incoherently explosive like a soda water syphon, with expressive hands when he suddenly speaks of something he feels strongly about'.

On Monday 5 January 1937, John broke the Barrymore record and on Tuesday that of an obscure American actor who had been discovered to have played 102 performances of *Hamlet*. John was now undisputed champion and made his first curtain speech. With the two runs in London, he had now given 400 performances of the part.

The run continued until the end of January and in the final week numerous parties were given for him. He met Stravinsky, Gloria Swanson and many American stars. At one party Helen Hayes told Mrs Pat that she wore her years like a crown, and Noël Coward spoilt it by saying 'I hope you keep it straight, dear.'

During the three-week tour of Boston, Washington and Philadelphia, John went with Lilian Gish to have tea at the White House. Mrs Roosevelt was 'gracious if a bit vague – a very plain keen-faced woman with a rather grating laugh. Beforehand we were taken in to see the President, who was charming, urbane and gracious, rather like Godfrey Tearle in manner.' There were ramps on the stairs and landings to allow Roosevelt's chair to be wheeled about the house.

The tour could have gone on longer but John was impatient to start work back in England on Emlyn Williams's romantic play *He Was Born Gay*. In the last two weeks of the tour he was counting the number of *Hamlet* performances like a schoolboy counting days to the end of term. Snow-bound in a Philadelphia hotel, he spent a lot of money cabling casting suggestions to Emlyn. Back in New York, he received several Hollywood film offers but refused them all.

Forced to be inactive on the voyage back, he suddenly realized how exhausted he was, and by the time he arrived in London he felt for the first time in his life that he had no desire to act, only to take a long rest. He went down to the cottage he had acquired in Essex, and went for long walks. Soon he was feeling eager for rehearsals to start.

2 1 The Queen's Season

In America it had seemed almost inconceivable that John's return to the West End could be anything but a triumph. But failure can be sobering and when Emlyn Williams's *He Was Born Gay* closed after twelve performances, he was forced to think very seriously about what he most wanted to do. Ever since he had seen the Compagnie des Quinze he had been savouring the idea of forming a company of his own and he had discussed the possibility with Michel St Denis when they were working together in *Noah*. The idea went on developing in his mind through his four years at the New Theatre but he had been too successful and too busy acting and directing to do anything else. But in June 1937, he wrote to Harley Granville Barker for advice. His reply went to the heart of the matter:

I am only afraid that any counsel – such as it would be – might increase and not lessen your distraction. For distracted – if I guess right – you must be; between two aims; the one, which is really forced on you, a personal career; the other, the establishing of a *theatre*, without which your career will not be, I think you rightly feel, all that you proudly wish it to be. It was Irving's dilemma; he clung on to one horn of it for a number of glorious years; then he was impaled on the other, and it killed him. It was Tree's, and he would have died bankrupt but for *Chu Chin Chow*. George Alexander, thrifty Scotsman, replied to me when I congratulated him on the twenty-fifth anniversary of his management: Well, I've not done much for the drama (though in a carefully limited fashion he had) but I've paid salaries every Friday night without fail, and *that's* to my credit. And it was. I won't say that there too was my dilemma; because I never had such a career in prospect, I should suppose. But I pinned my faith to the *theatre* solution; and finding it – with a war and a 'peace' on – no go, I got out. It must be your dilemma, I think; for you have rather the Irving than the Alexander conception of your job . . . The question is, have times changed? Can you yet hope to establish a theatre? If not the blessed 'National' Theatre (but names mean nothing) such a one as Stanislavsky's or even Reinhardt's of thirty years back? For that you'll gladly sacrifice as much of your personal career as need be – this I see; but naturally you don't want to make the sacrifice in vain. Is a compromise practicable? I don't know. Everyone English will be for compromise, just because they are English. And even the work has to be done in England. Perhaps one must accept there the fruits of the national virtue and failing combined. It makes for good politics but bad art. And so it is, you see, that the question (for me) opens up; no longer for me a practical question, therefore I can still say *Theatre or nothing* and not suffer. For you a devilishly practical one; so, who am *I* to counsel you? Only I'd say: do not expect to pick more than a few grapes from thistles and don't expect them always to be of the best quality!

Yours
Harley Granville Barker.

But you have given us some fine things and you'll give us more, I don't doubt – by whichever path you go.

Having liked almost everything about the Old Vic except the shortage of time and money, John was now able, at any rate for a season, to reproduce very similar conditions in a West End theatre but with a West End level of budgeting and long re-rehearsal periods. Today, with the National Theatre and the Royal Shakespeare Company, actors are used to long term contracts and long rehearsal periods, but in 1937 the actors could hardly believe it when they were offered nine months of security in the West End, with seven to nine weeks of rehearsal for each play. John and John Perry put up £5000 each and John collected an excellent company, consisting almost entirely of actors he had already worked with. Peggy Ashcroft was to be the leading lady and the others included Frederick Lloyd, Leon Quartermaine, George Devine, Glen Byam Shaw, Harcourt Williams, George Howe, Alec Guinness, Harry Andrews, Michael Redgrave and Dennis Price. The leading actors were paid on a percentage basis, as were the guest stars – Gwen Ffrangcon Davies, Carol Goodner, Angela Baddeley – who were engaged for only one or two of the four plays. Each play was to run for eight to ten weeks. *Richard II* was to open the season, followed by *The School for Scandal, Three Sisters* and *The Merchant of Venice*.

Peggy Ashcroft and John have always prided themselves on creating a pleasant atmosphere around them, though John by speaking impulsively has often upset people with his tactlessness. Once while he was reminiscing to his new company about his American experience, he said 'When I did Hamlet for Guthrie

McClintic, I had a rather poor Horatio. Oh it was you, Harry. Well, you've improved so much since then . . .'

John directed *Richard II* himself, with designs by the Motleys, who had already designed the play for him two years previously when he produced it for the OUDS with David King Wood and Vivien Leigh. The set had been simple but admirable; now they were more ambitious and the results were over-elaborate. One critic described their new garden scene as being 'exactly like a model of Dorothy Vernon's steps at Haddon Hall set inside a West End florist's'.

In his performance, too, John made the mistake of being over-elaborate. Basically he felt very confident about the part but having failed to please Agate with his Old Vic *Richard II*, he was determined to introduce a new subtlety which would win a good notice from him this time. But Agate behaved very unprofessionally. On the first night, he was seen in the foyer chatting to his friends after the curtain had gone up on the last act and he never returned to his seat. But before writing his notice he came back to see the last act at the midweek matinee, afterwards going round to apologize to John, and his review on Sunday said that his interpretation of the part 'has gained in depth, subtlety, insight, power since his Richard of eight years ago. Now indeed Mr Gielgud shows himself to be an actor at once *profond et reveur*.'

The other reviews were equally favourable. The *Manchester Guardian* reported that his vocal range was wider than ever and that he tended less to hysterical sharpness in his higher register. He was applauded for highlighting Richard's 'popinjay petulance' and for not trying to win the audience by playing for sympathy, as Tree, for instance, had done. Peter Fleming paid tribute to the ensemble playing. 'It might almost be a Russian company, so compact and smooth is the texture of a large cast, most of whom have bad parts.'

Granville Barker came to see the play. 'The performance is very good,' he told John, 'but I think you should act on the words and not in between them.' After this, John pared his performance down so much that he cut fifteen minutes off the running time. Although he had said nothing to the other actors about his intention of speeding up, no one appeared to be troubled by his change of tempo.

Barker also wrote to John:

I applauded you at first sight for so unselfishly hiding yourself in a corner. But I fear you were wrong to do so. I fancy W.S. thought of

the scene as a meeting of the Privy Council – Richard presiding . . .
But the point is that while W.S. doesn't begin to *write* Richard till he
comes back from Ireland (till he becomes himself, a *man* and not merely
a King) he does keep one wondering and guessing what sort of a man
he is up to that point and what the devil he will do next, and the more
we see of his cryptic face the better. You got that admirably during the
Lists scene – as good a piece of Shakespeare staging as I can remember.
But I'd like it done from the beginning. Richard, of course, carries too
much sail for his keel and so swings violently from side to side at any puff
of wind. But his stillness and silence in between . . . show us the poet
who is not really living in this practical world at all, but in one of his
own imagination.

All the 'plastique' of this part of the production and the blending of
the scene . . . all that scenic invention excellent. Gaunt's death scene
particularly and the colloquy afterwards (though damn all that crossing
and genuflecting and *Dies Irae*) first rate . . .

I thought during the first half of the play they were imitating each
other; then I found they were imitating you and your taste for sadder
sforzandi: good enough for Richard and clearly indicated for 'Down –
down I come – ' and 'No lord of thine, thou haught, insulting man – '
appropriate to him but quite wrong for Augustus Caesar–Bolingbroke
or Mowbray or the 'tenor' gallantry of Aumerle.

The thing got – I began to swear – more and more hung up as it
went on, and you began to play more and more astride the verse instead
of in it. The scenic invention of the deposition scene was again admirable. Bolingbroke on the throne, you wandering about below like a lost
creature – admirable (but *oh*, if you'd have let the marvellous and
sweet music of that verse *just carry you along with it*). The tune of that
'bucket and well' bit (again the business admirable) and even more of
the 'No deeper wrinkles yet . . .' It is like an *andante* of Mozart.
Shakespeare has done it *for* you. Why not let him?

For the second production, *The School for Scandal*, John had
engaged Tyrone Guthrie as director, but Guthrie, who was also
an actor at this time, was busy in a film called *Beachcomber*, with
Charles Laughton and Elsa Lanchester. The result was that he
came to very few of the rehearsals.

John had given him a completely free hand with the production
and, trustingly, had not even asked to see the designs. The
combination of cheerless, modernistic sets and 1797 costumes
(which Guthrie thought more amusing than those of 1777, when
the play was written) irritated the critics. Partly concerned to
show the grubbiness beneath the polished veneer of the social
scene, Guthrie also invented a great deal of funny but distracting
business and an elaborate dancing finale.

He found an enormous semi-circular sofa and had the actors bouncing up and down on it, which got a few laughs but effectively killed Sheridan's lines. For this kind of comedy, as John well knew, it is essential to place the characters far enough away from each other. The scandal scene is obviously meant to be played with them on small chairs, throwing each other the ball of conversation; Guthrie crowded them all together cheek by jowl on his large settee. And at the dress rehearsal John was disconcerted to find that during his first scene with Lady Sneerwell, there was a maid who was busy on the other side of the double set, making her mistress's bed and finally getting into it herself. Many good points were killed and many good situations never came to life. As Barker said, too much *bon ton* was sacrificed and Lady Sneerwell's salon became 'a bit of a bear garden'. The auction scene was played straight out to the audience, which did not tally with the convention of the rest of the production. Altogether there was too little gaiety and too much movement. What was welcome, though, was Guthrie's reaction against the Victorian tradition of bows and flourishes, snuff-taking and by-play with the cane, a tradition which had survived through Benson and Tree right up to Playfair's productions at Hammersmith.

Joseph Surface is a comparatively small role. He is not on stage for more than forty minutes, has only three scenes and very little to do until the screen scene. But by far the greatest success of the production was John's characterization – in spite of the fact that at his first entrance on the first night his mind went blank and he had to take the line from the prompter – an experience he had never had before.

Joseph Surface was very different from any part he had played – unsympathetic, sardonic, hypocritical, amused at his own corruption. John lightened the character's calculation with charm, embroidered his evil with elegance. He was laconic and languid, with a suave solemnity that beautifully underlined the hypocrisy. It was his first experience of Sheridan since RADA, and his comedy style suited both the part and the play. If anything was lacking, it was the gaiety and fun that the part requires and in trying to seduce Lady Teazle, he carried on too much as if he were involved in a serious discussion. But Desmond MacCarthy called it the best Joseph Surface he ever saw, and Laurence Olivier recently described it as 'the best light comedy performance I've ever seen or ever shall'.

John had invited Michel St Denis to direct *Three Sisters* and

approached Gwen Ffrangcon Davies to play Olga, the eldest
sister. He had discussed his idea for a season with her when
they were on tour together with *He was Born Gay* and naturally
she must have been disappointed that she was not invited to be
the company's leading lady. But when eventually she accepted
the part of Olga she quickly made friends with Peggy Ashcroft.
Both actresses were much too honest and generous-minded to
resent each other once they came to work together.

Carol Goodner was Masha and Peggy Ashcroft Irina. John
had thought of playing Andrey, the brother, but St Denis persuaded him to play Colonel Vershinin. John then cast Michael
Redgrave as Andrey but St Denis did not agree. George Devine
was given the part and Redgrave played Baron Tuzenbach.
After three days of rehearsals, St Denis accused him of giving
the Baron a personality. 'But surely an actor must try just that,'
Redgrave objected. No, said St Denis, the whole point was
that this man didn't make sense when he talked. 'Nobody
listens to him.' Thoroughly disconcerted, Redgrave just mum-
bled the lines. 'That's it,' St Denis enthused, 'that's the way this
man should talk.' And from this negative start, Redgrave was
able to build up a brilliantly understated performance.

Just as before, in his English production of *Noah*, St Denis
arrived at the first rehearsal with set ideas about every move and
every piece of stage business. John did not feel altogether at
home as Vershinin, but having once had the experience, as Noah,
of putting himself entirely into St Denis's hands, he did not feel
at all inclined to abdicate initiative in the same way, especially
now that he was master in his own theatre. But as the eight weeks
of rehearsals went on, he became more comfortable in the part
and during the play's run he gradually grew more satisfied with
his performance. Even more strongly than in his previous
experiences of Chekhov, he had the feeling that the acting
was independent of audience reaction. The stage was like a home
where the cast came every night to go through the same lines
and moves, with their timing unaffected by laughter and applause. All that mattered was that their behaviour should be truthful in relation to one another. By now the company had become
such a close-knit group that there was a harmony, almost a family
feeling, among the actors, which contributed substantially to the
atmosphere of the play. But John was disappointed when Michael
Redgrave decided to leave after *Three Sisters* to accept a film
contract he had been offered.

Altogether it was a brilliant production which made quite an extraordinary impact on the public. The play was the success of the season, and when John arranged a midnight matinee so that actors who were themselves performing in the evenings could come to see it, the company was given a huge ovation and he received dozens of enthusiastic letters from other actors. The great impresario C. B. Cochran wrote 'Not many times in my life have I seen anything as good, anywhere.'

He also had a letter from Constance Garnett. 'Ever since I began translating Chekhov – eighteen years ago – I've hoped and longed to see his plays adequately produced in England. Well, I had given up hoping for it. There have been some conscientious, painstaking efforts (as at the Old Vic) but it seemed impossible for solid English actors to enter into the liquid temperament of Russians. You have achieved it and I want to thank you for the great pleasure of seeing my dreams fulfilled.'

John directed *The Merchant of Venice* himself, as well as playing Shylock, but the strain of the season was beginning to tell on him and he found it difficult to give enough help even to actors he knew very well. He used to stand at the back of the pit and shout to George Devine, who was playing Lancelot Gobbo, 'For God's sake make me laugh.' But he tried not to be impatient or intolerant and because he was flexible and always alive with energy and ideas, (some good, some bad) he seemed never to lose the goodwill of his actors.

Scenically it was a pretty and ingenious production, moving swiftly in a semi-permanent arrangement of steps and curtains. But if the audience was expecting a patriarchal, Irvingesque Shylock, they were in for a disappointment. Because of what was happening in Hitler's Germany, the public would have been more likely to approve of a dignified, noble, martyred Shylock, but John could not feel that Shakespeare intended the Christians to emerge as villains. Following Harley Granville Barker, who wrote to him about 'the sordid little outsider, passionate, resentful, writhing under his wrongs – which are real – and the contempt of the Venetians,' John wanted to create a Shylock who was rather ridiculous in his villainy. He tried to suggest a Venetian ghetto-Jew, a mean little rat of a money-lender, lacking in dignity, a scavenger. With his clothes and his movements he gave Shylock a very strange shape, robes spreading like a gipsy's, hunching, crouching, lamenting, scrabbling about. He looked rather young, though almost bald, with straggling hair, straggling beard, and a ring in his ear. In no characterization since Noah had he got further away from his own personality, and Laurence Olivier counts this as one of the best performances John has ever given.

Still it was hard for him to direct himself, especially in the Tubal scene, which he played too hysterically. Needing someone to tell him where to use control and where to find the climaxes, he asked Glen Byam Shaw, who was playing Gratiano, to co-direct with him.

One reviewer complained that John's Shylock fell 'rather from the pavement to the gutter than from the mountain to the abyss' but the *New Statesman* praised his refusal to sentimentalize.

> When he is on the stage you can feel the whole house motionless under the painful weight of his realism. In the trial scene he obliged us to suspend disbelief in the impossible story, and when he stropped his knife upon his shoe, we were appalled, not by fear for Antonio, but by the sight of hatred turned to madness. His appearance throughout was extraordinary – gummy, blinking eyes, that suggested some nasty creature of the dark, and loquacious hands with as many inflections as his voice. 'But stop my house's ear,' 'I had it of Leah when I was a bachelor,' 'I am not well' – the intensity with which he delivered such phrases lingers in the memory.

The experience of working in such a good permanent company was enormously valuable for the actors in his season at the Queen's. The abnormally long rehearsal periods paid excellent dividends: as Gwen Ffrangcon Davies told Michel St Denis after seven weeks of rehearsing *Three Sisters*, 'I have never had the opportunity of working for such a long time. I thought I would be stale but it changes one's whole attitude to one's work.'

Of the four productions, *Three Sisters* had been the most expensive, costing £2200, and it was financially much the biggest success. The whole season showed a profit, which was very gratifying. John's first season in management was a success from every point of view.

During the run of *The Merchant*, John had also directed *Spring Meeting*, a play by John Perry and Molly Skrine, who had written several successful Irish novels under the pseudonym of M. J. Farrell. The play, too, was set in Ireland and two of the characters were based on John Perry's father and an eccentric aunt of Molly Skrine's. When Margaret Rutherford, who played the aunt, first read a script, she said 'What a pity it's such a sad part because people nowadays like to laugh.' But when she was on stage they were laughing almost incessantly.

John was totally unfamiliar with the background of horses and Irish country house life but he enjoyed working on the play and invented some very funny stage business. It ran for a year at the Ambassador's Theatre, though Harry Tennent, who presented it just before he died, predicted at the dress rehearsal that it would be a failure.

Meanwhile John had been offered a big salary to play in *Dear Octopus* with Marie Tempest, which was to start its pre-London tour in August 1938. He was sorry to disband his excellent company but he was tired of the anxieties of management and pleased to have the opportunity of appearing with Dame Marie, who had offered him co-star billing. Meanwhile there would be time for a long holiday in the South of France. The play was to be directed by his old friend Glen Byam Shaw, in association with the authoress, Dodie Smith. It was another H. M. Tennent production, with Hugh Beaumont as the new managing director of the company.

John rented the same villa he had had in 1936 and Peggy Ashcroft came down to stay, together with Glen Byam Shaw and his wife Angela Baddeley, who was to play the girl in *Dear Octopus*, which pleased John enormously. They had been friends ever since she played Mrs Cricket in *The Insect Play*.

He came back to England at the end of July to start rehearsals. Apart from Marie Tempest, John and Angela Baddeley, the cast included Valerie Taylor and Leon Quartermaine. The sets were by the Motleys. The play was a sentimental comedy about a Golden Wedding reunion. Marie Tempest had great difficulty in learning her lines. Beaumont had persuaded her the part would suit her and evidently she had read the rest of the play very perfunctorily. 'Are those some of my children?' she would ask. She was short and the sofa had to be firmly built up with planks and cushions. She always held her back very straight, with her tiny feet elegantly crossed in front of her. She was enormously skilful and John enjoyed watching her from the wings.

By the beginning of September 1938, when they were touring in the provinces, the war scare had become so serious that John was wondering whether they would ever be able to open in London. But on 14 September, two weeks before Neville Chamberlain met Hitler at Munich, the play was launched at the Queen's and it was soon obvious that in spite of the news from Germany, they could expect a very long run. John still remembers Noël Coward arriving at a party in Beaumont's flat, white with fury at the news of Chamberlain's meeting with Hitler at Munich.

In January 1939, John directed a series of eight charity matinees of *The Importance of Being Earnest* at the Globe, playing John Worthing himself, as he had at Hammersmith in 1930. Allan Aynesworth, Wilde's Algy at the première (14 February 1895) came to one of the matinees and said 'They've caught the gaiety and exactly the right atmosphere.' Beaumont now began to think of following *Dear Octopus* with a full scale revival of *The Importance* instead of the production of T. S. Eliot's play *The Family Reunion* which he and John had been considering, with John as Harry Monchensey. Eliot would have no-one but Martin Browne as director so John had offered to co-direct with him and suggested an initial series of matinees with Sybil Thorndike, Martita Hunt and May Whitty in the other main parts. He had lunch with Eliot and Browne at the Reform Club, but Eliot seemed very reluctant to answer questions about the play. Later he said that he did not want John to play the part because he did not have enough faith to understand the character's motivations.

John spent over ten months in *Dear Octopus*. His last performance was on 24 June 1939, when his contract allowed him to leave. Hugh Sinclair replaced him and the run continued for several months.

John was now invited to play and direct a new revival of

116

Hamlet to be given in the courtyard of the royal castle at Elsinore. The Elsinore Hamlet Festival had been inaugurated two years previously, when Laurence Olivier had played the part in Tyrone Guthrie's Old Vic production, with Vivien Leigh as Ophelia. The idea was to invite a different company each year and in 1938 there had been a German *Hamlet* with Gustaf Gründgens and his company. Now the Motleys designed a platform setting for the courtyard at Kronborg, flanked by huge banners, with a cur-tained inner stage in the style of an Elizabethan theatre. Fay Compton was Ophelia with Jack Hawkins and Laura Cowie as the King and Queen. Marius Goring, Glen Byam Shaw and George Howe were also in the company.

Before they left for Denmark, a week of performances was arranged at the Lyceum – Irving's old theatre, though much changed since his day – which was now due for demolition, though the decision was later reversed and it still survives as a dance hall. Meanwhile John had to adapt his open air production as well as he could for a proscenium theatre.

Harley Granville Barker happened to be in London for a few days, so before the play opened at the Lyceum, John asked him whether he would come to watch a run-through. He agreed on condition that there should be no press coverage or interviews. Next morning he invited John to see him at the Ritz, where he was staying with his wife. Barker sat there with a beautiful uncut copy of *Hamlet* on his knees and talked brilliantly, without notes, about the performance, cutting the pages as he went along. He asked John to be stronger and more deliberate at the beginning of the Closet Scene and then – in contrast – wilder, more dis-turbed and despairing after killing Polonius. 'Things are no longer working out as Hamlet planned. The appearance of the Ghost should then create a caesura in the scene,' Barker said. In the scene of Ophelia's funeral, he made the point that Laertes's behaviour in jumping into the grave is very much like Hamlet's own rash behaviour in his grief for his father at the beginning of the play. If Fortinbras represents one embodiment of what Hamlet might have grown into, Laertes is another – especially the noble, light-hearted youth that Laertes was at the beginning.

Barker's comments and criticism were invaluable, but after about three hours, his wife came in to take him away to lunch. John tactfully managed to keep her at bay for another half hour or so. He had called a rehearsal for two o'clock but he rang the theatre to say he would be late, and when he arrived he told the actors that Barker had given him some tremendously valuable notes which they could only hope to incorporate if they worked all day on Sunday. They agreed readily.

For John himself, the result was an altogether leaner characterization, with less business. He no longer broke the recorder across his knee after challenging Rosencrantz to play on it and he did not take the King's sword from him while he was trying to pray. Reviewing the performance, Desmond MacCarthy found that John was less effective in the distracted scenes (like the Play Scene and the Closet Scene) than in the soliloquies but remarked on his skill in stressing the words which illuminated the progression of Hamlet's thought.

When the company arrived at the hotel in Elsinore, two cannons were fired and a band struck up with 'It's a long way to Tipperary.' Rehearsals were rather chaotic. The weather was cold and gusty, and though an old actor had been appointed to act as interpreter, it was hard to communicate with the Danish extras, who pretended to understand more English then they actually did. But the set was effective in the stone courtyard, the acoustics seemed adequate and the weather looked as if it might hold. But it was impossible to ignore the signs of approaching war. As an old Danish lady, who was sitting next to John at lunch and smoking a small cigar, calmly remarked, 'If the Germans should come here they could walk straight in. We have no defences.'

For the first two nights the performances went extremely well. On the third night it was stormy, and heavy rain forced them to break off after Ophelia's mad scene. On the fourth night it was very black again and the actors were stopped by a downpour in the middle of the Ghost scene, to resume ten minutes later on a cold and rain-sodden stage. They got through to the end of the performance but the strong winds blew the actors' cloaks into their faces and the heavy banners flapped noisily in the wind. Audiences too were deterred by the bad weather, though only one performance was actually cancelled because of rain.

Also staying at the hotel in Elsinore were a lot of very strait-laced Danes and some Nazi naval officers, who were supposed to be there on holiday. In the hotel dining room there was a long table with the flags of all the nations, including the Swastika flag. One morning all the Swastikas had disappeared. Nervous of provoking the Nazis, the hotel manager came apologetically to

John. He would understand how important it was not to create an international incident. Reluctantly John spoke to the company, appealing that whoever was responsible should come forward. After a lengthy silence, Marius Goring said he had taken the flags. 'Would you mind putting them all back?' Marius Goring was very sorry but they had been cut up into small pieces and flushed down one of the hotel lavatories. The hotel manager found some replacement Swastika flags but by the following morning these too had disappeared. The manager was in despair. 'What are we to do? We've run out of Swastikas.'

On the whole, the audiences were extremely attentive: there was hardly any coughing. But one night, when it started to rain during the 'rogue and peasant slave' soliloquy, a woman five or six rows from the front put up an umbrella, only to have it snatched out of her hands by the man in the row behind, whose view she was obstructing.

Towards the end of the week the company broke out into a riot of outrageous practical jokes – putting cannons in the corridors and live chickens in people's beds. After the final performance of *Hamlet* there was a champagne party for which they all had to put on full evening dress. After the dinner and the dancing, someone said 'Let's go for a bathe,' and they all trooped down to the beach. It was the Motley girls who started it. They threw one of the actresses, still in her beautiful evening gown, into the sea. Then ceremoniously, systematically, one by one, each of the actors was thrown in. Dripping figures scrambled out of the sea and stripped down to their underclothes to assist with throwing the next one in. John watched until everyone else had been thrown. Then, just as it all seemed to be coming to an end, 'Isn't anyone going to throw me?' 'All right, John.' 'Just a minute.' And he took off his tail coat before he was thrown. The next morning, as they left, most of the company were clutching damp brown paper parcels. Many of the men in the company – including Anthony Quayle, Glen Byam Shaw, Jack Hawkins and Marius Goring – had played in John's companies since 1933. They must have sensed this was the last time they would be together before the war sent them off in different directions and the practical jokes were probably a kind of farewell to their youth.

In Copenhagen John met Baroness Blixen, who wrote *Out of Africa* and *Seven Gothic Tales* under the nom de plume of Isak Dinesen. She was a fascinating woman, tiny, with huge dark eyes which you could never see clearly because she always wore feathered hats with veils. In her deep voice with its appealing accent, she talked with great wisdom and devotion about Shakespeare. She said she loved reading his plays at night on the veldt when on safari shooting lions. 'If I had been a man,' she said, 'I would have loved to be Horatio.' She was to remain a friend of John's until her death: they often met in England, in Paris and in America.

Returning to England, John was faced by unrelieved gloom. War seemed inevitable, his father was ill and had to have an operation, his mother was in a state of anxiety. John tried to persuade her to go to Ireland as soon as the operation was safely over. John Perry's parents were willing to put her up in their house or could have arranged for her to live with friends. Nervous of air raids, which might start at any minute if war broke out, John took his most valuable books and pictures from his London flat down to his cottage in Essex.

It was here that the revival of *The Importance of Being Earnest* was planned. Edith Evans first read Lady Bracknell aloud one evening to the other guests and created a tremendous impression. She had strong feelings about the part.

> I know those kind of women. They ring the bell and ask you to put a lump of coal on. They *were* caricatures, these people – absolutely assured, arrogant, and that's the way they spoke. So many people said to me after *The Importance* 'It's exactly like Aunt Lucy' or 'It's just like Aunt Mabel.' They spoke meticulously, they were all very good looking and they didn't have any nerves. Nobody had nervous diseases at that time . . .

The Motleys thought that Lady Bracknell would be more imposing in a large early Edwardian hat than in one of the small bonnets worn in 1895. The furniture too was heavier and more ornate by about 1906, so they advanced the date of the play accordingly. Lord Alfred Douglas came round to see John, and described how he had been at Wilde's elbow during the original production but he seemed to remember very little of the way Wilde and George Alexander had directed the play. John suspected that Rose Leclerq, the original Lady Bracknell, had been smaller and less dominating than Edith Evans, and that his aunt, Mabel Terry-Lewis, (who played the part with him at Hammersmith in 1930 as a slim, elegant lady) was closer to Wilde's idea of Lady Bracknell. But she could not dominate the play as Edith Evans did, and having no sense of humour herself, had seemed quite surprised that the audience found the lines so funny.

John's inventions included a bird which warbled through the garden scene, interrupting Gwendolen, a church clock which heralded John Worthing's entrance in mourning and chimed four as tea was punctually served, and a step-ladder to climb when looking for the Army Lists on a high bookshelf. According to *The Times*, 'If the past theatrical decade had to be represented by a single production, this is the one that many good judges would choose.' And Tyrone Guthrie said that it 'establishes the high-water mark in the production of artificial comedy in our epoch'.

John's performance combined an accurate grasp of Wilde's language with an elegant restlessness. As at Hammersmith, he gave a subtle parody of his own seriousness in a tragic role, fully exploiting the comedy in putting on a display of unfelt grief. Agate wrote 'Throughout, the actor adopts the pose of John Philip Kemble, the abstracted air and elevated chin of one about to sneeze. And the result is irresistible.' (He was paraphrasing Hazlitt's description of Kemble as Coriolanus with 'the contracted eyebrows and suspended chin of a man about to sneeze'.)

John's father recovered from the operation and his mother resisted his efforts to make her go to Ireland. He then suggested they should both move into his cottage, where they would be safer than in London. But when he went down there for a weekend after *The Importance* had opened, he was worried by the amount of searchlight practice that seemed to be focused around the village and a large airfield was soon being constructed close by. Concluding that it must be on a direct route between London and the East Coast, he wrote to his parents in Somerset, where they were staying, urging them to stay on there if war should be declared.

John had already volunteered for Reserve service but was not expecting to be called up immediately. London was comparatively empty. The squares were being stripped of their railings so that the metal could be used to make ammunition, and Broadcasting House was surrounded by sandbags. John Perry had volunteered for A.R.P. work. Meanwhile *The Importance* went on doing surprisingly good business. The box office took £2200 during the first week and it was only at the end of the week that advance booking began to fall off. On 29 August John started rehearsing *Rebecca* in Daphne du Maurier's own adaptation of her novel, without feeling much confidence that the play would ever reach the stage. It was expected that the West End theatres would all be closed at any moment.

On 3 September war was declared and the Globe Theatre went dark.

23   War Conditions

John volunteered for active service before his age-group was called, but in October he was told he would not be enlisted for at least six months.

He abandoned *Rebecca*, which now seemed inappropriately commercial. He felt that if he was to go on working as an actor, it must be in classical work. Beaumont had quickly arranged a provincial tour of *The Importance* and this opened at Golders Green Hippodrome at a matinee on 16 September – the first full scale production of the war. It was taken on tour to twelve provincial towns and returned to the Globe to run there until the end of February 1940.

John also began to prepare a lecture with illustrative speeches under the title *Shakespeare in Peace and War*. The framework of the text was devised by Ivor Brown, and while he was on tour, John stayed on in each town to deliver it in the theatre on Sundays. He wanted to donate the proceeds to the Polish Relief Fund, but the organizers said they did not want anything until after Christmas, so he gave the money to the Red Cross.

In November, Rudolph Bing, who was then manager for John Christie at Glyndebourne, was making plans for a London production of *The Beggar's Opera*, which he invited John to direct, with Michael Redgrave – also an excellent singer – as Macheath. Audrey Mildmay, the Glyndebourne soprano, and wife of John Christie, was the Polly Peachum. The rest of the cast John had to take on Bing's recommendation, as he knew very few singers himself.

When he was planning the set with the Motleys, he told them

about an early Victorian engraving of a highwayman he had seen in an Edinburgh shop window. Working from this costume, they decided to post-date the opera to 1830, rather in the style of Cruickshank. This irritated the critics, and Michael Redgrave's costume, though very handsome, did not help him to look at all dangerous. John had hoped to create a more squalid and satirical effect in the whole production than he actually achieved.

After opening in Brighton and touring for eight weeks, the production arrived at the Haymarket. For four performances when Redgrave was ill, John appeared himself as Macheath, which involved much more singing – and much more difficult singing – than his part in *The Good Companions*. He spent a hectic week-end rehearsing the songs with the conductor. Fortunately, having always loved the opera and seen it at Hammersmith a dozen times, he already knew both his dialogue and his lyrics almost perfectly. After the performance, the company told him he had been doing what all singers did when they couldn't manage a top note – stamping his foot and clenching his fist in the air to distract the audience's attention.

24 'Lear' with Granville Barker

John was now involved in the first major theatrical event of the war – the re-opening of the Old Vic in a special Shakespeare season with Tyrone Guthrie as co-director. They decided to do two plays, *King Lear* and *The Tempest*. John was to lead a fine company – Jessica Tandy, Jack Hawkins, Fay Compton, Cathleen Nesbitt, Marius Goring, Robert Harris, Lewis Casson, Nicholas Hannen, Harcourt Williams and Stephen Haggard.

Guthrie and John invited Granville Barker over from France (which had not yet surrendered) to direct the play. He refused to have his name on the programme but agreed to come for ten days to direct some of the rehearsals.

First he spent a weekend in London to confer with Roger Furse, the designer, and make the preliminary arrangements with John, Guthrie and Lewis Casson. Casson, an old friend who had played in many of Barker's productions, was to take the early rehearsals with Guthrie, basing them on Barker's Preface to *King Lear*. John went to meet Barker at the Queen's Theatre and read the whole of Lear's part to him in the manager's office. In one of the emotional outbursts, John started to weep. 'Too soon! You haven't got there yet. You should merely be peevish and cross.' Later Barker asked him why he had not wept. 'But it's too late now.' When John had finished, Barker said drily 'You read exactly two lines correctly. Now we'll begin to work. Lear is an oak and you are an ash. We must see how this will serve you.' At the end of the session, John's copy of the play was thickly covered with notes.*

After Granville Barker went back to France, Lewis Casson began to rehearse the play, using the ground-plan Barker had devised, with simple patterns of levels and entrances, and diagrams showing how the furniture should be placed. There were several days of rehearsal before Barker came back to London, this time to stay for ten days and for once without his wife. John and Guthrie went to meet him at the Athenaeum, where he had taken a room. He came into the hall of the club in a bowler hat and demanded 'Who sent me freesias?' They had been sent by Guthrie.

'From the moment he stepped through the stage-door at the Old Vic,' John has written,

he inspired and dominated everyone like a master-craftsman, and everyone in the theatre recognized this at once . . . he . . . began to work with the actors, not using any notes, but sitting on the stage with his back to the footlights, a copy of the play in his hand, tortoise-shell spectacles well forward on his nose, dressed in a black business suit, his bushy red eyebrows jutting forward, quiet-voiced, seldom moving, coldly humorous, shrewdly observant, infinitely patient and persevering.

But he immediately changed everything that John, Guthrie and Casson had already set. He had clear ideas about the way each character should be played but he made no attempt to force these on the actors. He had the groupings and a great deal of the stage business already worked out, but he seemed to improvise the moves from the simple and significant arrangement of the few necessary pieces of furniture and the positions of the entrances and exits.

He did not want a Lear who seemed mad from the beginning,

* These notes have been printed fully in the Appendix to *Stage Directions* by John Gielgud. Heinemann Educational Books, 1963. I am also grateful for being allowed access to an unpublished manuscript by Hallam Fordham, *Player in Action*, a detailed account of the production, with notes by John himself.

but a sullen, twinkling old man who could sulk and intimidate his daughters and his court, then change his manner, becoming smooth and charming. In the first reading and later at the rehearsals, Barker encouraged John to find as much humour as possible in Lear. It should even become something of a mischievous game for him to see how far he could get away with his behaviour towards his daughters. He should remain urbane while being cruelly ironic to Burgundy about Cordelia – 'Schoolmaster showing up dunce' runs the note. In the fourth scene, at Goneril's castle, he is robust and jolly when he stamps in from the hunting, singing and throwing things about as he sits down hungrily to table. When Kent trips Oswald up, Lear roars with laughter, but the entrance of the Fool induces a different mood. Immensely fond of him, Lear gives him food and shows him off to Kent.

The curse on Goneril should come as a surprise to the audience. 'Strange, not loud. Deadly. Ride it.' Lear stands with his arms outstretched, palms upwards, as if receiving the curse from heaven. On the words "Away, away", he makes a slow exit. His abrupt return was staged as a deliberate anti-climax to counteract the solemnity of the curse and to show that his sanity is at breaking point. His speech is broken and despairing, in contrast to the earlier mood. On seeing Goneril, he bursts into tears before gathering his forces for the curse.

Arriving at Gloucester's castle, weary after the journey, to find Kent in the stocks, he is deadly, his pride hurt. 'Too indignant to be angry.' The insult to his messenger has knocked away the last prop to his pride and there is rage and hysteria in the sequence which follows. At the end of it, before Regan's entrance with Cornwall, he must find an entirely new voice. 'Pay no attention to the Fool. Closed eyes, hand to head.' In the exchanges with Regan he is exhausted by his own rage. When Goneril arrives, to be welcomed by her sister, he is more moved than ever as his knowledge of the truth grows. The notes on "I prithee daughter do not make me mad" and "Or rather a disease that's in my flesh" are 'Physical. Real. Turn swift' and 'Rash mood. Then suffer in the head.' With "O reason not the need" he drops it right down, ironic and dignified. At the end of the scene he collapses with an onset of the rash mood. His rages are self-devouring. Ignoring his own physical symptoms, he towers into a passion of fury, threatening revenge against his daughters as he backs away towards the outer gateway, but his strength gives way, his tone suddenly becoming feeble and plaintive as he calls to the Fool in a frightened premonition of oncoming madness before they rush out together into the night.

At the beginning of the first storm scene, he pitches his voice in a low key, every word impersonal. Then, in the great speeches which follow, the actor must use the full gamut of his voice to create the storm, like an organ in an oratorio. When his wits begin to turn, he must go for the reality, not the pitifulness of his situation. The lines to the Fool give him a chance to be kind and casual, enfolding him tenderly in the cloak. 'Hold on to the edge of security. Leave stage on a high, unfinished note.'

In the second scene on the heath, he is really mad. 'Living in purely metaphysical world.' And his disintegration continues gradually in the hovel scene. By the end he is a 'tiny, trembling, old man, childlike, tottering about.' He must play the whole scene quietly, giving equal value to the real and the imaginary characters.

Then for the scene on Dover Cliff he is the 'Happy King of Nature. No troubles. Tremendously dignified.' He carries a branch, walking with it as he did with his staff in the opening scene. He is almost jolly in the "Let copulation thrive" speech, swinging his branch above his head. In this scene Barker helped John enormously by showing him where to find moments of lightness. There is comedy in "To't luxury pell mell" and Lear can be coy on the line to Gloucester, "Do thy worst blind Cupid", changing his key, his tone and his pace immediately afterwards. "Your eyes are in heavy case" is a joke but he is a bit impatient with the old man on "Get thee glass eyes". He is 'serio-comic' on "When we are born, we cry that we are come/To this great stage of fools" and 'very light' on "This, a good block" as he carefully feels Gloucester's head.

The recognition is very gradual. There is a danger of sentimentality in what follows and Barker told John to act in a key and tone removed from the emotion of the scene, so as to contribute a contrast each time he spoke. In the final scene with Cordelia, "Come let's away to prison", he is really happy. Barker told John to 'dance the whole speech like a polka' and to use every possible variety of tone, 'but lightly, like a boy of nine telling a fairy story to a girl of six'. He leaves the stage triumphantly, hand in hand with her.

Even after her death there is one point where he can be jolly, standing firmly above her body as he says, "I have seen the day, with my good biting falchion / I would have made them skip". But he breaks suddenly on "I am old now". In the passage with Kent, he forgets Cordelia, which provides an opportunity to find her body again with the rope around her neck on "And my poor fool is hanged". He dies joyfully, looking at her lips.

John suggested that one of the soldiers in the final scene should still be carrying the rope that had hanged Cordelia. At first Barker was against the idea. 'It's too much like Beerbohm Tree business.' But then the next day 'Try it, it might be good.' John took the rope from the soldier's belt and Barker liked the effect. But John was too overwhelmed by the genius who was directing him to put forward any other ideas of his own. He was told how to stand with his legs apart for the curse and where to put his hands.

Barker was a perfectionist. He spent a whole morning on the King of France (Alan McNaughton) who has only a few speeches in the opening scene. Unfortunately there were only ten days.

Stephen Haggard was the Fool and Barker, who knew his father in Paris, where he was British Consul, would ask him out to lunch. John, who would have liked to use the lunch hour to talk about the play in greater detail, never got the chance. Barker left after the first dress rehearsal and never saw the play in performance, but he sent John a note from the Athenaeum.

My dear Gielgud. Lear is in your grasp.

Forget all the things I have bothered you about. Let your own now well self-disciplined instincts carry you along, and up; simply allowing the checks and changes to prevent your being carried *away*. And I prophesy – happily – great things for you.

Yrs.

H. G. B.

Some months later, in a broadcast,* John summed up the differences that Barker had made to his Lear, encouraging him to characterize more, while being less declamatory, holding more emotional power in reserve. In the first scene, for instance, Lear can afford to be quieter than John had previously realized. The actor, Barker said, does not have to use volume to indicate the majestic authority, which can be established quite adequately by the processional entrance.

The play ran for over three and a half hours with only one break, but the press was generally favourable, though some of the critics had their reservations. Agate, writing under the pseudonym of Richard Prentis in *John O'London's Weekly*, complained that the madness was less poignant than the anticipation of it, and

* On 31 January 1941.

Desmond MacCarthy argued that the part needed a voice of greater compass than Gielgud's. He was at his best, MacCarthy said, in the opening scene, in the hunting scene, when delivering the curse – quiet, merciless, with a superb yet modulated crescendo – and when lashing the hypocrisy of the world. He was moving in the recognition, but the "Howl" entrance was beyond the compass of his physical energy and the death needed better framing. *The Times* said that John 'was acting with a nervous force which . . . seemed at times to fall something short on physical toughness', but that he succeeded in charting 'with brilliant exactness Lear's progress from worldly to spiritual authority'.

Edith Evans wrote a letter saying 'There is so much that you do that is *new* in your work that I wanted to rejoice with you at your growth. I believed in your parenthood. I believed that you were a widower. You had eliminated to an amazing extent all your Johnisms . . . You never once let go because it would be a nice thing to do and keep the show going. It was such a beautiful bit of *character* and so piteous in some scenes, *not* self-pity, such a very different thing, so humble and altogether lovely the scene with Cordelia in the tent, you in the red cloak – I never wanted you to be a young man again. I wanted to come up and share your mood and sorrow, I wanted to be *in it* with you, not as an actress but as a woman.'

Once *Lear* was under way, *The Tempest* went into rehearsal, directed by George Devine and Marius Goring. They asked Barker for his advice but he demurred: it was not a play on which he had anything to offer, he said. He had warned John against his old habit of letting his eye rove about the stage and into the audience; now he had the assurance of Esmé Percy that he had at last succeeded in checking it. 'You had the fixed contemplative compelling eye of an hypnotist. I actually felt the power of it through my Edwardian opera glasses.' As before, when he played the part at the Vic, he never looked at Ariel, seeing him only in his mind, and far from destroying the feeling of contact between the two actors, this gave a strange intensity to it. But in other respects his Prospero was very different from this turbaned Eastern conjuror of 1930 – ascetic, irascible, robed like a priest, thin hair cut short, a slender moustache and neatly barbered beard. George Devine and Marius Goring wanted a vigorous Prospero still at the height of his powers and full of passion for life. His decision to renounce the world of affairs is then very different from what it would be if he were a weary old man.

The Times described John's Prospero as a 'scholarly Italian nobleman of middle age, lightly bearded and, though accustomed to reading spectacles, well-preserved . . . voice always attuned to the royal note of the verse . . . never . . . the preaching patriarch'. Uncertain of whether he had improved on his Old Vic Prospero of 1930, John was delighted when T.C. Worsley wrote to him 'I remember your Prospero of ten years ago quite well . . . I think you need have no fear that you have not grown in it in the time. I remember well those productions – they had the lyric quality – irrevocable – of youth. But now there's a dignity – a result of understanding and experience which is greater. I also remember fearing that in the intervening time you would fall into the trap of exploiting your personality – and that must be the greatest temptation for the actor. All fear of that is gone with this season.'

Making extensive use of gauzes, Oliver Messel's designs imparted a dreamy shimmer to the production, and though the effect was a little cold, the memory of Dunkirk gave a strange emotional impact both to Prospero's reconciliation with his enemies and to his speeches of farewell. After the final performance of *The Tempest* on 22 June 1940, the Old Vic went dark until it was hit by a bomb eleven months later. There had been talk of taking the Shakespeare productions to France, but the French government capitulated on the actual day the London run ended, so the company broke up in a very depressed state.

25   Entertaining the Troops

In July, John started touring the military camps with a programme of three short plays – *Fumed Oak* and *Hands Across the Sea*, both from Coward's *Tonight at 8.30*, together with John's own adaptation of Chekhov's *Swan Song*, in which he played the part of an old actor spouting Shakespeare in an empty theatre with the old prompter for an audience. He re-titled the piece *Hard Luck Story*. With Beatrice Lillie and Ivy St Helier he visited Birmingham, Abergele, Nottingham, Rhyl, Ross-on-Wye, Oswestry, Chester, Newmarket and Manchester. He also gave his Shakespeare lecture on the tour, raising substantial sums with it, but the more pacifistic passages seemed inappropriate now, and this involved certain rearrangements. He wound up, of course, with "Once more unto the breach" from *Henry V*, which never failed to go down well with both the troops and civilian audiences.

Besides performing in theatres, the three of them gave concerts in camps and hospitals. The performances themselves were less of a strain than the endless travelling, the packing and unpacking and what Beatrice Lillie called the 'social sprightlies' – standing about in huts and tents before and after the performances, drinking sherry on an empty stomach and making polite mindless conversation with the officers and their wives, one of whom said that the French catastrophe was 'a jolly bad show'.

John found he needed to use a different technique, almost as in vaudeville, first of all to win the audience's attention, and then to hold it. The men had to pay from threepence to a shilling for admission, when even threepence was a considerable sum for them. Whenever they were given a free show there was a far bigger audience.

In many camps the plays went badly. The men were not used to listening to dialogue and would have preferred a pretty girl with an accordion. They loved singing themselves and Bea Lillie and Ivy St Helier did their best, leading them in *Land of Hope and Glory* and *Lily of Laguna*. But much of Bea Lillie's comedy was received as if it were deadly serious, though oddly enough one of her most successful performances was at a Roman Catholic convent school at Ross-on-Wye, where the audience consisted of priests, small boys aged seven to fourteen and an evacuated girls' school from Ramsgate.

This was the time of the invasion scare and it seemed futile to carry on making theatre plans. The news in the papers was almost incessantly bad, but there were rumours among the troops that more damage was being done to Germany than was reported. John was using what leisure he had on the tour to study *Macbeth* for a new production he was vaguely planning and to fill gaps in his reading – *Moll Flanders*, *Tom Jones* and *The Brothers Kara-mazov*.

Wanting to lengthen the bill they had been playing in the camps and in some of the provincial theatres, John asked Gordon Daviot whether she would let them include the Darnley murder scene from *Queen of Scots* as a one-act thriller, only playing about ten minutes. She gave her permission but when they had to appear at

Manchester they needed still more new material because Fay Compton and Edward Chapman had just done *Fumed Oak* there in a variety bill. So John altered his programme, substituting Shaw's *The Dark Lady of the Sonnets*, with Martita Hunt as Elizabeth. This went so well that he kept it in the programme.

26   Disraeli and 'Dear Brutus'

While he was in Scotland, he received an offer to play Disraeli in a film called *The Prime Minister*, subject to satisfactory make-up tests. Thorold Dickinson was to direct and Diana Wynyard would be Lady Beaconsfield. The script was uninspired but John liked the part and accepted, though he knew it would be hard to rival George Arliss's famous characterization of Disraeli in the play and the film.

As John afterwards discovered, the new scenario had been written for Hollywood and been turned down by various film stars. It now had to be made on a very small budget – only two small studios were available, with a couple of pillars and an arch that were moved around for exteriors, and grass matting for a stagey-looking garden. 'When in doubt,' Thorold Dickinson said, 'we make it a night scene.'

John's father had once met Disraeli in the eighties at a reception given for Irving, and John had never forgotten his description of 'that fabulous old man making his entrance on the arm of his secretary, Montague Cory, with his dead white face and jet black hair, his white gloves and the paint under his eyes, and his odd little wife fluttering along behind him'. Actually Lady Beaconsfield was fifty-six when he married her, thirteen years older than he was, but of course she had to be glamorized in the film. In the latter scenes Diana Wynyard wore a white wig and a lot of painted wrinkles, but only succeeded in looking more beautiful than ever.

John worked with an enthusiastic make-up man who covered his face with some kind of fish skin, preventing his pores from breathing and bringing him out in a skin rash which stopped him working for several days. In his make-up as the old man he came to look more and more like his father. During the filming he asked him whether there was any Jewish blood in the family and was rather disappointed to be told 'No, not a drop.' As he soon saw from the rushes, the clothes and the wig helped to make him look convincing and distinguished, but it was very difficult for him to achieve the necessary continuity. Often he had to play young scenes in the morning and old scenes in the afternoon. Fay Compton played Victoria and managed to look very much like the old queen, but she and John could not take their scenes very seriously and ruined several takes by giggling.

Conditions of working were far from ideal. John had to get up at 6.45 every morning for seven weeks. The blitz was just starting, so the extras were anxious to finish at Teddington early, in time to get home from the studios before the raids began. Scenes were therefore set up and filmed very hastily and John did not get sufficient time to study his lines, many of them long excerpts from political speeches. The art director was cramped for space and the research had been skimped. After pointing out two mistakes – there was no photograph of the Prince Consort in the Queen's room and her writing-paper had no black border – John suggested that James Laver should be called in to advise on the detail.

John's best scene was a quiet one sitting in an armchair, reading his wife's letters after her death. For almost the first time in his experience of filming, John had the screen to himself for a sequence in a relaxed mood. All too often in the past he had either found that the camera favoured the pretty star who was playing opposite him or that he himself was spoiling his chances by trying too hard. Perhaps the fact of playing in costume – which was always a hindrance to Leslie Howard – was a help to John. In any case here was a scene which made him aware of how effective he could be as a film actor, though it was not until the sixties that this side of his talent came to be exploited more fully.

In January 1941 he made his return to the West End, where only nine theatres were open. Most of them, after closing in panic when war was declared, had re-opened by the beginning of 1940, only to be closed again because of the blitz. The news of John's return was reassuring and one critic said that it looked 'as though the London theatre was approaching something like stability again with Mr Gielgud back in the fold'.

But it was no time for the classics. Donald Wolfit was cutting down Shakespearean plays to a running time of about an hour and a quarter for lunch-hour performances and the only full-scale classical revival of 1941 was Tyrone Guthrie's production of *The Cherry Orchard* at the New. The play John chose was *Dear Brutus*, by J. M. Barrie, which had been such a success in the war-weary London of 1917. It is a whimsical fantasy about an enchanted wood which can give the characters the illusion of having a second chance in life. The wood appears magically on Midsummer's Night outside the house of a strange gnome-like creature, called Lob, whose age is uncertain. "They do say in the village that they remember him seventy years ago looking just as he does today." Lob's butler, Matey, is about to be arrested for stealing jewellery from the house-guests, and they all turn out to be involved with each other in fantasies of how much better they might have done with their lives. John played Dearth, a disillusioned artist who feels that his life with his beautiful wife (Margaret Rawlings) could have been so happy if only they had had a daughter, while his wife wishes she had married another man. In the enchanted wood Dearth acquires a daughter, but at the end of the play he realizes she is only a fantasy and returns to his wife.

In 1917 and in the two successful revivals, Gerald du Maurier had played Dearth. It was one of his finest performances and John had been particularly impressed by him in the scene with the child in the enchanted wood – a scene which Barrie was said to have founded on George du Maurier, Sir Gerald's father and the author of *Trilby*. But the audience of 1941 could not accept this scene, in spite of Muriel Pavlow's charm as the young girl, and John became self-conscious in it. Altogether his admiration for du Maurier made it difficult for him to arrive at a new interpretation of the part and he knew it would have been fatal to imitate du Maurier's. It might have been easier for him – or so he felt afterwards – if someone else had been directing him. And as in *The Maitlands*, he found himself unable to convince either himself or the audience in the drunk scene.

Graham Greene, reviewing the production for *The Spectator*, decided that 'the lines have dated no more than Wilde's', but Desmond MacCarthy had reservations both about John's Dearth and about the play. 'In the first act he appears far too well pulled-together, too smart and attractive. In the scene in the wood between the painter and his dream daughter, his charm lacks the *crispness* of Gerald du Maurier's personality and acting, so necessary in counter-acting the sentimentality.'

But the audiences seemed to enjoy the play and after the run at the Globe, which lasted till the middle of May 1941, the company went on tour to the provincial theatres and then, for ENSA, to the camps, staging the play in huts and recreation halls. In his curtain speech in Manchester, where there had just been a heavy air-raid, John said 'I'm sorry to see your beautiful city laid waste.' The audience laughed and in the morning, one of the papers said that it was the first time anyone had called Manchester beautiful since the eighteenth century. Liverpool too had been hit badly by the raids and John felt guilty to be staying in Princes Park with rich friends who gave him luxurious dinners after the play.

On Sunday he went back to Manchester, to see a dress rehearsal of Noël Coward's *Blithe Spirit*. He liked it but was not at all sure whether it would succeed in London, and he found Margaret Rutherford so real and touching in her heartiness and enthusiasm as Madame Arcati, the medium, that it seemed almost offensive when Elvira (Kay Hammond) told her she was a silly old bitch.

At Nottingham, the editor of a local paper took John to meet an old man called Willie Hopkin, who had been a close friend of D. H. Lawrence's. 'He was quite a character,' John wrote, 'and jabbered away for about an hour and a half in a very stuffy little room with no windows open – showed us photographs of Lawrence and his wife with the Huxleys and Katherine Mansfield... He also told us that the original of Lady Chatterley was – whom do you think? – Edith Sitwell! ! ! ! And that the scene of the story was laid in their home – Renishaw Park – but that Miss Sitwell had no idea of it herself.'

27   The Wartime 'Macbeth'

It was in January 1942 that John's long-planned production of *Macbeth* opened in icy Manchester. The music was by William Walton and the sets by Michael Ayrton in collaboration with the brilliant young painter John Minton – his last work before being called up. Inspired partly by Tchelitchev, the set looked impressive and Arthurian, rather like a mixture of Burne-Jones and Beardsley. Gwen Ffrangcon Davies came back to England after cutting short a tour of South Africa to play Lady Macbeth. Leon Quartermaine played Banquo and Milton Rosmer Macduff. For the rest it was a makeshift company, for the supporting parts are unrewarding and it was hard to find men of the right age because of the call-up. But the young Alan Badel, who was playing one of Macbeth's servants, was already showing great talent and proved invaluable in stirring up the extras to bring the necessary excitement to the discovery of Duncan's murder. Later he also took over as Lennox. The morning after he was told he must replace another actor in this part, he came to rehearsal word perfect and had already planned his make-up. But he was called up soon afterwards, before the long provincial tour was over.

John devised a mask-like make-up for himself with spidery eyebrows, derived partly from Nikolai Cherkassov's Alexander Nevsky in Eisenstein's film. In Manchester John had good advice from the Guthries, Ivor Brown and Alec Guinness. They all made constructive suggestions, and Alan Dent, a friendly drama critic who had been working for many years as personal assistant to Agate, wrote John a long letter. 'As happened with Laughton, you are at your best in the Banquet ... the wide gesture with the red robe, for example, is superb, just after your first shriek.' He complained of lack of light on John's own face. 'So far as we can *see*, you come out of Duncan's chamber after the murder with no more expression on your face than anybody shows on coming out of a lavatory ... You do wonders here – and everywhere else – with your voice and hands. But I want to *see* more horror here ... You really do not have to be *quite* so violent, so loud all through the last two scenes ... (Incidentally and to my great delight you have lost – I hope for good – the high hysterical pitch which I used to object to in Hamlet. The forte quality is now a fine sound.)' He asked for more perplexity and less indignation in "Why do you dress me in borrowed robes" – 'You know, dear heart, you always tend too easily to indignation.' 'There was also too much indignation with the murderers,' he said. A colder contempt was needed.

The opening week in Manchester was very exhausting, with rehearsals every day, a photo call which lasted most of Friday, and then on Friday evening, a brave old actress, Beatrix Fielden-Kaye, who had rehearsed as the Third Witch but had been too ill to play, died in the hotel of a heart attack. In spite of her illness she had insisted on coming each day to the chilly Scala Theatre where she sat in the wings, wrapped in rugs, watching the rehearsals. John had not expected her to come to Manchester, but she arrived in a limousine, saying she'd have died if she'd stayed in London, where there was no-one to look after her and where she had to go down to the front door each morning to get the milk. John was told of her death on the Tuesday morning after the first night. As so often before, *Macbeth* was proving an unlucky play.

In Scotland, several of the matinees were disturbed by school children. In Glasgow there were screams of laughter through the sleepwalking scene and through the "Tomorrow and tomorrow and tomorrow" soliloquy, and in Edinburgh it was worse. When Lady Macbeth greeted her returning husband by throwing herself into his arms, there was a howl of laughter which would not stop. Gwen Ffrangcon Davies whispered 'Get on, John, get on' but, refusing to come out of character and speak to the audience, he tried to quell them with baleful glares and Macready pauses. As he said later at an official lunch, he would have been less surprised if the children had laughed at the Witches or the Ghost. Surely they were used to seeing their parents kiss each other good morning. He was much amused by a letter which appeared later in *The Scotsman* saying that possibly Mr Gielgud was unaware it was not the custom in Scotland for husband and wife to kiss at breakfast time.

There was also a disturbance when a party of boys in the gallery bombarded the girls in front of them with ice-cream cartons, whistling and making cat-calls. Afterwards there were letters in the press about the incident.

> 'Stands Scotland where it did?' In good manners and ordinary intelligence, young Scotland certainly does not . . . It is surprising that the company carried on. In the interest of the good name of Edinburgh, I demand that there shall be no repetition of this hooliganism at subsequent performances.
>
> DISGUSTED.

Alan Dent came to see the play again in Edinburgh and thought it much improved. 'He even gains in facial expressiveness,' he wrote in his newspaper review, 'which was always one of his weaker points. At least he comes out of Duncan's chamber . . . with some inkling on his face that he has just done a deed of dreadful note.'

It was a hard winter, playing eight and sometimes nine performances a week, and moving to a new town every fortnight, with the lighting to rehearse in each new theatre. And on Sundays John often fitted in extra concerts for the troops. He was in Leeds when spring arrived and he celebrated by going to his favourite building, Fountains Abbey. 'There were sheets of snowdrops,' he wrote, 'and the pink stone and green grass were looking most beautiful in the first spring sunshine – the sky quite blue through those huge empty windows and the rooks cawing and swooping about.'

Milton Rosmer had two bouts of illness, leaving him too weak to go on playing, and Francis Lister was engaged to replace him as Macduff. Then the Duncan, Marcus Barron, had a sudden attack of angina and died shortly afterwards. The old actor who was first employed to replace him could neither remember his lines nor read them without wearing spectacles, which ruined three important scenes until Nicholas Hannen took over the part. But the company was still a weak one. John had to call endless rehearsals and to bring the Banquet Scene to life he kept having to turn his back on the audience in order to harangue the army rejects who played the unhappy guests.

At Birmingham the press was largely favourable, despite one critic's witticism about 'a Thane with a public school background', while another felt that 'the characters take on a Southern subtlety that tends to enervate the whole. Mr Gielgud deals with Macbeth's quieter moments with a sardonic intensity that gives an Italianate complexion to what should be "bold and resolute" in the Northern manner.'

In July 1942 the production opened in London at the Piccadilly Theatre. *The Times* found the performance 'lacking in soldierly quality' but Agate – who had already seen it in Bournemouth, where he told John that both Gwen and he were miscast – wrote that 'every Macbeth worth seeing must fail with the problem of reconciling Bellona's bridegroom with the hag-ridden neurotic.' John 'gave Macbeth at his first entry a swashing and martial outside, though low in tone, gaunt and sombre like an El Greco. Having discharged the formal reply to his sovereign with the gloriously delivered "Stars hide your fires" Mr Gielgud dropped the warrior and bent up each corporal and intellectual agent to the terrible feat of interpreting the most poetical of all murderers.' John spoke the verse beautifully, he said, and described his collapse after the murder as a 'masterpiece of nerves'. He spoke of his 'magnificent virtuosity' in the Banquet Scene, his still finer achievement in the Apparition Scene, and of the final moments which overtopped even this.

On the day before this review appeared in the *Sunday Times*, he also wrote a letter to John, prompted by the review in the *Daily Telegraph*.

> Darlington was talking nonsense when he said your Macbeth isn't as fine a piece of acting as your Hamlet. It is much finer, though less successful. It contains more sheer acting ... I never admired you more ... (You) are the best Macbeth I have seen, except perhaps old Mollison, who hadn't much poetry but remained a soldier. Your Macbeth is an introvert; he wakes up from his nightmare to get rid of it by action. Not, I think, Shakespeare, but very fine Gielgud. In my mind your Shakespearean roles are Hamlet, Richard II, Macbeth, *Wolsey*, Iago (!), Brutus, Lear, Coriolanus – you have the pride and the breeding for this non-burly patrician – Hotspur, Romeo, Mercutio, Malvolio, Leontes. But not Othello, Antony, Richard III ... Anyhow you moved me very much on Wednesday, almost to crying in the 'Tomorrow' speech and in the earlier despair before the Banquet Scene.

Macbeth ended its run on 10 October and after a single week's rest John opened at the Phoenix in another revival of his production of *The Importance of Being Earnest*. He now had a new Algernon in Cyril Ritchard, who had previously worked mainly in musical comedy and revue, but readily adapted his style to John's direction.

Seeing the production, Vyvyan Holland, Oscar Wilde's son, wrote to John saying 'I never enjoyed any play so much' and enclosed a copy of the *Playgoer* which contained a photographic souvenir of George Alexander's revival in 1909.

Now that he was getting to know the play so well, John became more alert than ever to the dangers of too much speed. Played too fast, he found, the dialogue could lose its period flavour and sound too much like Coward. Years later, when John directed the second act for a charity matinee to help the OUDS, he found the muffin scene became much funnier when taken very slowly. It then occurred to him that he had always been inclined to sacrifice the farcical deliberateness Wilde intended. Shaw had attacked this tendency in his review of an Edwardian revival, complaining that the actors had ruined the end of the play by gabbling the last act as if they were afraid of losing the audience.

The production ran until 12 December and on Christmas Eve
John went to Gibraltar via Lisbon, together with Edith Evans,
Beatrice Lillie, Elisabeth Welch, Phyllis Stanley, Jeanne de
Casalis and Michael Wilding, to entertain the garrison there. They
flew out of blacked-out Britain in a blacked-out plane and when
the shutters were finally drawn back, it was thrilling to see the
necklaces of lights underneath them and then to wander through
Lisbon streets bright with illuminated shop windows and Christmas decorations. Because of the fuel shortage the streets were
empty of cars but crowded and brilliantly lit. The hotel was cold
and the food poor, but fruit, so rare in England, was plentiful and
whisky only ten shillings a bottle. After going to a Portuguese
cabaret and an American night club, they ended up standing in
the shadows of the packed cathedral for Midnight Mass.

On Christmas day they flew on to Gibraltar, where Anthony
Quayle and John Perry, both now officers on the staff of the
Governor, General Mason McFarlane, were at the airport to meet
them, and they all went to a Christmas dinner at Government
House.

The pretty little theatre held about 750 people and it was
packed at every performance, officers and men all sitting together,
which created a better atmosphere than in the English camps
where they were always separated.

After an opening chorus in which the others were introduced,
Edith Evans appeared in the Millamant costume Oliver Messel
had designed for a scene from *The Way of the World* which she
had played with John at a charity performance in London a few
weeks before. She spoke a poem specially written by Sagittarius
of the *New Statesman*, (Olga Katzin, wife of the actor Hugh
Miller). Then the coloured singer Elisabeth Welch, standing in
a black dress against a white satin curtain, sang 'Prayer for Rain',
'Begin the Beguine', and 'Solomon'. John played the Proposal
Scene from Act One of *The Importance* with Edith Evans and
Jeanne de Casalis, and Beatrice Lillie sang some songs, including

one called 'Early Morning' in which she sat on a windowsill with a shutter that banged in her face after every other line. John later appeared in a dinner jacket to speak a comic poem, 'Mussolini and the Eagle', Housman's 'Bredon Hill' and the Henry V speech, 'Once more unto the breach'. He also sang in a quartet with Bea Lillie and Michael Wilding, and towards the end of the programme, dressed in an old trilby hat and a raincoat, recited a patriotic poem by Clemence Dane about Nelson and the bombing of St Paul's in the Blitz.

Most of the troops had been there for two years, garrisoning the town and having a very dull time, so they were a magnificent and grateful audience. Recognizing the actresses in the streets outside the theatre, they would shout out 'Evening Edith', 'Hello Bea'.

There were two performances every night, including Sundays. During four weeks there, the company gave forty-eight shows in the theatre, as well as several forty-five-minute concerts in two of the local hospitals and some on board battleships and aircraft carriers, with sailors sitting cross-legged on railings and bridges and stokers peering from the funnels with grimy faces and coloured rags tied round their necks. It was strange to be reciting Shakespeare at 11 o'clock in the morning, but John found the audiences amazingly responsive. Once, when his voice was nearly drowned during the Nelson poem by the noise of a passing aeroplane, the Commander rushed to the telephone to reprimand a neighbouring aircraft-carrier which had sent it over at that moment.

While John was playing in Gibraltar, Leslie Howard was lecturing in Portugal for the British Council. Returning to England, John flew from Lisbon on a neutral Portuguese airline that had never been attacked by the Germans. Two weeks later, Leslie Howard flew back on the same line and was killed when his plane was shot down. His accountant was with him, a stout man whom some German agent may possibly have mistaken for Churchill. Back in England, a few weeks later, John was offered a film that Howard had contracted to make. He started to read the script but was embarrassed to find that the story seemed to have been custom-tailored around Howard's private life, so he refused it. Altogether, with the period of understudying Howard in *Berkeley Square* and with the rivalry over *Hamlet* in New York, their careers were oddly linked but they never got to know each other.

Meanwhile, *The Doctor's Dilemma*, which had opened in March at the Haymarket, was still running with Vivien Leigh as Jennifer Dubedat. When the actor playing her husband was suddenly taken ill, John learned the part over the week-end and played it for a week. During the death scene he kept a script in his lap, concealed under the rug which covered his knees in the wheel-chair. In 1936, when Vivien Leigh had played the Queen in *Richard II* at the OUDS, John had only taken rehearsals himself at the week-ends and had hardly got to know her. But now he became devoted to her and their friendship lasted till her death in 1967.

29 'Love for Love' and Eric Linklater

After using two painters, Ayrton and Minton, for his *Macbeth* set, John, who has always kept a lively eye on the art galleries, had the inspired idea of inviting Rex Whistler to design the scenery for *Love for Love*, which he was eager to revive, remembering its success nineteen years before at Oxford. Whistler was training for the Guards, and too busy to design the costumes, but he contributed some splendid ideas in the few meetings he had with John. His realistic sets, with a Thornhill mural in Forsyte's house and a cluttered, shabby room for Valentine's lodgings, were exactly right.

He insisted that the windows should have neither curtains nor pelmets, only shutters, and explained how in the eighteenth cen-tury there was no arrangement of furniture in the middle of the rooms – one large sofa perhaps, and stools round the walls which were brought forwards to make conversational areas. This allowed great variations in stage picture and grouping.

It was the first West End revival of *Love for Love* for over seventy years and one of John's problems was that of having to think in terms of very large theatres in the provinces and London. He wanted the production to be very much less stylized than Guth-rie's *School for Scandal* or his own *Beggar's Opera* of 1940, and he found it was necessary to cut the text more than Fagan had at Oxford in 1924. John asked Leon Quartermaine to direct but found him unwilling to accept the responsibility, though he gave valuable help over cutting the text and with many production ideas, as well as contributing a very stylish performance in the part of Scandal. The cast also included Yvonne Arnaud, Angela Baddeley, Rosalie Crutchley, Cecil Trouncer, Miles Malleson and Naomi Jacob. The casting of Tattle was problematic. John begged Robert Morley to play the part but he firmly refused to take the risk of failing in it. One night in the BBC's bleak wartime studios in Elgin Avenue, hearing a distinctive voice over the loudspeakers, John knew he had found his Tattle. The voice belonged to Leslie Banks – an outlandish piece of casting which justified itself in a brilliant performance.

Yvonne Arnaud played with great brio, enormous charm, infallible comic timing, and a precision of style which from the first rehearsal onwards helped to inspire the rest of the company. Later, in performance, when another actor failed to get an exit laugh which the text seemed to demand, she easily won a big laugh and a round of applause by making a false exit and then sweeping back into the next scene.

Rehearsing his old part of Valentine, John was astonished to find that after eighteen years he could still remember the exact wording of some of his speeches. He was particularly good in the mad scene, which became a riot of comic invention, interrupted by a moment of complete stillness when Angelica, after coming in with Tattle, challenged the seeming madman, "Who am I?" Everything stopped. For a perfectly judged moment of serious feeling amid the burlesque madness, John gazed at Rosalie Crutchley in absolute stillness, and sustained a realistic sadness all through the ensuing speech:

> You're a Woman – One to whom Heav'n gave Beauty, when it grafted Roses on a Briar. You are the reflection of Heav'n in a Pond, and he that leaps at you is sunk. You are all white, a sheet of lovely spotless Paper, when you first are Born; but you are to be scrawl'd and blotted by every Goose's Quill. I know you; for I lov'd a Woman, and lov'd her so long, that I found out a strange thing: I found out what a Woman was good for.

Then when Tattle joined in the dialogue, "Aye, prithee, what's that?" John resumed his mad movements on his answer, "Why to keep a Secret."

After a five week tour, the production opened at the Phoenix in April 1943. The audience responded to the play enthusiastically and, unlike the Oxford audience of 1924, did not seem at all shocked by the innuendo and coarseness of language. John himself was most pleased at Alfred Lunt's reaction to his performance: 'It seemed to me about as near perfection as anything can be in the theatre.'

Shortly after the transfer, Bernard Shaw, with his usual good-humoured arrogance, tried to woo John away to star in a film of *Caesar and Cleopatra*. On 29 August he wrote:

> Gabriel Pascal who is in America for the moment asked me whether he might film my *Caesar and Cleopatra* this winter for deferred production after *St. Joan*. I said he might if he could secure you for Caesar.
>
> I am now informed by Nicholas Davenport that you cannot undertake the part just now. May I take this as settled? If it is, I must turn down the whole project as I know no one who could follow Forbes Robertson in the part with any chance of getting away with it except yourself. As you are now playing the worst part in a very obsolete play I had hoped you would like to try the best part in a comparatively modern one. The dialogue in its Victorian idiom is as musical as Congreve's, and even more easily learnt. You will have to play Caesar some day, just as you have had to play Hamlet and Macbeth. You owe him to your repertory.

But if Shaw had a genuine intention of refusing to allow the film to be made without John, he must have changed his mind, for it was Claude Rains who eventually starred in it with Vivien Leigh.

Love for Love ran for over a year at the Haymarket and, as usual, John fitted a great deal of other work into his schedule. His brother Val was now Head of Drama at the BBC and John's radio performances included a very moving Christian in *The Pilgrim's Progress*. He spoke the commentary for a filmed tribute to General Sikorsky called *Unfinished Journey* and he directed a play called *Landslide*, which opened in October, and a revival of Sierra's *The Cradle Song* with Wendy Hiller and the young Yvonne Mitchell.

His next production owed its origin to one of his radio performances. In May 1943 he had played in Val's production of Eric Linklater's radio play, *The Great Ship*. Linklater was profoundly affected by hearing John's voice in his play and on 6 June he wrote:

> I've discovered (I mean you have discovered for me) an old truth – that words are meant to be spoken, that paper's a cold thing, that the human voice can be not only lovely to the ear but mighty significant to the mind . . . I now want to write for the stage – the play's the thing – and you have done this. You have dislodged me from my placid novelizing and tilted me towards the fearful difficulties of the theatre. It's a dreadful prospect – thank you very much for it.

The result of Linklater's decision was a play called *Crisis in Heaven* which, naturally, he offered to John, who agreed to direct it, but it did not have much success, in spite of a starry cast and decor by Cecil Beaton.

30   The Haymarket Season

Meanwhile *Love for Love* was still doing such excellent business at the Haymarket that questions were asked in Parliament about the earnings of the actors who, like John, were on percentages. Beaumont suggested that John should build up a repertoire season to keep it in the bill, using the same actors in three other plays. At first John was not at all keen on the idea and he might have done better to resist it. His company was neither young enough nor versatile enough and it was a crucial period in his career. Olivier had hardly been a serious rival in the thirties but in 1943 he had directed and starred in *Henry V*, the first of his three Shakespeare films, and in 1944, while John was preparing for his season in which *Hamlet*, *A Midsummer Night's Dream* and Somerset Maugham's *The Circle* were chosen as the other three plays, Olivier and Ralph Richardson had joined forces at the Old Vic, gathering around them a very strong company which included Sybil Thorndike, Margaret Leighton, George Relph, Joyce Redman, Nicholas Hannen and Harcourt Williams. *Hamlet* started a five-week provincial tour on 12 July; the Vic season opened with *Peer Gynt* on 31 August.

Not wanting to direct *Hamlet* again himself, and feeling in need of a fresh approach, John enlisted George Rylands, a Cambridge don who had directed many undergraduate productions, including an impressive *Antony and Cleopatra*. Nevill Coghill, a don at Exeter, who had played a corresponding role in undergraduate theatricals at Oxford, was engaged to direct *A Midsummer Night's Dream*. But things did not work out quite as John had hoped. Experience with undergraduate actors is not always the best preparation for directing in the professional theatre and Rylands soon found that the *Hamlet* cast did not respond with the unquestioning obedience he was used to, while the actors found him didactic and unhelpful in answering their questions about motivation. He was strict in telling them what inflections to use, but he would sit in the stalls at rehearsal with his eye fixed on the script, scarcely looking at the stage. The result was that the company kept appealing to John for his advice, which he was reluctant to give behind the director's back.

The whole production was rather formal and static. Rylands, it seemed, cared less about the visual flow than the diction and verse speaking. Peggy Ashcroft was moving as Ophelia, but Leslie Banks – so excellent as Tattle in *Love for Love*, though he did not much enjoy playing the part – was unhappy as the King. He said himself it was too late in his career for him to start experimenting with the classics. Francis Lister, the Horatio, had been a fine actor but was no longer at his best.

About his own performance John was not altogether happy: Rylands's production made him uncertain whether he should try to approach the part as if he had never played it before or try to incorporate everything he had learnt in his three previous productions, and especially from his session with Granville Barker before the Lyceum-Elsinore production in 1939. He felt he was giving something of a hotch-potch of his earlier performances, confused by the different directors he had worked with, as well as by critics and friends, and he no longer found himself as fresh or confident as he had been before. What was hardest of all was to be consistent about age. At forty he could not possibly emphasize the young student in Hamlet as he had when he played the part at twenty-six. But vestiges remained not only from his 1930 performance but from his three other Hamlets, and Rylands was unable to show him how to integrate these disparate elements into a coherent whole.

In Hamlet's first scene, he felt less happy as he was now placed, sitting in a chair, facing the audience, than he had been when Barker made him enter after the King had begun his speech and sit scribbling at the council table till he broke in with his first line.

For the middle section of the play he discarded the traditional black in favour of a dark red doublet and hose to mark his assumption of feigned madness, but no-one (critics or audience) seemed to notice the innovation. He no longer repeated the business he had invented of taking the King's sword into the Closet Scene, though it was used both by Robert Helpmann in Tyrone Guthrie's Old Vic *Hamlet* of 1944, and by Michael Redgrave when he played the part in 1949, directed by Hugh Hunt. This is the way in which theatrical tradition is created.

But despite John's own misgivings, his 1944 performance was remarkably good. He had more power, dignity and authority than he had ever achieved before and he still had a youthfully energetic attack. His flashes of triumph were electrically exciting, following on the heels of the more thoughtful passages, and the quick changes of mood were fascinating to watch. He still sustained the long complex progression of the part with an admirable clarity, never over-emphasizing or losing his lightness of touch.

Agate, who judged this to be John's best Hamlet, said that he had 'acquired an almost Irvingesque quality of pathos, and, in the passages after the Play Scene, an incisiveness, a raillery, a mordancy worthy of the old man . . . The middle act gives us 90 minutes of high excitement and assured virtuosity . . . In short I hold that this is, and is likely to remain the best Hamlet of our time.' In the *Telegraph*, Darlington made the point that he was now not so much a sensitive youth, aghast at the wickedness of the world, as a sophisticated man to whom wickedness was no surprise.

Some critics were disappointed to be deprived of the old-fashioned emphasis on Hamlet's madness. Partly thanks to John, it is now taken for granted that Hamlet is not at all mad. 'What Mr Gielgud plays down,' Desmond MacCarthy wrote, 'is Hamlet's mask of madness. He excels in interpreting his impetuous but sane emotion – his greeting of Horatio must have made many hearts in the audience leap.'

Elsie Fogerty, still Head of the Central School and an acute judge of acting, wrote to John that he was 'the most satisfactory Hamlet I have ever seen: a Hamlet who belongs to the play as a whole, to Fortinbras as well as to the Ghost . . . The quality and tone of your speech is better than I have ever heard it. Full of personality, but not strained – as Irving's always was.'

John also received a letter from Tyrone Guthrie, who had directed Olivier's Hamlet of 1937 and Alec Guinness's of 1938, as well as Helpmann's of 1944.

The production is good but lacks courage . . . the formality of setting and grouping were half-hearted . . . the lighting should either have aimed at mere illumination without alteration or realistic flummery, or else have gone full-bloodedly for atmosphere and spectacle. It was a compromise, in good taste, so was the choreography . . . You stand quite alone, in my opinion, as a speaker of verse. It was a distinguished, sophisticated, masterful, gracious and imaginative performance of this majestic concerto. The lack of youth is more than counterpoised by the authority and sophistication of maturity. I don't think you were sufficiently directed for mannerism of movement and various awfully unfunny funny bits.

After five weeks of *Hamlet, Love for Love* was revived at the end of August, when the company was at Bournemouth, and then *The Circle* was brought into the repertoire at Edinburgh in October, 1944, with Yvonne Arnaud as Lady Kitty, Leslie Banks as Lord Porteous and John in the comparatively small part of Arnold Champion-Cheney. After two weeks, the repertoire was brought to London.

The Circle (directed by William Armstrong) was probably the best of the three new productions. Yvonne Arnaud was an immensely vivacious Lady Kitty, Leslie Banks excellent as Lord Porteous and John, always in his element when given the chance to apply his comedy timing to priggish parts, considered Arnold his best performance in the season, apart from Hamlet.

A Midsummer Night's Dream was added to the repertoire in January 1945, but without incorporating any of the ideas John had discussed with Rex Whistler in 1942. Nevill Coghill's production had designs by Hal Burton, who used Jacobean costumes.

Coghill was scarcely more at home with professional actors than Rylands had been. Partly no doubt because he was not happy at rehearsals, John had rather neglected his own performance as Oberon. At the dress rehearsal he was still very uncertain. After the first night he changed his whole conception of the part, discarding his Greek helmet and his greenish make-up, which was disastrously ageing. Agate reported he was 'terrifying, with a make-up like the Ghost of Hamlet's father . . . he treated Titania as Mr Murdstone treated Clara'. Later he made himself as handsome and youthful as he could, appearing clean-shaven, with golden hair. This was an improvement but he still felt that at forty he was too old for the part and that his Oberon at the Old Vic had been altogether lighter and more relaxed. At the Haymarket he let himself be carried away by the beauty of the lines, indulging himself both vocally and emotionally. Edith Evans told him as his voice broke with emotion at the speech "I know a bank whereon the wild thyme blows", 'If you cry less, the audience will cry more.'

The critics, too, took him to task for being too involved in his own voice, while Philip Hope-Wallace was unable to forgive the moment when 'John Oberon and Peggy Titania did a pas de deux à la Novello and Dickson.' This had been one of John's pet inventions and it was rehearsed under the expert supervision of Frederick Ashton. As Bottom, Leslie Banks was effective but not very individual. The lovers and Theseus and Hippolyta were all uninspired, while Max Adrian was too old and heavy as Puck. The final effect was laboured and plodding.

The last production of the season was *The Duchess of Malfi*, also directed by Rylands. It was a play John did not greatly care for, though he grew to admire it by the end of the run. It had not been staged for many years, except for some special performances by the Phoenix Society in the twenties. Again Rylands found it difficult to give the actors the confidence they needed. When John asked whether his relationship with the Duchess was incestuous or not, Rylands replied 'Just follow the text and it'll all come out.' Leslie Banks could only play Antonio (the Duchess's steward and lover) as an English gentleman while John as Duke Ferdinand was trying to be as Italianate as possible. Leon Quartermaine, who played the Cardinal, the Duke's brother, hated his part. Generally, as Peggy Ashcroft told John, the company felt unsympathetic towards the play. John passed this on to Rylands, who, at the following morning's rehearsal told the actors that this was a play which must be *understood* and played in a particular way which they had not been able to *understand*. But he seemed to be unable to explain it and it was hard for them to work with him in an atmosphere of mutual distrust.

His attitude is reflected in a letter he wrote to John later in the year:

> It was your sweetness of nature, your distinction and your enterprise – and nothing else – which made the season (from *Love for Love* to *Malfi*) a success – both with the highbrows and with the Great British Public. What a team you had to work with! Oh dear, oh dear! No one but you could have stuck it and have held them together. Lack of brains cannot be helped nor perhaps lack of taste but it was in the moral qualities that they were nearly all so shamelessly deficient and that in the midst of a world war . . . As Ferdinand you were always a little uncertain and patchy. Your best moments could not be bettered although they were not always coincident with Webster's highest spots. Something inside you disliked or feared the part so it was always a struggle for you. If we had had more time and you had been fresher and the other players had not been so tiresome, we might have achieved a unified result. But who knows?

One of the best appreciations of John as Ferdinand came in a letter from Coghill:

Your performance was at important moments better than stage madness . . . especially in those passages that speak of your sister as *damned* for what she has done, for here you created the sense that you knew all about Hell and believed in it . . . The Duke believes in Hell deeply and is in it without knowing it . . . and that deep horror and passion appeared in you with real fanaticism in those moments, at such moments I was able and even forced to forget that you were John Gielgud, and if there is any higher praise for an actor I do not know it.

31 Around the World with ENSA

On the night the peace treaty was signed, John gave a dinner party at his house for the Granville Barkers, Lady Cunard and Hugh Beaumont. Because of Barker's wife, there was more discussion about her dog in quarantine and a book of poems she had written than about the theatre but, knowing they had been to see *Hamlet* at the Haymarket, John told Barker 'Anything that's good in my performance I'm very much aware that I owe to you.' Barker, who seemed to have aged considerably since they last met, had forgotten giving John the notes about *Hamlet* in 1939 and disappointed him by saying 'I had no recollection of seeing you in the part before.' Altogether it was an uncomfortable evening. Because of the peace celebrations it was impossible to get a taxi when the Barkers wanted to go home. They had to wait for a long time and sat in the kitchen listening to the radio, with Barker almost falling asleep.

But on 15 August 1945 he wrote his last letter to John:

I'm ashamed that I had forgotten the 'Lyceum' (yours) performance of Hamlet. I knew that I *had* seen you at it before but I could not remember when, and that 'extraordinary' occasion escaped my memory. I don't think I told you last night how well it seems to me to have matured. All the difficult bits: the Ophelia, Gertrude, Rosencrantz and Guildenstern ones. These especially which *seem* so easy: I suppose there's no one at present who can touch you at them. All that it struck me to criticize was the late saner part: from the Gravedigger scene onwards. I'd like the intellectual continuity kept clearer (he is now, past dispute, sane.' I was troubled now and then by rather (?) forced emotion, passages on the brass: they spoil what a musician would call the melodic line, in this case break the intellectual continuity. We can be held – at least, you, I am sure, can hold us by quiet, or at any rate controlled tension. And of course I'd like you as detached from the background as possible, you as much among us, so that we share your thoughts. He has thought his problems out, is pretty cold blooded about them now . . . And he is ready to die himself. All quite cool and calm. Only that sudden vain heartrending pang for Ophelia and all that is gone. Yes, I'd say take full advantage of the change from student's age to the stressed 'thirty'.

Within a year Barker died. John, Lewis Casson and Nicholas Hannen wanted a memorial service to be held for him in London but Mrs Barker refused her permission, so much had she always disliked her husband's connection with the theatre.

The war was over but John's work for ENSA was not. He was soon rehearsing Charles in *Blithe Spirit* and a new production of *Hamlet* for a five months' tour of the Middle and Far East. John Perry, who was promptly demobilized by the R.A.F. in September, was to go with them as company manager.

John had moved into a Queen Anne house in Cowley Street, Westminster. The neighbourhood appealed to him particularly because it was so close to Westminster School, the Abbey and the streets around it, which he had known so well when he was a boy.

After flying out to Cairo, John and John Perry went to see the theatre, which had been built for the first performance of Verdi's *Aida* and a visit of the Empress Eugenie in the sixties. The next day they stopped at Lydda, in Palestine, flying over the Jordan to Baghdad. After an all-night flight, touching down only once or twice for an hour, they reached Karachi. John's letter from Bombay said 'There are bits of Beau Geste, Chu Chin Chow, Charing Cross Station in a fantastic jumble – the worst is the smells and beggars and ugliness and squalor, the best the wonderful touches of colour – mostly in the scarves and sashes and turbans, all washed and washed till they are the most exquisite shades of blue and yellow and crimson, and those colours stand out with unexpected and dazzling brilliance against all the rest which is cheapjack and sordid and often depressing.'

In Bombay there were two performances of *Blithe Spirit* and

As Shylock in *The Merchant of Venice*
(1938)
(Gordon Anthony)

As Benedick, with Diana Wynyard as Beatrice, in *Much Ado About Nothing* (1952) *(Radio Times Hulton Picture Library)*

As Konstantin
in *The Seagull* (1925)

As Trigorin with Peggy Ashcroft as Nina in *The Seagull* (1936)

As Gaev in *The Cherry Orchard* (1961)
(Royal Shakespeare Theatre Company)

As Trofimov
in *The Cherry Orchard*
(1925)
(Alan Trotter)

As Vershinin
in *Three Sisters*
(1938)
*(Radio Times Hulton
Picture Library)*

As John Worthing
in *The Importance
of Being Earnest*
(1930)

As Ferdinand
in *The Duchess of Malfi*
(1944)
(Cecil Beaton)

As John Worthing in
*The Importance of
Being Earnest* (1939)
(Angus McBean)

As Jaffier in *Venice Preserv'd* (1953) (*Angus McBean*)

As Valentine in *Love for Love* (1944) (*Cecil Beaton*)

As Mirabell in *The Way of the World* (1952) *(Angus McBean)*

As Joseph Surface in *School for Scandal* (1937)
(Radio Times Hulton Picture Library)

As Cassius, with James Mason as Brutus, in the film of *Julius Caesar*
(M.G.M.)

Laurence Olivier as Richard III, with John as Clarence,
in the film of *Richard III*
(London Screen Distributors)

As Lord Raglan in *The Charge of the Light Brigade*
(Woodfall Films)

Pamela Brown as Jennet and John as Thomas
in *The Lady's Not for Burning* (1949)
(Angus McBean)

As The Headmaster in *Forty Years On* (1968)

In New York,
listening to the playback
of a recording
of *The Ages of Man*
(1959)

then *Hamlet* for the rest of the week. But ENSA allowed no civilians to attend the performances, which antagonized the press. In any case the troops made money by buying tickets and selling them to the Indians, and even the boxes were full of turbans and saris.

The actual performances of *Hamlet* were unexpectedly exciting for John. It was fascinatingly different to play the part to an audience that did not know what was going to happen next.

In Madras he had to share a tiny dressing-room with eleven other actors and the theatre was a kind of circular speech-room with the auditorium stepped in a rising ring of seats. The stage was built so far back from the auditorium that he was afraid the actors' voices would be drowned by the monsoon which was raging outside. Fortunately there were planks available and he had the orchestra pit quickly covered over. Although he had only six hours for lighting and re-rehearsing the play to fit the new space, he hurriedly revised the whole production, bringing every scene out onto the improvised apron. Inevitably there were a great many hitches during the first of the three performances, but John, who had never before been so near to his audience while playing Hamlet, found it very exhilarating, particularly for the soliloquies, in which it was a big advantage to feel so closely in touch with them. He ended some scenes by running up the aisle, making his exit through the auditorium. These performances of *Hamlet* were, he feels, among the best he ever gave.

There was only one theatre in Ceylon big enough to take *Hamlet*, so they gave three performances of it in Colombo and ten of *Blithe Spirit* in the other two towns in Ceylon, Kandy and Trincomalee. John stayed on in Colombo after the others to give his lecture recital on 'Shakespeare in Peace and War', which raised £400 for the Red Cross. Together with Marian Spencer, who played Gertrude in *Hamlet* and Ruth in *Blithe Spirit*, he then travelled in the ward-room of a flying boat to Singapore, a twelve hour flight of over sixteen thousand miles.

They stayed in an ugly ramshackle hotel where the water was cold and the electric light rationed. One evening they went to a fair. There were three Chinese theatres in it with female impersonators, squealing orchestras and garish drop-scenes. Outside there were punch-balls and penny slot machines. The crowd was very motley – Dutch and British soldiers mixing with the Chinese and Malayans.

The theatre had a seating capacity of six hundred, but a

thousand people were packed into it for each performance and
the unfortunates who had to stand were only allowed in just as
the curtain was going up, so they were still clattering to their
places through the opening scene. Altogether it was hard for the
actors to concentrate. The windows had been blown out, and at
the back of the theatre there were no doors, only curtains, so all
the street sounds came in, while twittering swifts swooped in
and out of the roof. Solomon, the pianist, was playing at a concert
in the equally windowless hall next door. He must have been
as distracted by the bursts of applause for *Hamlet* as the actors
were by the applause for him and the shouts of 'Encore' which
continually interrupted their concentration.

As a child, Solomon had played a sailor in a performance of
H.M.S. Pinafore at Mathilde Verne's school in Cromwell Road
when John's sister Eleanor had acted and sung Little Buttercup
and John had only been a sailor in the chorus. He had afterwards
seen Solomon playing at the Albert Hall, a child prodigy in a
velvet suit. Now in Singapore, a balding man of about John's
own age, he was playing at a Sunday concert with the local
orchestra, which included a large proportion of natives and many
ex-prisoners-of-war. Some, whose hands had suffered in captivity,
had only been regaining the use of them gradually during the
last three months. 'I stood out on the balcony at the very back
of the circle,' John wrote, ' – again they made no attempt to shut
the doors – and watched the darkening of the harbour to one
side of me, with the lights coming on in the ships, while on the
other side one could see the packed hall – with men in uniform
sitting, standing and crouching in every nook and cranny – on
window sills and parapets – the birds sailing in and out under
the lights and the distant orchestra sawing away like mad.'

On 27 December the company flew from Singapore to Saigon
in a twin-engine Dakota. Over the China Sea they came into
terrible weather. Buffeted violently about by the winds, the plane
was now at an altitude of ten thousand feet, now only a few yards
above the sea. Afterwards the pilot said 'I never thought we'd
make it.' But John sat stolidly in the middle of the plane doing
The Times crossword and frowning whenever anyone was sick
too close to him. 'Were you frightened John?' John Perry asked
in the evening. 'I don't know really. I thought it was better to
concentrate on something.'

To fly to Hong Kong they got up at 5.45, dressing and
packing in the light of a hurricane lamp. They had been warned

to expect a difficult flight but, unlike the last one, it was easy. At three in the afternoon they made a perfect landing in between two ranges of mountains.

They stayed in a comfortable hotel in Kowloon, across the ferry from Hong Kong. Rangoon, where they flew next, was a sorry contrast, much of the town in ruins, every house-front flecked with bullet-marks, pot-holes in the roads, tottering tele-graph poles, shops and bazaars empty.

The rectangular auditorium of the theatre reminded John of a congregational chapel. Hazel Terry, Irene Browne, Marian Spencer, John and John Perry were given a 'V.I.P. Bungalow' at the edge of the slow-moving river; the others were put in a hotel nearby. After ten days in Rangoon, they had six days in Delhi, where John stayed in Government House with Lord and Lady Wavell, in the last splendour of the English Raj. Much as John disliked Cawnpore, the next town, which was arid and dreary, he was very glad afterwards to have gone there. The troops, weary and dreading another hot summer there, were responsive and grateful. There had been a mutiny in the camp and John put his foot in it by saying in his curtain speech 'I do hope you got what you wanted.'

After a fortnight at Karachi, the tour ended at Cairo. On 7 February, in a press interview there, John remarked that he did not intend to play Hamlet any more. He never went back on his decision.

32 Raskolnikoff

Unfortunately a plan for him to join forces with Olivier and Richardson at the Old Vic came to nothing, but John immedi-ately threw himself into preparations for a production of Rodney Ackland's new dramatization of *Crime and Punishment*, with Robert Helpmann as Raskolnikoff. After the exhausting ENSA tour (eighty performances in eighteen weeks) John had felt he could do with a holiday. But he had only just gone away when the news came through that Helpmann had been taken ill and ordered by his doctors to rest. John cut his holiday short to come back to London for a conference with Beaumont. They decided that John should play Raskolnikoff himself, and Anthony Quayle was asked to direct. As he later wrote to John, 'three-quarters of this production came from the evenings we spent in Cowley Street and without your help then the play would have been nowhere. You were as tactful, too, in withholding advice as you were in giving it – and God knows there must have been times when your producer's fingers itched. But always you helped me to maintain my position with the company and set them a wonderful example of a disciplined actor.'

Edith Evans played Madame Marmaladoff but she was not altogether happy in the part. Audrey Fildes was Sonia and Peter Ustinov played the Chief of Police. Paul Sheriff designed a brilliant multiple set to contain the whole action in four rooms and a staircase.

Obviously John was hardly ideal casting for the poverty-wracked Russian student. He was too old and found the part extremely difficult. Like so many adaptations from novels, the play lacked shape. The emotional climaxes were unprepared, there was too much detail and too many distracting minor characters.

The pre-London tour opened in Manchester in May 1946. A good deal of tightening was still needed, both in the production and in John's own performance. He wrote in a letter 'I hope to get less mannered as I gain confidence – it was already simpler last night and I know better now what to begin to eliminate – especially some of the gulps and snorts and my standing positions.'

The process of paring the performance down continued through the rest of the five week tour. The play opened at the New on Wednesday 26 June. After seeing it again on the Thursday, Quayle wrote to John about his performance:

> It is subtle and it is lucid, it is nervous and it is relaxed, it is delicate and it is absolutely sure. There are the few melodramatic movements of which I spoke to you tonight, which I do not like. (Vocally you have achieved a perfect economy but in movement there is here and there the redundant twist and turn) . . . I think too that you can improve the last 'soul's dead' scene with Sonia. I watched this scene very closely tonight and I do not think you were feeling it truly. I did not get from you the feeling of stark terror that Raskolnikoff should have. I think he should be like a little boy who has stuck a pin into himself and found to

his horror that no blood comes. You have very nearly got it but as it is the very climax of the part I think it is worth striving for. Beyond these two criticisms I have nothing but admiration.

Most of the critics were less critical. Agate was sure it was 'the best thing after Hamlet he has ever given us'. But some reviewers found the first act better than the rest, and in the *New Statesman*, Stephen Potter was altogether less enthusiastic: 'Perhaps Mr Gielgud acted too much on one note, the quiet I-must-be-calm-voice followed too quickly, too often and too regularly by the nervous staccato outbreak. One longed for a moment of quietness while one marvelled at the ability to keep at strain.'

33   Eighteen Months in America

For his tour of *The Importance* and *Love for Love* in Canada and the United States, John's company included Robert Flemyng as Algy, Margaret Rutherford as Lady Bracknell, Pamela Brown, Jane Baxter and Jean Cadell. They opened with *The Importance* in Ontario, touring for five weeks before the first night in New York at the Royale Theatre in March 1947.

John was apprehensive because the two plays were neither well known nor highly thought of in America. It was eleven years since he had appeared there himself and the first time he had taken his own company, but Brooks Atkinson immediately remarked (in the *New York Times*) on his success in achieving a unity of style in the playing. 'Notice how all the actors hold their heads high as if they were elevating themselves above vulgarity. Notice how they greet each other with dainty touches of the fingers, avoiding at all costs the heartiness of the handshake.' Other critics were equally welcoming and John Chapman of the *Sunday News* commented that in these days of Marshall Aid 'it is quite a comfort to discover that Britain can send us an ambassador whose mission is, simply and gloriously, to give'.

At a Russian-style Easter party John had a long talk with

Greta Garbo, 'who is the most extraordinary individual – little girl face and now quite short hair tied with an Alice ribbon, hideously cut dress of beautiful printed cotton to her calves and then huge feet in heel-less black pumps. Lovely childlike expression and great sweetness – she never stopped talking but absolutely to no purpose – said her life was empty, aimless, but the time passed so quickly there was never time to do anything one wanted to do! All this with twinkling eyes and great animation, not at all the mournful tones of her imitators – charming slight accent. But I couldn't make out whether her whole attitude was perhaps a terrific pose.'

After their success with *The Importance* in New York they then opened with *Love for Love* in Washington during a May heatwave. But it went fairly well, though the performance was rather jerky and uncertain. Before it began, John and Robert Flemyng had rashly drunk two mint juleeps each, deceived by their mild flavour into thinking them innocuous, but they felt the effect as they reeled back through the stage door. It was also a big theatre with an old-fashioned deep stage which set the action too far away from the audience for projecting comedy. Everyone was afraid of playing too fast for Congreve's elaborate sentences to be understood. Some of the older actors underplayed through nervousness, while others were inclined to force the laughs. But the reception was warm and the press good.

Against the advice of the Theatre Guild, which was presenting him, John took the production on to Boston, where it was well received and the whole week was rapidly sold out. But it was a staunchly religious town and after the first night the City Fathers insisted on the omission of words like 'pimp' and 'whore' but, failing to understand several of the coarsest jokes, they failed to censor them. They were particularly strict about any anti-religious implications, jokes about the Pope and so on. These were all piously cut for the week in Boston.

The New York notices were very disappointing. Brooks Atkinson was less enthusiastic this time about the ensemble playing. He judged that the other actors were playing in a 'higher style' than Gielgud himself and 'the pallor of his acting throws the whole performance out of balance'.

Meanwhile back in England both Laurence Olivier and Ralph Richardson were knighted. But Olivier wrote to John saying that he felt embarrassment at being given preferential recognition. Ralph Richardson wrote in the same vein and John was very touched by their letters. Had he wanted to compete with the prestige and popularity that Olivier was now so rapidly winning in England, John should have put in an appearance on the West End stage immediately following the run of *Love for Love*. As it was, rumours were spreading that he had decided to stay in the States and to take American citizenship.

Actually he had already promised to direct Judith Anderson in a new translation of Euripides' *Medea* by Robinson Jeffers, which was to go into rehearsal at the beginning of September 1947. It was not his original intention to play in it himself, as he did not feel particularly suited to the part of Jason, but he could not find anyone who was ideal for it and when Judith Anderson took immense pains to persuade him to play in it at least for the first eight weeks, he gave in, partly as a gesture to her and partly because the part might be quite an effective contrast to the two comedy roles he had just played. 'If I could get a really striking make-up, wig and clothes,' he wrote, 'and play it as a character part – a sort of young Macbeth – I think the strength of the character would be very effective for me . . . It is something a bit different from anything I've done and that always tempts me.'

As he worked on the part, he became interested in the visual possibilities. His original intention was to play the first act in armour, changing into a white tunic for the second, to appear romantically scorched at the end, his face, arms and hair blackened by the fire – 'a dark broken figure sprawling on the steps – when she comes out in a light dress stained with blood and goes down a rocky decline towards the sea carrying the bodies of the children.'

For the set, he gave the designer, Ben Edwards, an idea which had been in his mind ever since he had seen Komisarjevsky's production of *The Snowman*, in which the audience was shown the same room from a different angle for each act. To push forward the temple portico in *Medea* was expensive, requiring a great many stage-hands, but it did produce a kind of close-up on the most violent part of the play in which she killed the children.

Despite all his hard work, the notices were disappointing. George Jean Nathan said he was 'a tenor Siegfried cast as a bass Hagen'. Nor was his direction praised, though in fact he had, as the cast recognized, done good service for the play. As the chorus he had three women of contrasting ages and personalities.

But it would have been almost impossible to devise a good production that was also a good framework for the emotional hurricane of Judith Anderson's performance. As Alan Downer wrote, 'He has tried, through grouping and movement, to suggest the temper and attitudes of the classical society which the original suggested. When Miss Anderson is not on the stage he succeeds but with each of her entrances the focus inevitably shifts and the play, as a play, is destroyed'.

But Judith Anderson had a prodigious personal success as Medea and the play was doing excellent business. Toscanini came to see it twice and Mrs Roosevelt was very complimentary to both John and Judith Anderson, who was grateful enough to give John a first edition of *Little Dorrit* in the original fortnightly serial parts. But she was very hurt when he left the cast to take a holiday before starting rehearsals for *Crime and Punishment*.

Komisarjevsky was now living in New York where he was running a drama school. Partly to do him a good turn, and partly because he thought it was likely to improve his own performance, John arranged for him to be asked to direct *Crime and Punishment*. He accepted readily and, as usual, asked only a low fee, but he was an old man now and his behaviour was more perverse than ever. The London set had worked very well but though Komisarjevsky accepted it for use in New York, he obviously felt he could have designed a better one himself. He also seemed to distrust Rodney Ackland's dramatization of the novel and insisted on making a lot of changes. He wanted to cut Katerina's part down and reduce the importance of the lodgers, but to improve John's part, giving him less hysteria, more variety and a good scene in the first act.

At first John was pleased with these ideas but wondered how Rodney Ackland would react after his original script had been so successful in London. Ackland was still in England and on reading Komisarjevsky's new version of Act One he said he would not come to New York. But eventually he arrived, stayed in John's apartment, and got on very well with Komisarjevsky, agreeing to a number of changes, though rather against his own better judgment.

Komisarjevsky added ten parts for students of his school and made difficulties about the entrances. How did people get into the house without a key? he demanded. So he introduced a doorbell and a housemaid who went down to open the door each time a new character arrived, adding to the conglomeration of distractions on the side-lines of the action. Ackland had built his dramatization around Marmaladoff's death. Komisarjevsky insisted that no previous dramatization which included this episode had ever succeeded. Unable to persuade John or Ackland to cut it, and taking an unreasoning dislike to the actor who was playing the part, he compromised absurdly by putting Marmaladoff downstage in a dark corner with his back to the audience.

Auditions were protracted and embarrassing, mainly because Komisarjevsky was unpleasant to the Jewish and German actors who came to read for the Russian parts, turning his back whenever one appeared. John had to use all his tact, but it failed him with one girl whom he turned down by saying 'I'm sorry dear. You're not blowzy enough.'

Rehearsals were chaotic. For the first week Komisarjevsky made them sit around reading from scripts and when the time came to put in the movement, he spent a disproportionate amount of time working with the students from his school. A well-known actor had been cast in one of the most important parts but after rehearsing for ten days, he was so obviously going to be bad that he had to be asked to give up the part amid stormy scenes created by the famous actress who was his wife. He was replaced by Vladimir Sokoloff, a Russian actor Leslie Faber had talked about during the run of *The Patriot* in 1928. Sokoloff was then working for Max Reinhardt in New York, playing Puck in *A Midsummer Night's Dream* and Robespierre in *Danton's Death*. He was a very small man with great charm and a wizened cat's face – a physical contrast to John which proved extremely effective in the interrogation scenes. Although he had only ten days to rehearse, he gave a brilliant performance.

There was a lot of disharmony among the cast. At the dress rehearsal, John's patience finally gave way and he took charge of certain scenes, while Komisarjevsky sat passively watching. On the Sunday they worked till 4 a.m., with a final dress rehearsal from two till five on the day of the first night.

Despite these setbacks, John felt that Komisarjevsky had helped to make his performance better than it had been in London. But once the play had opened to a fairly critical press, Komisarjevsky stayed away and the management and the actors had different opinions about which passages needed tightening. Robert Whitehead, the producer, wanted John to take over and rehearse the whole play afresh. At first he refused to alter anything except his own scenes, but finally he agreed and a rehearsal was called. Just as John was about to start working, Komisar-jevsky strolled in through the auditorium and in a long and bitter tirade, told the assembled company that none of them was any good, except a few, whom he mentioned by name, John, Lilian Gish (Madame Marmaladoff) and Dolly Haas (Sonia). He said that the American public was lucky to have such an interesting play on Broadway and of course couldn't appreciate it. He then took the rehearsal himself.

Vladimir Sokoloff later wrote an article in the *New Yorker* about the experience of working with John. 'We played *Crime and Punishment* for forty performances and each performance to me was just like a first performance. Gielgud is so flexible, so hospitable to each nuance that you give him, that there was always something new to find in what you yourself did. I enjoyed the way he would take it and answer it. In our three big scenes, I felt as though we were playing tennis with the audience, the ball going to the audience and then back to the stage . . . We were playing doubles with the audience and we always won. It was such bliss to act with a man like that.'

In order to prolong the run, the actors were all willing to accept cuts in their salary. John would have preferred not to go on since the play was not really liked, but he did not want to put the cast out of work, so the play survived until 14 February.

Terence Rattigan, who had wanted him for the part of Sir Robert Morton in *The Winslow Boy* (which was eventually played very successfully by Emlyn Williams) had written two one-act plays for John – *The Browning Version* and *Harlequinade*, which was partly a skit on the Lunts, with whom he had recently been working. Rattigan also drew on his memories of John as the director of the 1932 OUDS production of *Romeo and Juliet*, and if he had appeared as the ageing actor who plays Romeo, John would have been able to introduce some amusing self-parody. But neither he nor Beaumont was enthusiastic about *Harlequinade* and they both thought the idea of a double bill was dangerous. During a walk in Central Park, John tactlessly said to Rattigan 'I have to be very careful what I play now.' Although it had been announced that he would star in the Rattigan double bill in the autumn, it was later presented very successfully by another management, Stephen Mitchell, with Eric Portman scoring heavily in both parts.

Meanwhile John was thinking about a new production of *King Lear* in London, and some visits to Martha Graham's ballets got him fascinated in the possibility of using stylized movement and abstract settings for the play. This started the train of thought which led to the 1955 *Lear* with designs by Isamu Noguchi,

34 The Return of the Prodigal

John did not work in London again until the end of June 1948, when he was preparing his production of Tennessee Williams's *The Glass Menagerie*. At first he had been reluctant to direct it, thinking the play too American for him, but a recent visit to New Orleans had given him a feeling for the atmosphere, and Helen Hayes, his leading lady, persuaded him that the types were universal and encouraged him to trust the American cast to provide all the national colour that was needed. John had not seen the New York production but he was given the use of Eddie Dowling's original prompt copy and Tennessee Williams, who came to the London rehearsals, seemed to approve of the direction. But the production was not a great success.

John had reached a point at which it was harder than ever to plan his career. He had never taken the position which Granville Barker had summed up in his 1937 letter as 'theatre or nothing' but had compromised by running a company of his own for limited seasons. The Queen's season of 1937–8 had succeeded brilliantly, setting new standards of performance and production for the West End. But even if he had tried to keep that company together, the interruption of the war would have been fatal, and his Haymarket season of 1944–5, though a commercial success, attained nothing like the same standard of ensemble work.

So what should he do now? Irving had gone on playing the same parts in the same plays until he was too old for them. Fred Terry and Martin-Harvey had followed his example, touring the provinces with their old successes and giving occasional short seasons in London, till they were quite old men. There was, as always, a shortage of good new plays, and John, who had built up and maintained his reputation largely with the classics, had by now played all the great parts which most attracted him. It is easy for an actor and for a company to become stale, and at this crucial phase it could have been disastrous for his prestige if he had revived one of his previous successes unsuccessfully. In any case, he wanted to find something new, not to repeat himself. But he was more apprehensive than ever about making the wrong choice and for eight months he did not act at all.

As soon as *The Glass Menagerie* had opened at the Haymarket, John went to work on another production—*Medea*, again in the Robinson Jeffers version but this time with Eileen Herlie as Medea, Ralph Michael as Jason and Cathleen Nesbitt as the Nurse. After the try-out at the Edinburgh Festival, John felt pretty sure that the production ought not to be brought into London at all and on its first night he went to see another play, arriving back at the Globe just in time to see several of the H. M. Tennent staff come hurrying out of the bar to help swell the applause at the final curtain. The critics were hostile, cavilling at the translation and comparing Eileen Herlie unfavourably with Sybil Thorndike, who had played Medea in Gilbert Murray's translation.

For his own reappearance after a two year absence from the London stage, John chose *The Return of the Prodigal* – a choice which sounded apt but turned out to be unfortunate. The play had first been produced in 1905 and four years later the author, St John Hankin, had drowned himself at the age of thirty-nine. Lewis Casson had understudied and walked on in the original production and Sybil Thorndike had retained an enthusiasm for the play which she had now passed on to John.

But *The Return of the Prodigal* was a Radical play which led up to a scorching denunciation of society by Eustace Jackson, the character John played. This speech was now cut and in Peter Glenville's hands, the play became less abrasive and rather over-elaborate, with beautiful costumes, three attractive sets by Cecil Beaton and a starry cast which included Sybil Thorndike (as Eustace's mother), Irene Browne, Audrey Fildes, Walter Hudd, David Horne and Rachel Kempson. Reviewing for the *Evening Standard*, Beverley Baxter called it 'the best dressed and best acted bad play in London'. Two of the critics said that in his fair wig and knickerbockers, John reminded them of Danny Kaye.

At the last minute John was asked to take over the direction of *The Heiress*, an adaptation by Ruth and Augustus Goetz of Henry James's *Washington Square*. Peggy Ashcroft and Ralph

Richardson had leading parts and the director, who was in great difficulties with the production, had to be replaced about five days before the pre-London tour opened in Brighton. With so little time in hand, John was very uncertain whether he would be able to do anything to help. When he arrived at the theatre, Ralph Richardson, who was unhappy about the sacking of the director, murmured darkly 'We have today assisted at the murder of Julius Caesar.' John immediately saw that the furniture was very badly placed for the long scenes of formal dialogue and when he had watched the actors rehearse a few scenes for him, he felt that every move and position was wrong. The characters had all been made to stand about as if they were waiting for a train. The sedate Jamesian dialogue demanded just the opposite treatment. Rather nervously, John began to try different moves and groupings. Soon the scenes began to run more smoothly and he seemed to win the confidence of the company.

Peggy Ashcroft was apprehensive that despite the shortage of time he might want to try things out in too many different ways. But, as so often in an emergency, he rose to the occasion, proving that he could work rapidly, without his usual changes of mind. Within four days he had brought the play to life. At the Brighton first night the reception was overwhelmingly enthusiastic and the Goetzes said that the play worked far better in John's production than it had in New York, where Jed Harris had directed it with Wendy Hiller and Basil Rathbone.

35 'The Lady's not for Burning' and 'Much Ado About Nothing'

When it was announced at the beginning of March 1949 that John was going to star in Christopher Fry's *The Lady's not for Burning*, the headline in the *Evening Standard* ran 'Gielgud has new chance of No. 1 place.' In the article which followed, the critic went on to say 'Olivier is a first class actor and producer. But in my opinion Gielgud is the one genius of the contemporary English stage.'

John had been in New York when *The Lady's not for Burning* had been produced at the Arts Theatre with Alec Clunes, but Kitty Black and Daphne Rye, who worked in the Tennent office, had both seen it and kept saying it was an ideal part for John. Alec Clunes had an option on the play but a few months later he was suddenly willing to sell it.

Fry, who was now forty-one, had previously written several verse plays, but they had mostly been done at festivals and at little theatres. *A Phoenix Too Frequent* had been staged at the Mercury Theatre in 1946 and *Thor with Angels* in the Chapter House of Canterbury Cathedral. Before the war he had written sketches, but between the ages of seventeen and twenty-eight he had not written at all. Pamela Brown, for whom he wrote the part of the suspected witch in *The Lady's not for Burning*, had first met him at the Oxford Playhouse when she was in the company there. He had arrived with sketches and lyrics for a revue they were rehearsing and these were such a success that he was invited to stay on as resident producer. He had always thought that he wanted to write verse for the theatre but it was John's performance as Richard II which started him actually doing so. As he put it much later, 'Instead of the old sweep of rhetoric, Gielgud played his part in a minor key with clear precise enunciation.' After the old Bensonian style of Shakespearean acting, which was all Fry had previously seen, John's performance had been 'a revelation. You saw a mind creating a world as if it were a writer writing . . . The whole approach was of our time. He showed it was possible to be speaking not *as* verse, and yet in verse.' So it was curious that two of the best parts John ever had in modern plays, Richard of Bordeaux and Thomas Mendip in *The Lady*, derived directly or indirectly from the stimulus he unwittingly gave to two playwrights with Richard II, which he had only played about fifty times – at the Vic in 1929–30 and at the Queen's in 1937.

When John read the script he liked it enormously, though he found it hard to understand. He had persuaded Beaumont to buy the play for him but before it went into rehearsal he became more and more dubious about its chances of success. The pre-London tour began at Brighton and various problems arose. Thomas had a striking entrance, leaping in through a window, but for the next ten minutes he had very little to say or do. The audience was bewildered and he had somehow to explain himself. In the second act, John felt that the lovers, meeting again for the first time after Jennet (the suspected witch) had been thrown into prison and Thomas had been tortured with the thumbscrews, ought at least to ask each other what had happened while they were separated. Fry carefully considered all John's suggestions and gradually made improvements during the eight week tour.

Oliver Messel's beautiful sets and costumes helped to evoke a mediaeval atmosphere. As John said, 'The stage looks like an Italian primitive or one of the early Pre-Raphaelite pictures.' It was only after a year of playing in it that he wondered whether the designs were too romantic for the basic attitude of the writing. Beneath the elaborate surface of the verse there was a bitterness that might have been more interesting to capture in the production than the enchantment which Messel's designs helped to create. John was also, it seems, rather misled by a remark of Harcourt Williams. 'It's beautiful, original and striking. But if you do not play it with artlessness, the simplicity of children, you will be lost.' Fry himself was diffident about making suggestions, thinking that once a play had been handed over to a director, it was for him to interpret it, and that by interfering he might possibly destroy effects that would be valuable. And of course it is quite possible that a production which reflected his intentions more accurately would have been less popular.

Once again John collected an excellent cast: Pamela Brown, the twenty-four-year-old Richard Burton, Claire Bloom, Esmé Percy, Harcourt Williams, and Eliot Makeham, who was very funny indeed and touching too, as the Chaplain. John asked Esmé Percy to help him with his own performance by watching him from the front and generously gave him a credit as co-director. Richard Burton already had an extraordinary instinct for timing. His performance was charming and modest, though in rehearsal he annoyed John with fits of yawning whenever they were late in breaking for lunch.

John was already committed to directing Diana Wynyard and Anthony Quayle in *Much Ado about Nothing* which was to open at Stratford on 20 April. This meant he had to travel to Stratford and back each day from wherever he was playing *The Lady's not for Burning*, letting the *Much Ado* actors go on rehearsing by themselves when he had to leave at about four o'clock each day. Fortunately during the rehearsal weeks, all his touring dates were nearby. In spite of – or perhaps partly because of – having so little time, he did an excellent job on the production. Having no time to change his mind, he built up the production consistently and imaginatively, working with a Spanish designer, Mariano Andreu, who contrived an ingenious set with screens and walls which could be manœuvred by eight page-boys who changed the scene by moving them in and out like pages in a picture book.

This was the first production Andreu designed at Stratford. John had noticed his work years before in a Fokine ballet of Don Juan at the Alhambra, when he had been particularly struck by the black costumes and built-up head-dresses of the four shrouded women who drew huge white curtains with Beardsley motifs embroidered on them. During the war, when John was planning his production of *The Cradle Song*, he had wanted a Spanish designer but finding it impossible to trace Andreu, he had used another Spaniard, Grigorio Prieto. Later, hearing there was a possible part for him in Montherlant's play *Le Maître de Santiago*, John went over to Paris one Sunday night to see it. Unfortunately the performance was cancelled because the leading actor was ill, but seeing from the bills in the hotel that Andreu was the designer, he got in touch with him. Their collaboration was enormously successful, though Andreu spoke hardly any English.

On the Sunday before *Much Ado* was to open at Stratford, John took three or four members of *The Lady's not for Burning* company to see the dress rehearsal of *Much Ado*, which lasted all day. Monday was a Bank Holiday and that evening *The Lady* was opening in Leeds. A train was due to leave at noon from Birmingham but when John and the other actors arrived at the station, they found the whole platform packed with people. Two trains had been cancelled and if they waited for the next, they would not have arrived at Leeds till nine o'clock. Desperately they asked a taxi driver how much he would charge to drive them to Leeds and after an anxious, uncomfortable journey across the Yorkshire moors, they arrived at the stage door just in time for the curtain.

During the provincial tour of *The Lady's not for Burning* a great deal of tightening was done. Lines and jokes were cut and though not much new material was added, the alterations helped to make the play far easier to follow. Most important of all, John had discovered that the whole thing was less romantic than he originally thought. It was only when it was first played in front of an audience that he realized how much comedy there was in it and on the tour he worked continually to sharpen and solidify the whole production.

As always, John changed his mind a great deal about moves,

and at one point the Stage Manager pleaded with Fry to make him finalize them. She had rubbed out her pencil notes so many times that she had almost gone through the pages of the prompt copy. At the next rehearsal, Fry was sitting behind John when he changed a move he had already set. Fry tapped him on the shoulder, but the protest died on his lips when John turned round and said 'It's always better when it's different.'

The play opened in London on 12 May 1949. It was a very successful first night but despite the persistent shouts of 'Author', Christopher Fry would not appear.

John went on making changes after the play had opened. At one point he asked Esmé Percy to sit down in a different chair, apparently forgetting that Nora Nicholson was sitting in it and forgetting to tell her about the change. The result was that Percy, who only had one eye, sat down in her lap. Fortunately it was not entirely out of character for the drunken tramp he was playing.

There were a few critics who objected that John was lacking in male assertiveness, but the consensus was overwhelmingly favourable, though Fry felt that the embittered soldier in Thomas Mendip did not quite get a fair showing in John's performance. Though he was excellent in the passages involving self-mockery, he was not quite able to turn the mockery outwards or to show how Mendip's nature compels him to mock all the things he most cares about. In fact he was better at showing self-disgust than disgust at the outside world. But James Bridie wrote to tell John that he had never seen him better, and to point out how difficult things were made for Pamela Brown 'who has to make us fear for her almost single-handed because her persecutors are so funny'.

As usual, John went on working at the production all through the run. A bad production of *Love's Labour's Lost* (which he had neither seen before nor read) gave him what he called 'a great lesson in how not to carry on when speaking verse . . . Nora and I haven't *moved* our hands on the stage since'. He went on calling occasional rehearsals to simplify and refresh the performances, including his own. He now started the first act with more detachment and less pace, feeling that this made it clearer. He also slowed down the opening of the love scene 'to give a truer feeling of awkwardness and gradual awakening of interest and familiarity'.

In September, when John directed Sybil Thorndike at the

Apollo in *Treasure Hunt* which John Perry had written (again in collaboration with M. J. Farrell) three of his productions were running simultaneously in the West End. *The Heiress* was still playing to good business and *The Lady's not for Burning* survived into 1950, despite the general theatre slump.

36   Stratford-on-Avon

John had been disappointed not to be invited to Stratford in the thirties, but the standard had been lower then and it was a great compliment that because he was to lead the company now, the 1950 season was planned to open a month earlier than usual. Despite the severe winter and the petrol shortage, Anthony Quayle, who was now Artistic Director, was quite confident that John could fill the theatre for him, even in an unpopular play like *Measure for Measure*. He was right. Nearly 20,000 seats were sold before the season opened.

For *Measure for Measure* the director was the twenty-five-year-old Peter Brook. This was John's first experience of working with him, though he had known him since he was an Oxford undergraduate and had arrived at the Haymarket one day with a friend to ask whether he could use John's *Love for Love* sets in a film he was making of Sterne's *Sentimental Journey* on a budget of £250.

Ever since he had seen Charles Laughton as Angelo in the Old Vic season of 1933–4, John had wanted to play the part. In Guthrie's production, Laughton had made Angelo an outright sensualist in a billowing black gown with wide sleeves, roaming the stage like an obscene bat. But John saw Angelo as a repressed Puritan, concealing his sensuality under a mask of piety. Working on *Measure for Measure* was completely different from working on *Macbeth*, *Hamlet* or *Richard II*. Both the play and the part were almost unknown territory to him. There were no pieces of traditional business to be remembered or discarded.

Though he had designers working with him, Brook had conceived most of the ideas for the costumes and the set, which allowed the action to move very quickly, making clever use of a kind of cloister stretching upstage in two directions from a central point. Much of the action was lit by torchlight and the costumes, based on ideas derived from Breughel, also helped to create an exciting theatrical atmosphere. It was the first time that Brook had taken all the different sides of a production into his own hands. Even the music for the Page's song he wrote himself.

From the beginning, he got on very well with John. 'Between us,' Brook has said, 'there was a very deep intuitive understanding from the second we began to talk to one another. Both of us work very empirically: neither of us believes in starting from a set plan. Work would be experimental, high-speed. As John has this endless series of ideas, he immediately sees every possibility. In this sense he belongs completely to the most free and modern school. He might say, for instance, that this character is no doubt ferocious at this moment, and as he begins to speak the line ferociously, that gives him the idea that the character might be meaning to say that line in a very gentle way, and he does it, tastes it by doing it. So in the course of two or three days, an enormous number of possibilities have been explored.'

Brook was also aware that

John's highly developed sense of responsibility to an audience is greater than his responsibility to himself, and so, of the two integrities, John, unlike a number of actors, will sacrifice not only himself but the reality of his own work for the sake of not letting the audience down. The moment he hears a cough, he'll sense that the house is restless and produce a brilliant but well-tried stage trick to catch the audience's attention. That's where his great professionalism and his enormous experience are both a virtue and a vice. So a director can help by concentrating on him in a way that he won't concentrate on himself, creating for him a climate of selfishness that he won't create by himself. What you do is gradually build a glass wall around him with an intense spotlight in the middle of it. When the intense spotlight of his own creativity turns inwards on his own work, it has a shedding effect, as it has with all artists, always, because all artists, as their work develops, start to shed the unimportant to get closer to the essential. Submerged in each one of John's performances is a core which is pure, clear, strong, simple and utterly realistic. The act of working rightly is, for him, to come towards that core. Where, historically, his Angelo seemed so striking was that there was more of the essential John in it than had been seen for a long time, and less of the superficial, extravagant and tricksy John that had been seen in plays where he had been concentrating on everything except his own inner work.

John found that Brook immediately began to check his tendency to facile vocal and emotional effects and did not try to force his interpretation but seemed to like the thin-lipped hauteur he brought to the part. John played Angelo not as a conscious hypocrite, but as a man who really thought himself incorruptible until he met Isabella and found out how unscrupulous he could be under the impulse of a sudden lust. In this way he acquires much more of the stature of a tragic hero. John made his hubris lie in an over-estimation of his own self-control.

He had ordered a fair, shoulder-length wig and Brook and Quayle were both in the stalls when he first appeared in it. 'Oh John, you look marvellous,' Brook said. 'You look twenty-five.' John of course was delighted. Then Brook went on: 'But it's absolutely wrong for your performance.'

The idea of a close-fitting black cap was evolved overnight. It made Angelo look spiritually clean-shaven, unromantic and very strict. At the same time, the original grey velvet robe designed by Brook was replaced by a serge gown falling in heavy folds.

Playing opposite him as Isabella was the nineteen-year-old Barbara Jefford. She had auditioned several times for the part, finally being chosen in preference to two actresses who were quite well known. Naturally she lacked confidence and John was generous in the help he gave her, often encouraging her to take a dominating upstage position when otherwise she would not have dared to. He found her excellent to work with and the scenes of attempted seduction were highly effective.

The way he played his first meeting with Isabella was well described by the actress Gwen Watford in a letter headed 'in the queue Friday morning': 'It was a purely mental process, he made no physical movement at all but it seemed as if a tremendous force had suddenly gripped every muscle in his body and numbed his brain. There was a timeless pause as the shock lessened and he found sufficient strength to move down to the table and sit. And then the tremendous relief when he heard his own voice speaking steadily and under control. I must confess I found myself gasping under the impact.'

The last act is so full of improbabilities that most directors accelerate the tempo to give the audience as little time to think as possible. Brook was confident enough to take the last act very slowly, introducing several substantial pauses, of which the most striking was a very long one while Isabella was making up her mind whether or not she should plead for Angelo's life to be spared. After hesitating, Barbara Jefford had to walk downstage to Alan Badel (who played Claudio), and then fall on her knees in front of the Duke (Harry Andrews). John gave her courage to take all the time she needed and she found that the length of the pause scarcely varied from night to night.

T. C. Worsley wrote in the *New Statesman* 'The problem for a romantic actor, as his youth begins to evaporate behind him, has always been difficult. Mr Gielgud has continuously been haunted by his own Hamlet: he has never before, it seems to me, entirely shed the last vestiges of that part, though it has not been for want of trying. Now with his Angelo he makes a break – it may be a complete break – with his past. In this characterization of a thin, spinsterish walking Legality there are no traces of the romantic gestures, no echoes of the youthful tones. His Angelo, as meticulous for the letter of the regulations as a bloodless civil servant, yet harbouring in the inner recesses a hidden ambivalent itch, cuts a clean swathe of sense through the beginning of the play such as is not often given to it.'

Next came a revival of *Much Ado about Nothing*, John's production from the previous year, but this time he was to play Benedick himself. Having seen so many rehearsals with Quayle in the part, he now had to decide exactly where he wanted to repeat points he had suggested to Quayle and where he must devise other tactics for himself. Peggy Ashcroft had joined the company to play opposite him – the first time they had worked together for five years.

Her Beatrice was very much her own invention and at first John could not see what she was driving at. With Andreu's help she evolved her own clothes, much simpler than Diana Wynyard's, and her performance began to grow into something like a development of her coltish Juliet. It was a very touching, truthful characterization of a woman who was always putting her foot in it – rather in the way John did himself – not at all the conventionally comic sophistication of a bluestocking scoring witty points over all the other characters. As she saw it, Beatrice was 'above all an Elizabethan – an eccentric girl rather than a witty woman'. She felt that the 'great lady' Beatrice was a Victorian invention. Altogether, the Victorians damaged the Shakespearean heroes and heroines by refining them, though Irving and Ellen Terry must have had more of the common touch than Forbes-Robertson and Mrs Patrick Campbell.

In rehearsal, Peggy Ashcroft was worried that John was not

devoting enough time to their scenes together. As always, when
he was directing, he tended to neglect his own part, but his
performance emerged brilliantly on the first night. From then on
Peggy Ashcroft found that playing opposite him 'was like
having a marvellous partner in a dance'.

That John made such an enormous success of Benedick, both
in 1950 and in the revivals of 1952 and 1955, is all the more
remarkable when you consider how far he is from ideal casting
for the part. Benedick is a soldier, bluff, tough and a woman-
hater, as rough-hewn as Petruchio. Shakespeare obviously
intended a much coarser fibre in Benedick's blunt ripostes, less
polish and a different sort of assurance. Benedick is probably
meant to be in his early twenties; John was forty-six in 1950 and
fifty-one in 1955.* But though two critics detected flickers of
The Importance in his reading of certain lines, he succeeded in
exploiting the comedy for all it was worth and altogether he gave
a remarkably effective performance. Richard Findlater described
it as 'one of the most enjoyable evenings I have spent in any
theatre', and he liked John's 'succession of remarkable hats –
blancmange mould, floral cartwheel, tarboosh – worn with an air
of amused disbelief'.

One of the difficulties of the play is to avoid getting a laugh
on Beatrice's line "Kill Claudio" and Benedick's volte face "Ha!
not for the wide world." At first John was unable to avoid a laugh
on his reaction; later he succeeded by facing the difficulties
squarely and he ended the scene brilliantly, retreating on "Enough
I am engag'd; I will challenge him." Then, halting, as if arrested
by a premonition, he spoke the words "I will kiss your hand and
so I leave you. By this hand, Claudio shall render me a dear
account." About to go, he still hesitated. "As you hear of me, so
think of me." And then he took another lingering pause before
"Go comfort your cousin; I must say she is dead; and so farewell."
Shakespeare may have envisaged a Benedick who threw himself
into action more impetuously than this, but by playing on his
own personality, John used the pauses to indicate an amusing
mixture of reluctance and determination.

Another excellent pause was on "Lady have you wept all this
while?" after which Beatrice and Benedick look at each other in a
long pause full of understanding and sympathy.

Eleanor Farjeon came to see John five times as Benedick and

---

* Irving seems to have been equally miscast as Benedick. He was forty-four when he
first played it opposite Ellen Terry's Beatrice at the Lyceum.

finally wrote to him 'The upshot is – and I confess it with the greatest reluctance – Henry Irving is the second-best Benedick I have ever seen.'

The third production of the season was *Julius Caesar*, co-directed by Anthony Quayle and Michael Langham, with Andrew Cruickshank as Caesar, Harry Andrews as Brutus and Quayle as a Mark Antony who shouted the "Friends, Romans, countrymen" speech with his back to the crowd. John had asked to play Cassius rather than Brutus and this time Quayle was of great help in directing his performance. In *Crime and Punishment* he had left him to play it very much in his own way. But now, seeing that John's instincts were carrying him towards too romantic a reading of the part, Quayle fought hard to make him play Cassius more realistically as a tough soldier, and a bitter one at that. 'Go and station yourself between Whitehall and Pall Mall,' Quayle said, 'and watch the hard-bitten faces of the men trained for action and responsibility when they come out of the War Office. Look at the bowler hats and the red complexions. Cassius is a soldier up against a better soldier than himself in Caesar and he's bitter, like Iago, because he's been passed over. If you could play him with a tight lip and a clipped moustache, so much the better.' At first John's reaction was that he could only play the part in his own way and he asked Quayle not to force him in another direction. Quayle persisted, knowing that the Cassius he wanted was within John's range and about half way through the rehearsals, his performance started to come to life in the way Quayle had conceived it.

John was not altogether happy with the production as a whole but he surprised himself on the first night when his nerves made him play it with a violent rhetorical attack which to him seemed melodramatic and uncontrolled. But *The Times* reported that he had 'never before shown such sustained vehemence', and that he drew the audience's eyes to him in each of his scenes, while according to the *Evening Standard*, his 'burning sincerity made Brutus and even Mark Antony seem a puny pair by comparison'. J. C. Trewin's verdict was, 'It is the performance of the season, and – I would say – the Shakespearean performance of the year.'

Still he did not look forward to the Julius Caesar evenings. It was a strain for him to make himself audible above the restless crowd of Roman citizens, and to hold the audience's attention with so much activity all round him. With no prose to speak and long passages of verse to sustain, it was tiring and difficult to play the unvarying rhetorical lines in a large theatre, particularly at the high emotional pitch he had set for himself.

The final play of the season was *King Lear*, which John directed with Quayle in a composite set designed by Leslie Hurry, with an ingenious suggestion of a portcullis to frame the scene of Gloucester's torture and candle-lit side scenes which facilitated continuity. John of course based his production on what he had learnt about the play from his two previous perform-ances and especially from Granville Barker, to whom he made acknowledgment both in his programme note and in his first night curtain speech.

Peggy Ashcroft was Cordelia, Maxine Audley and Gwen Ffrangcon Davies played Goneril and Regan, with Leon Quarter-maine as Gloucester, Andrew Cruickshank as Kent, Harry Andrews as Edgar and Alan Badel as the Fool. Badel did not agree about the Barker characterization of the Fool. It seemed to him that what was wanted from him was a pretty, happy, dancing, singing boy. Badel, who was feeling his way in rehearsal, felt he needed to go very much more slowly than John wanted him to. What emerged for him was the idea of a boy from the kitchen, timid but unable to tell a lie. John saw that he was best left to himself and for the last two weeks of rehearsals made no attempt to direct him. The performance which emerged was a brilliant and memorable one, which surprisingly enough, fitted in per-fectly with John's performance as Lear. At the final dress rehearsal John gave a magnificent performance which had several of the other actors in tears, but on the first night he was tired and nervous, and there was some trouble with the storm effects, which were turned up too loudly, drowning some of his speeches. Nevertheless, the notices were very good. Ivor Brown praised him for going in for 'no embroidery of character acting in Olivier's way. He is the text incarnate and what more should anybody ask of Lear? . . . Goneril's refusal to play up Lear's folly at the start leads to the grander finale; Olivier's Lear less justified Kent's and Cordelia's loyalty.'

According to W. A. Darlington's notice, 'the emotional tension slackened' after the storm; according to Alan Dent's, 'from the thunderstorm onwards this is a great Lear'.

One or two of the critics like T. C. Worsley and Richard Findlater sensed that something had gone wrong, causing the performance to miss the mark that night. After spending the night in Stratford they went to the play again the following day and saw a performance which was quite excellent. Worsley was able to write his *New Statesman* review under the headline 'A Great Lear'. 'If Mr Gielgud is the great tragic actor *par excellence* of our generation, is it not by virtue of his ability to exhibit the particular kind of simplicity that lies at the heart of passion in highly conscious, complicated personalities? Both Mr Wolfit and Sir Laurence Olivier strike harder, clearer, louder at the note of the majestic or the terrible. But they oversimplify ... It is the weight Mr Gielgud gives to the ironies, the irresolutions, the subtleties, that gives the still moments when they come their extra turn.'

John's mother, now eighty-two, came to see the dress rehearsal and the first night. 'I can only be thankful,' she wrote, 'that I lived to see John so wholly master of his Art and his public, great actor and great artist. To have heard his voice break in "Howl, howl, howl, howl" and die in infinite tenderness on a final "never" of utter desolation is to hold a memory unspeakably exquisite. Earlier he is the primitive man at bay, opposed, frustrated, battered alike by the world and by the Elements, forsaken by Cordelia, hounded adrift by his daughters and their faction, his fight for power, for life itself rises and falls as the force of a great tide against breakwaters.'

Angelo, Benedick and Cassius are all taxing parts, but it was only after *Lear* opened that John fully remembered how much better it was to be playing in repertoire rather than attempting the same performance eight times a week. He was not in *Henry VIII*, the fifth play of the season, so he had some evenings free and with all four performances in such contrasted characters he was able to go on refining, paring down, improving the transitions, strengthening the spine of the characterization as he worked to eliminate unnecessary movement and vocal indulgence.

The Stratford season broke all records. Having started a month early, it was also extended by four weeks at the end, but it was still impossible to accommodate all the people who wanted to see the plays. Towards the end of the season there were all night queues every night for the unreserved seats. On the final Friday over fifty people were queueing before midnight. By the end of the season, 350,000 people had bought tickets.

Most important of all, the Stratford experience had been a watershed in John's development as an actor. Worsley was not alone in thinking that he had made a breakthrough with Angelo, becoming less of a romantic actor, widening his vocal and emotional range as he felt it less necessary to play for sympathy. Richard Findlater, too, wrote that as Cassius, Angelo and Lear he 'deepened and widened his acting range, ripening his fine sensibility, intelligence and skill'. Of Lear he wrote 'it has the profundity of common experience, lit by the incandescent fire of maturing genius'. This seems to me an accurate summing up. John's genius had come of age.

37 'The Lady' in New York

When John took *The Lady's not for Burning* to New York there was a warm welcome for him and for the play. The press was highly favourable and box office business was better than for any other serious play of the season. But whereas in London there had been laughter all through the play, here some of the comedy got very big reactions, some none at all. The lines quoted in the press seemed to get the biggest laughs. As one American said to an English newspaperman, 'Well, it's hard enough understanding the accent without understanding the words.'

On the whole it was the physical images which came off best, like the description of the moon as a "circumambulating aphrodisiac". There was a big laugh when Peter Bull (as the Justice of the Peace, Edward Tappercoom) was asked how something struck him and replied "With a dull thud". But the jokes about figures of speech — like John's "Tell that to a sailor on a horse" failed to appeal to the Americans, though he got a huge laugh on his Act One curtain line, "I demand fair play for the criminal classes," and the Chaplain amused the American audiences with his reference to a ladder "made of diminished sevenths" and with "That's all Greek to me. Except of course that I understand Greek."

John found the noise of New York almost overpowering. 'It seemed like a gigantic monster waiting to swallow one up and I suppose my nervousness exaggerated the feeling. It seemed as though the traffic down below drove right through my bedroom the first night I slept there — and the taxis drive with terrific exhilaration.'

By now he had spent over twelve months playing Thomas Mendip, so it was a relief when the management announced the decision to close the play in the middle of March 1951 after 151 performances. The reason given in the papers was that John had been ordered to rest by his doctors, but in fact he was perfectly well. He had to tour with the production for a month in Washington and Philadelphia before he could take a holiday. But first he had the satisfaction of breaking the house record at the Washington theatre. Previously it had been held by the Lunts, but in both the weeks he was there, John did even better business.

38   'The Winter's Tale' and 'Much Ado' Again

After his holiday John arrived back in England in the middle of May 1951, feeling fit and ready to start work on *The Winter's Tale* for the Festival of Britain. Peter Brook had been in New York, staying for three weeks in John's flat, making plans for the new production. Despite the telephone calls, which had been incessant as the New York hostesses bombarded the bright twenty-six-year-old director with invitations, John had very much enjoyed his company. But together they had decided against Brook's intriguing idea that John should double Leontes and Autolycus. Their next idea for Autolycus was Robert Helpmann, who was not available, but they managed to contract George Rose for the part and the two actresses they most wanted for Hermione and Paulina – Diana Wynyard and Flora Robson.

It had been the success of *Measure for Measure* which made John anxious to play another unsympathetic part in another of Shakespeare's less familiar plays. Again he had the same feeling of starting with a clean slate. As with Angelo, he had seen one performance of the play and had fallen in love with the part. Peter Brook seemed the ideal director to produce the necessary momentum in the divided interest of the action and the right imaginative framework to persuade the audience into a willing suspension of disbelief. Again John was at his best under Brook's direction and he was able to carry on from where he had left off at the end of the Stratford season. Possibly his range had always been wider than he knew; possibly he had only just succeeded in widening it. In any case, he consolidated his achievement, using his new-found powers to great effect.

He spoke the lines about cuckoldry in Act One Scene Two straight out to the audience, which was something very seldom done in the early fifties, even when the lines themselves require it, as here:

> There have been
> (Or I am much deceiv'd) cuckolds ere now;
> And many a man there is (even at this present,
> Now, while I speak this) holds his wife by th'arm
> That little thinks she has been sluic'd in's absence
> And his pond fish'd by his next neighbour – by
> Sir Smile, his neighbour

And this is how Arthur Sprague* remembers his reaction to the Oracle's revelation:

He seemed at first stunned, then staggered across the stage (the boards sounded), then sank upon the throne and groaned once. Some great actor of another age, a Macready, say, or a Kean, might have been puzzled by Mr Gielgud's Hamlet. He would, I am sure, have understood and admired his Leontes.

'I cannot remember him in better form,' Beverley Baxter wrote, and Cecil Wilson of the *Daily Mail* confirmed that 'Mr Gielgud has never looked more handsome, never spoken or moved more nobly', while Stephen Williams praised him for 'deploying the most resonant baritone I have ever heard from him'.

After a week in Brighton, Beaumont took the production to the Edinburgh Festival, and at the beginning of September it opened at the Phoenix Theatre where it played for 166 performances, the longest run the play had ever had. Previously the record had been held by Forbes-Robertson's 1887 production at the Lyceum, when Mary Anderson, the great Victorian beauty, had doubled the parts of Hermione and Perdita.

John stayed on at the Phoenix in a revival of *Much Ado About Nothing*, this time with Diana Wynyard as Beatrice. Fortunately there was no personal rivalry between her and Peggy Ashcroft. They had been very good friends ever since school, where they

* Arthur Colby Sprague, *Shakespearean Players and Performances*. A. and C. Black, 1954.

had once appeared together as Brutus and Cassius in the tent scene from *Julius Caesar*. They still sometimes performed it together as a party piece.

As Hero John cast the twenty-one-year-old Dorothy Tutin (whom he had seen in Christopher Fry's *Thor with Angels*). The production ran for 225 performances and again John broke the record, which was held previously by Irving and Ellen Terry.

John was now invited to direct *Macbeth* at Stratford with Ralph Richardson and Margaret Leighton, who were leading the 1952 company. John had to rehearse there during the day while still playing eight times a week in London. He designed the scenery himself in collaboration with Michael Northern – the first he had designed since *A Roof and Four Walls* in 1922. He wrote a programme note which ran

> I am producing *Macbeth* in this new manner because I've come more and more to the conclusion that Shakespeare never intended it to be done as a strictly historical play set firmly in the eleventh century, encumbered with melodramatic horned helmets, cloaks falsely baronial, bagpipes, tartans and the rest of it. The less 'realistic' we can make it the better.

But while it was a good idea to avoid scenic elaboration, his choice of a background of black velvet overstressed the basic point about evil and it blended rather uneasily with the furniture and the properties brought on for the banquet. The production was not much liked.

39   Cassius on the Screen

When Joseph Mankiewicz offered John the part of Cassius in a film of *Julius Caesar*, he was no longer hostile to the idea of Shakespeare on the screen, and *Julius Caesar* struck him as one of the most suitable of all the plays for filming. Despite some inevitable cuts, the script was impressively faithful to Shakespeare's text and generally so promising that John thought the play might come over even better than on the stage. After seeing

All about Eve, he also had a high regard for Joseph Mankiewicz, who had written and directed it. John was offered a very high salary and the rest of the casting was promising: James Mason as Brutus, Marlon Brando as Antony, Louis Calhern as Caesar, Deborah Kerr and Greer Garson as Portia and Calpurnia.

He was installed in a suite at the Hotel Bel Air, Los Angeles – two large and luxurious ground-floor rooms on a patio surrounded by a lush garden with a swimming pool. Rehearsals started on 7 August 1952 and they worked slowly and methodically. Shooting was due to start on the 18th and the whole film was scheduled to be made in twenty-five days but Mankiewicz decided to allow an extra week for rehearsals in the unfinished sets before the actual filming started.

At first Mankiewicz wanted Cassius to have a beard, but after some tests had been made, they agreed it was better for John to be clean-shaven, as he had been at Stratford. He found James Mason enormously helpful and generous. Brando he described as 'a funny, intense, egocentric boy of twenty-seven with a flat nose and bullet head, huge arms and shoulders, and yet giving the effect of a lean Greenwich Village college boy. He is very nervous indeed and mutters his lines and rehearses by himself all day long. Very deferential to me, and dragged me off to record two speeches of Antony on his machine, where he listens to his own voice and studies records of Larry (Olivier), Barrymore, Maurice Evans etc. to improve his diction. I think his sincerity may bring him to an interesting performance. His English is not at all bad . . . but I think he has very little humour.'

One evening Richard Burton, who was filming in *My Cousin Rachel*, drove John over to a cocktail party at the house of David Selznick and his wife Jennifer Jones at Malibu Beach. Charlie Chaplin was there. 'He is weary and neat, with carefully waved white hair and wonderful little expressive hands, and alternates between rather pretentious philosophical generalities and sudden bursts of very natural sweetness and warmth . . . He suddenly gave a fantastic imitation of an Italian actor. How he went to see Duse and this actor – he mimed the whole thing – gave the most skilled and voluble speech which fascinated the house – twirling a chair, sitting down astride it, hands on the back, the gestures, and a marvellous imitation Italian dialogue, made up to sound like the language – and suddenly there was a stirring behind the piano, and an old lady appeared from a curtained door and by her utter simplicity, as she first moved some flowers on the piano, slowly sat down, and held her wonderful hands towards the fire, the actor who had been so effective was completely blotted out and forgotten by the audience in a moment.'

John was invited to many Hollywood parties. 'One begins to scent the jealousies and disappointments and ambitions, much as in the theatre – only rather more concentrated out here – like actors crossed with Anglo-Indian civil servants who have a perpetual chip on their shoulders.'

Shooting actually started on Tuesday 26 August and watching the first scene with real sheep, pigeons, dogs, goats and dirty water running in the gutter, John felt that 'Herbert Tree's ghost must have breathed approval'. John asked why the pigeons did not fly away. 'Their wings are clipped,' he was told. One day a pigeon fluttered down from the balustrade to the floor of the studio. A large cowboy in overalls rushed to put it back, muttering 'Get back. Don't you want to work today?'

John found some of the actors' American English difficult to accept but this had not seemed to matter in his New York *Hamlet* and most of Cassius's scenes are with Brutus, which was fortunate, for James Mason was not only English but sympathetic and relaxed. John was greatly helped of course by having played the part in the theatre. Knowing the line of Cassius's development from scene to scene, he was much less worried than he would otherwise have been by having to play episodes out of sequence. He knew exactly where the climaxes came, where a scene went up and where it came down. But the other actors did not know the progressive line of their parts as well as he did. Brando lost his voice two or three times during the filming and Mankiewicz went ahead shooting crowd reactions in the forum scene to break up Antony's big speeches. Brando tended to play every speech almost full out, and though the cutting produced variety, it did not reproduce Shakespeare's superb shaping of the scene. Everyone was impressed by John's speed and accuracy in the long tirades, but both vocally and emotionally he had to lower the tone in many passages and he sometimes found it hard to underplay without losing urgency.

Soon they were three or four days behind schedule. In the murder scene time was lost because the actors had to wash the blood off, change their togas and make up all over again after each take.

When John saw the rushes of the tent scene he felt reasonably pleased but also self-critical. 'I blink and fidget still in close-up and my eyes wander as if I was looking to see if a policeman was coming to arrest me. Mason is so steady and clear in his facial acting that I get very jealous.'

John liked Brando and thought him extremely flexible as well as talented. One day he asked him 'Why don't you play Hamlet?' Brando looked at him hesitantly: 'Would you direct it?' John said he would. But nothing came of the idea.

Mankiewicz made good use of close-up details like Casca's sweating forehead as he pushes through the conspirators to strike the first blow at Caesar and there was a good cut from the sunlit stadium scene to the atmospheric night scene with Cassius and Casca whispering their plans for the murder, standing on the slippery cobble-stones against a background of flapping shutters. Then the camera glides on to Brutus pacing undecided in the garden, amongst the debris of broken branches after the storm.

Of course it was easier to achieve the right balance in the crowd scenes than it had been in the theatre. Mankiewicz could fill the screen with a vast, milling, noisy crowd, then pan or cut to let the leading characters fill the foreground, subduing the background sound as much as necessary, while the camera could focus the audience's attention, making each important detail of action and facial expression stand out clearly. John felt that the naturalness possible on film and the freedom (especially in close-up) from any need to over-project made it possible to suggest that verse might really be the natural speech of the characters.

The last two days were spent on location shots for the battle at Phillipi in a dusty quarry in the Hollywood Bowl under the scorching sun. John was, as usual, unhappy on horseback. In his heavy armour and boots he could only get on to the horse with the assistance of three men, and a cowboy had to ride ahead, leading his horse by a string attached to the bridle. Not wanting to undergo the cumbersome business of dismounting and remounting, especially in front of the infantry extras, John stayed in the saddle for several hours. When he was finally helped off the horse he was stiff all over and almost bow-legged. He then had to play a scene of jumping up from the ground from under his horse, which was supposed to have thrown him, dodging a shower of arrows and engaging in hand-to-hand fighting with shield and broad-sword. It struck him that the battle scene may have been left till last because of the danger of injuries. Afterwards it took four baths to wash off the dust and grime.

During the final weeks of filming, John had already been making plans for a season of three plays at the Lyric Hammersmith, including Thomas Otway's *Venice Preserv'd*, a play he had read a long time before. Venice had been his favourite city ever since he went there in 1939, and after seeing the superb designs Craig had done for a Berlin production in 1905 at the Lessing Theater, John was convinced the play could still be highly effective in the theatre. It had first been produced in 1682, when Otway was thirty. Betterton had played it at Drury Lane, where Garrick later revived it, and in the nineteenth century Macready was equally successful with it at Covent Garden, but since that time it had been almost completely neglected. When John suggested it to Peter Brook, he was intrigued by the idea and they worked together on the script, not only cutting, but editing and rewriting here and there, though without making any major changes.

The season at Hammersmith was to open with *Richard II*, which John had at first intended to play again himself. Fearing he might be thought too old for the part, he suggested Paul Scofield. As he realized later, it might have been wiser to engage another director than to ask Scofield to work under him in a part he had made so much his own. At first he tried to give Scofield complete freedom, but two days before the Brighton opening, feeling that he had been holding back, John made a lot of suggestions based on what he had done himself in the part. The result was not altogether happy. The performance did not have the edge it might have acquired had Scofield been able to work more freely on his own lines. Nevertheless, at the Lyric Hammersmith, the play took a record £1,936 in one week and Scofield's performance was widely praised.

The second play was *The Way of the World*, which opened in February 1953. John played Mirabell, Scofield Witwood, Pamela Brown Millamant and Margaret Rutherford Lady Wishfort. The cutting was very successful and the plot, which can be difficult to follow, emerged very clearly under John's direction. But he was deeply depressed at the time by the death of his brother Lewis. He could not find a definite character as Mirabell, and though he had only been twenty when he saw it, he was still too much under the spell of Edith Evans's Millamant to give Pamela Brown the help and the confidence she needed to recreate the character in her own way.

But Tynan, who was normally more critical of John and Richardson than of Olivier, was well disposed towards the production. 'What glorious contrasts Mr Gielgud has provided!' he enthused. 'Having assembled what I heard described, in an enviable slip of the tongue, as "a conglamouration of stars", he has let them have their heads. The play sails into life with pennants flying.' He praised Paul Scofield ('a beautifully gaudy performance, pitched somewhere between Hermione Gingold and Stan Laurel') and Margaret Rutherford ('the soul of Cleopatra has somehow got trapped in the corporate shape of an entire lacrosse team'). But he found the all-important scenes between Mirabell and Millamant unbalanced. 'Mr Gielgud, an impeccable Mirabell in plum velvet, has Pamela Brown begging for mercy almost before the battle is joined.' Like *Much Ado*, the play needs a heroine clever enough to prevent her affection from spilling into the open until the end of the play.

Reviewing the Hammersmith production for the *New York Times*, Brooks Atkinson neatly summed up its virtues and its faults. 'As an exercise in stylization, the acting is immaculate, satirically mannered and accomplished (but) in perfecting the style Mr Gielgud is omitting the life. Both Mr Gielgud and Miss Brown . . . are sacrificing the fun to the technique. Mr Gielgud's Mirabell is too scholarly and Miss Brown's Millamant lacks force.'

It was *Venice Preserv'd* which became the critical success of the season, though oddly enough it was the only one of the three plays to lose money. It was now hailed by Tynan 'as the last great verse play of the English language'.

Together Peter Brook, John, and Leslie Hurry, the designer, created a murkily claustrophobic atmosphere, ideal for the involved melodramatic story about a plot to overthrow the Venetian senate. The curtain went up on what looked like the top of a heavy archway laid flat on the small stage. It rose slowly and, as it did so, two huge chains attached to bolts on either side of the arch fell with a dramatic clatter, while the play of light on them suggested the ripples on moving water. The whole stage effect gave the feeling of a gondola passing under a bridge. For the scene in the Doge's palace, Leslie Hurry designed a backcloth with a crowd of people painted on it in perspective, and for the conspiracy scene he used an idea John suggested. At the Palazzo Dario in Venice he remembered seeing how a gondola could be propelled through a watergate into the paved hall of the house so that guests could be brought indoors dry-shod. John suggested a similar cellar for the conspirators' meeting – a scene which was known by the company as 'the Gondola Garage'.

Venice Preserv'd is one of the few tragedies which, like *Othello*, has two male parts of almost equal importance. John played Jaffier, a noble but impoverished Venetian secretly married to Belvidera (Eileen Herlie), who has been disowned by her father, a senator. Scofield's part was Pierre, a cynical foreign soldier who exploits Jaffier's disaffection to recruit him for a conspiracy against the Senate. But when the leader of the conspirators tries to seduce Belvidera, Jaffier betrays the plot to the council and the play ends with madness, an execution, a suicide and a ghost scene.

Tynan had one reservation. 'The play's major flaw is that Otway allows Jaffier far too much self-pity, a mood of which John Gielgud, as an actor, is far too fond. The temptation sometimes proves too much for him: inhaling passionately through his nose, he administers to every line a tremendous parsonical quiver. But pictorially, if not emotionally, this is a very satisfying perform-ance.'

The last sentence implicitly contradicts Tynan's most famous dig at John – made à propos of his 1957 Prospero: 'bodily inexpressive and manually gauche, he is perhaps the finest actor, from the neck up, in the world today.' In 1930, reviewing his novice's Romeo, Ivor Brown may have been justified in objecting 'Mr Gielgud from the waist downwards means absolutely nothing.' But Tynan's jibe was unfair. Except as Noah and Shylock, John has done almost nothing to disguise his body in a physical impersonation and little to disguise his face. Olivier can magnetize an audience with his physical plastique, using his body as a dynamo of animal strength. But John is very unaggressive in the theatre and has never been able to play on his own sexuality. If Olivier is a Dionysian actor, John is an Apollonian, seldom convincing as a soldier and as a lover more lyrical than erotic. But it is absurd to call him 'bodily inexpress-ive'. On the contrary, he is capable of characterizing very effectively with his whole body. The nobility of his Hamlet, the age and sturdiness of his Lear, the brisk buoyancy of his Jack Worthing, the viper elegance of his Joseph Surface could only have been produced by an actor with a highly expressive body and very considerable skill in managing it.

Thanks to Olivier and Richardson, who personally persuaded Churchill, John's knighthood, long overdue, was announced in the Coronation Honours List on 2 June 1953. It was apt that this was during the run of *Venice Preserv'd*, for Jaffier's first line is "My Lord, I am not that abject wretch you think me." On the eve of the Coronation, there was such a prolonged burst of laughter, cheering and applause after the line that John had to pause for several minutes.

Paul Scofield made his first entrance shortly after John. That night he was waiting in the wings when John went on stage and he remembers how 'the audience exploded into wild cheering and applause. When, a long time later, I came on, John's face was streaming with tears and the whole theatre was charged with a high emotional excitement. It seemed as if the whole world was glad for him and he was overwhelmed by this quite unexpected and clamorous revelation of public affection. And it was his own humility and vulnerableness that was most moving. It was also quite funny, because it wasn't easy after that to get on with the play!'

After the season at Hammersmith, John went to South Africa to play Richard II himself in the Rhodes Festival. With John Perry, who was managing the company, he travelled separately from the others in a Comet, which had to refuel every three hours. After a bad landing in Rome, where the under-carriage was damaged, and a difficult landing in Khartoum in the middle of a sandstorm, they were late in arriving at Livingstone. But John still took the first opportunity to see the Victoria Falls. The huge cloud of spray above the waterfall dominated the view and baboons were crawling about by the roadside. He was driven through the Game Park and round the top of the Falls. 'The most lovely light every moment,' he wrote, 'two or three rainbows at a time spanning those great gorges where the vast heaps of water hurl themselves – down below grey heaving clouds of spray like the bottom of a gigantic cauldron and rocks and slopes of trees that make the dramatic impact still finer.'

At Bulawayo it was surprisingly cold and John had only brought summer clothes with him. The theatre was huge and newly built, laid out in a wide, treeless plain, where the wind howled unceasingly. The dressing-rooms were heated but the stage and the auditorium were icy-cold, so the dress rehearsal, which lasted for eight hours, was extremely uncomfortable. Still deaf from the noise of the plane, John could hear his own voice inside his head. On the vast stage, the simple screen scenery from Hammersmith looked toylike and ineffective, while all the moves had to be rearranged because it took so long to cross from one side to the other.

The Monday evening audience had to sit huddled in rugs and overcoats for 3¼ hours, but they were very enthusiastic. For most of them it was the first chance for several years to see live theatre.

The house was usually fairly full but it was hard to know where the people came from. During the day, the streets were oddly empty, and so were the Exhibition Grounds. The Rhodesians who spoke to John were pathetically anxious to seem welcoming and appreciative. He was never told 'We enjoyed the play' but always asked 'Are you pleased with your reception?'

What disappointed him most was the actual experience of playing Richard II. Ever since 1937 he had been longing to act the part again, especially when he was directing Scofield in it. But in Bulawayo he found that all he could do was an imitation of the performance he had given at the age of thirty-three. Sixteen years experience of life and an improved technique seemed to be of no help. Like Hamlet and Romeo, Richard II had been a splendid milestone in his career, but one he could not return to.

41 'A Day by the Sea'

The playwright John Whiting had been an actor in *The Winter's Tale* and in the season at the Lyric Hammersmith. When his play *Saint's Day* had won a competition organized by the Arts Theatre for the Festival of Britain, it had been savagely mauled by the critics but there were letters in *The Times* from Tyrone Guthrie and Peter Brook, professing their faith in Whiting's talent, and, two weeks later, from Peggy Ashcroft and John, who wrote 'We found it moving, beautiful and fascinating.'

Whiting had an enormous regard for John, and wrote *Marching Song* in the hope that he would play the leading part, a German general who is released from seven years of imprisonment to find that there is no place for him in the new apparently democratic society. John liked the play and it was announced in the papers that he would star in it in the autumn of 1953. But before he was fully committed, he was offered *A Day by the Sea* by N. C. Hunter, whose first big success, *Waters of the Moon*, with Edith Evans, Sybil Thorndike and Wendy Hiller, had been filling the Haymarket Theatre for a year. Ever since the war, John had been unable to find a single new play he wanted to do, except *The Lady's not for Burning*, and now there were two possible parts at the same moment. *Marching Song* was far more original and far better written, but it was a difficult play and it did not succeed when it was produced the next year. One of the attractions of *A Day by the Sea* was the possibility of assembling an extremely starry cast. John also saw exactly how he could direct it and, encouraged by Beaumont, this was the play he chose.

It was the first time he had played a prose part by a contemporary writer since the 1946 ENSA tour of *Blithe Spirit* and it was hard to adapt to the rhythms of modern dialogue. 'I am afraid of talking as quickly as I do off the stage,' he told a journalist.

When the play opened at the Haymarket, Tynan called it 'an evening of unexampled triviality . . . It was like watching a flock of eagles and macaws of magnificent plumage jammed for two hours into a suburban birdcage.' Ivor Brown summed up John's production by saying that he 'directed the play's inaction with a clever capacity to keep the immobile seemingly important'.

All the same, *A Day by the Sea* was a huge success with the public and the actors settled down for what was obviously going to be a long run. But in May 1954, while he was working at the Lyric Hammersmith, on a production of his own adaptation of *The Cherry Orchard* with Trevor Howard and Gwen Ffrangcon Davies, John was taken ill. He only missed a couple of performances of *A Day by the Sea* and he insisted on taking the dress rehearsal of *The Cherry Orchard*, but he had to go back to bed immediately afterwards and he went on suffering from double vision for some weeks.

The part of Julian in *A Day by the Sea* was not a rewarding one, but again John was able to find comedy in priggishness. Ralph Richardson was excellent as an unhappy doctor and Sybil Thorndike, Lewis Casson, Megs Jenkins and Irene Worth were all contributing fine performances. This was John's first experience of working with Irene Worth, a splendid actress who was also to become a close friend.

42   Three Shakespeare Plays

As early as 1947 John had been trying to conceive a production of *Lear* based in some way on stylized movement. He did not apply this line of thinking to his 1950 *Lear* at Stratford, which was still influenced by Granville Barker, but he returned to it in his Stratford production of *Macbeth* in 1952, using simplified settings and costumes to avoid any attachment to place or historical period. The result was disappointing, but convinced that the idea was sound, he made a more determined effort to realize it in a 1955 production of *Lear*, designed by Isamu Noguchi, the Japanese sculptor who had produced such impressive sets for Martha Graham's ballets on Greek themes.

John did not know that Noguchi had never designed costumes. He was still in the United States when he accepted the commission to work on the production. When, after sending over his set designs, he at last arrived in England, he was surprised to be asked where his costume designs were. The fee he was getting was so high that it was impossible to engage a second designer, and in any case no Westerner could have devised costumes that could be worn against the background of Noguchi's scenery. He had to do the work hurriedly but he came back with tiny wooden boxes containing exquisite dolls dressed in miniature versions of the costumes. The designs were hastily made up but a few weeks later, after a single half-completed dress parade, Noguchi had to leave in order to design a garden for UNESCO in Delhi, without even waiting for the first dress rehearsal.

The scenery, consisting mainly of abstract blocks of contrasted shapes and colours which slid into different positions, apparently self-propelled, might almost have derived from Craig's idea of

building sets of manœuvrable screens, but the costumes turned out
to be disastrously difficult to act in. They imposed a surrealist look
on the production and, to be consistent with this, the actors would
have had to conceive their movements in terms of a stylized
balletic technique, which they could not possibly have learned
in such a short time, even if the whole production had been conceived to accommodate it. Everyone was unhappy about the
costumes, and at the dress rehearsals some of the actors very
nearly refused to wear them. John's own costumes were so heavy
and cramping it was impossible for him to give a performance of
anything like the depth and expansiveness he had achieved in the
1950 Lear. He even thought of scrapping the costumes altogether
and dressing the actors in rubber sheets, made into cloaks, with
heavy simple folds, to produce a Blake-like effect, but he decided
this would be unfair without Noguchi's consent.

The basic intention was clear from the programme note:

> Our object in this production has been to find a setting and costumes
> which would be free of historical and decorative associations so that the
> timeless, universal and mythical quality of the story may be clear. We
> have tried to present the characters and the places in a very simple and
> basic manner for the play to come to life through the words and the
> acting.

This is admirable in theory. In reacting against the tradition of
detailed pictorial naturalism, John's ambition was to achieve a
scenic simplicity which would let the words and the acting speak
for themselves. But the unfamiliar Japanese doll-like wigs and
the kimono costumes were distracting and eccentric, with holes
in John's cloaks that got progressively larger. 'I see,' Emlyn
Williams said when John explained that the holes symbolized
Lear's disintegration, 'it's a sort of Gipsy Rose Lear.'

The scenery too was designed symbolically. Lear's world was
encompassed by an arch and there was a black shape to represent
doom. Noguchi intended his large floating wall as a symbol of
'time' or 'history' while two smaller moving screens were meant
to denote elements of evil human will, to be identified with
Goneril and Regan. In the first scene there was a blue diamond
shape which signified Lear's dominion, but the shade of blue was
also intended to suggest a link with France and the distance to
which Cordelia is banished. In the next scene the shape was reversed and shown in red. As Noguchi explained in his Designer's
Note for *King Lear*,* 'This is Edmund's perversion of nature,

* The Folio Society, 1956

like the cone of the approaching cyclone. Its shadows appear in the storm. It is the blood of Gloucester's eyes. The shift of symmetry gives a sense of unbalance – much as Gloucester is unbalanced by his righteousness.' The triple diamond shapes in the final scene were meant to show 'the resurgence of British dominion, red with battle and violence. Out of its red evil must come the new good.'

Both the scenery and the costumes might have been effective in a ballet, or even in an opera, but it is hard to conceive of any decor which could have done more to frustrate the basic intention of bringing the play to life through the words and the acting. Nevertheless Peter Brook later said that he would never have arrived at his enormously successful production of *Lear* with Paul Scofield in 1962 if John's 1955 Lear had not prepared the way.

In April John directed *Twelfth Night* at Stratford-on-Avon with Laurence Olivier as Malvolio and Vivien Leigh as Viola. Alan Webb played Sir Toby Belch, Keith Michell Orsino and Angela Baddeley Maria.

John wanted his old friend Glen Byam Shaw, who was now director at Stratford-on-Avon, to play Sir Andrew, and managed to drop four bricks in his attempt at persuasion.

'But John, I haven't acted since 1938, and I've got gaps in between my teeth.'

'That would make it all the funnier.'

'No I really couldn't.'

'After all,' John persisted, 'there's practically no verse speaking in the part. And you'd have nearly all your scenes with Angela and Alan Webb. You know them both very well.' Glen had been married to Angela Baddeley for twenty years. When Glen said he'd talk it over with her and accept if she was in favour, John made one last attempt at encouragement. 'It's the sort of part you should have played before the war, only nobody asked you.'

Angela Baddeley was decisively against the idea and Glen finally engaged Michael Denison for the part.

Since Fagan's production of *Twelfth Night* in 1919, John had seen the play a great many times and, with a blur of affectionate memories in his mind, he had no clear idea of what he wanted to do with it. The sight-lines at Stratford have always been bad, and instead of solving the problem (as Peter Brook had in 1950 with *Measure for Measure* and in 1955 with *Titus Andronicus*) by using a V-shaped set which forced the action downstage, John's designer, Malcolm Pride, gave him a formal garden with symmetrical side wings and a palace at the back, with windows which lit up. Unfortunate people sitting in the side aisles could only see half the scenery. John also set the comedy scenes too far upstage, which prevented the actors from involving the audience sufficiently.

Vivien Leigh had a romantic quality and a boyish charm which was delightful in the Cesario scenes, but her voice was rather lacking in lyrical power and her personality in comic vitality, though she might have been more successful in a smaller theatre. Afterwards she said to John 'I know you thought I was awful.' 'Why didn't you cry?' he asked. 'All my leading ladies cry.' 'I did, but not until I got home.'

Olivier came to the first rehearsal having already calculated exactly what he wanted to do with the part and John did little to change what he had invented for himself. Olivier found John worryingly apt to change his mind about what had been set – so much so that Olivier asked for the cast to be left alone for three days. 'We promise not to change anything but just leave us to ourselves so we can get set.'

The notices were polite but not enthusiastic. Olivier was praised, but the production was criticized as not having enough fun and spirit in it.

While *Twelfth Night* was still playing at Stratford, John was preparing a revival of *Much Ado* to take on a European tour together with the Noguchi Lear. Peggy Ashcroft now played Beatrice again, as well as Cordelia. Some of the *Much Ado* costumes were remade on simpler lines, and John gave up his own extravagant hats. He was trying to make Benedick less of a popinjay, rougher, more uncouth, and he obviously succeeded. Before the tour began, both plays were produced at the Palace Theatre for a short season starting in July, when T. C. Worsley noticed a 'robuster swagger in his carriage' and Richard Findlater wrote 'In making his Benedick more soldierly, Sir John has blunted the sharp perfection of orchestration heard in 1950 and 1952. The performance is more emphatically in character – at Stratford, Sir John was always, with infinite subtlety, detached from Benedick's predicament – but less delightfully in voice.'

Both plays were performed in Berlin as part of the 1955 Festival. Arriving there, the actors were all keen to see Brecht's Berliner Ensemble in the Russian sector and at Friedrichstrasse underground station on the way back, although they had been warned not to take the Potsdam train, which would carry them into the Russian Zone, John rashly leaped into a train standing at the platform and the doors slammed shut behind him, leaving the others gesticulating on the platform. He speaks no German, had no money on him, no passport and no papers. He got out at the next station, hoping the others would be following him on the next train. But the next train to come in was empty. He knew the station they had set out from in West Berlin was called the Zoo. So when a train came in going the other way, he said the word 'Zoo – zoo' to two old ladies waiting on the great empty platform. They nodded and he boarded the train. To his relief the actors were still waiting for him on the platform when the train arrived at Friedrichstrasse.

John preferred Austria to Germany, but he was ill for most of his week in Vienna. Although his performance could not but suffer, there was a huge crowd outside the stage door after *Much Ado*, applauding in the street. Both productions were also played in Zurich, Amsterdam, The Hague and Oslo. Some of the foreign critics welcomed the uncompromising boldness of the Lear production, but for most of the actors the costumes remained an embarrassment and a handicap.

43   'The Chalk Garden' and 'Nude with Violin'

When Enid Bagnold showed Hugh Beaumont her play *The Chalk Garden*, his first reaction was 'I can't stand all this allegorical stuff.' In fact she had not intended the chalk garden to stand for the dryness of the characters' minds and she did not even understand what he meant, though of course she was pleased to find the parallel was there. But the play was rejected by him and by several other London managements. It was only after she had put in two years work on revising the script and after Irene Selznick, who collaborated on the rewriting, had presented the play very successfully on Broadway, that Beaumont asked John to direct it in London.

When he first read the script he did not like it. 'I've just read a most disgusting play,' he told Peggy Ashcroft, giving her a copy to read when they were together on a train. She did not find it disgusting but extremely funny.

Edith Evans, who had not been well, was in a vulnerable and nervous state. She had always been inclined to baulk at John's changes of mind in rehearsal, but this time he promised Beaumont 'I will not change my mind and Edith will not be disturbed.' He kept his promise, handling her so well that afterwards she said 'I never want to be directed by anyone except Johnny.' After three weeks in the provinces, the play opened in London on 11 April 1956 but when it had been running for three months she was taken ill again. Beaumont telephoned Los Angeles to speak to Gladys Cooper, who had played the part on Broadway. Fortunately she was free and at once agreed to come. She arrived at London Airport after twelve hours of flying at 11.30 on Tuesday morning and at one o'clock she was in the Haymarket Theatre, talking to John and Beaumont. When John asked her when she would be able to take over, 'Tonight,' she said without hesitation. 'I will rehearse with the company now and the hairdresser will be here this afternoon.' They rehearsed intensively for some hours and she remembers a moment when in the middle of telling her how to play a line he checked himself with a blush. 'I shouldn't be telling you how to say a line.' 'If not you, then who?'

At 7.30, Felix Aylmer, who was playing the old Judge, made an announcement to the audience and a few moments later, Gladys Cooper appeared at the window with a gardening hat on her head. 'Are my teeth on the table?' She played the part quite differently from Dame Edith but sailed confidently through it without a mistake. Afterwards she told John she had at once seen what she was doing wrong. 'You've produced it as the House of Regrets and we produced it as the House of Cuckoos. We must rehearse again in the morning.'

John's next appearance as an actor was in a part Noël Coward had written for Rex Harrison. When he heard that Harrison was not going to do *Nude with Violin*, John asked Beaumont what had happened to it. 'Oh Noël's changed the part into a woman for Yvonne Arnaud.' But presumably she refused it. Finally John was shown the original version and decided to appear in it.

He was eager to so something lighter than usual, and Sebastian, the valet, was the last sort of character that anyone would expect him to play, though the dialogue was so characteristic of

Coward that John was slightly apprehensive of giving an imitation of him, as he had in *The Vortex*. Peggy Ashcroft did not care for the play and John himself had reservations. 'It's very broad and a bit vulgar,' he wrote in a letter, 'but full of surefire situations and brilliant curtains, and I think it could not fail to be a success – but I should have to be rather clever at creating a character out of a "type" which does not really exist in life.'

If Coward had come to England, it would have cost him £25,000 in income tax, so John spent a week-end in Paris with him, talking about the play. They arranged to open the pre-London tour in Dublin so that he could 'supervise' the production with impunity.

The Olympia Theatre was repainted for the occasion and the price of the stalls was put up to a guinea for the first night. The demand was so great that spivs were hawking tickets in the streets for £5 each. After two dress rehearsals earlier in the day, John and his cast were too exhausted to be at their best on the opening night. The performance was so late in beginning that impatient galleryites folded their programmes into paper darts which they aimed at the safety curtain. The play went fairly well, but there were many passages where cutting was needed, and some of the Irish critics complained that the play was too chatty. When Coward arrived the next day, he found that John, as usual, had neglected his own performance for the sake of the rest of the production and he helped him to build it up, adding lines in two of the scenes. But though he took some rehearsals in Dublin and saw the play every night, he did not do nearly as much rewriting as John had been hoping for.

One of the parts was hastily recast and there was a great deal of rehearsing on the rest of the tour. But on 7 November, when the play opened in London, the audience was unresponsive and the press decidedly hostile to the play. 'Billed as a comedy,' the *Evening Standard* said, 'it emerged as a farce and ended as a corpse.' But Tynan was unfair to say 'Sir John never acts seriously in modern dress; it is the lounging attire in which he relaxes between classical bookings; and his present performance as a simpering valet is an act of boyish mischief, carried out with extreme elegance and the general aspect of a tight, smart, walking umbrella.' T. C. Worsley disagreed. In a letter to John he wrote that the performance was 'absolutely dazzling . . . Every gesture, movement, inflection in perfect style, a little triumph, I thought.'

Despite the bad press, the play enjoyed a very long run, though

John received few letters and comparatively few visitors to his dressing-room. But he stayed in the play for nine months, leaving in June 1957 to start rehearsing at Stratford-on-Avon in Peter Brook's production of *The Tempest*. His part in *Nude with Violin* was taken over first by Michael Wilding and later by Robert Helpmann.

44   Directing 'The Troians'

Meanwhile John was invited to direct the first production at Covent Garden of Berlioz's opera *The Trojans*. Previously it had either been heavily cut or spread into two parts, *The Fall of Troy* and *The Trojans at Carthage*. This was the first time that an almost uncut version was ever performed, anywhere, in a single evening, as Berlioz intended.

It was a massive undertaking for John – the first opera he had directed. There were two orchestras, 22 principals, 40 extras and a chorus of 180, quite apart from the five Irish wolf hounds specially engaged for the Hunt Scene. The whole rehearsal routine was unfamiliar. The scenery was set up on the first day of rehearsal but only for a limited number of hours. The moves and groupings had continually to be checked by the conductor and chorus master and altered if John had put the singers in the wrong relationship to each other for the voices.

Mariano Andreu, who at John's suggestion was invited to design the production, still spoke little English and the budget was limited. Many of the costumes had to be taken from stock, and though John had insisted on an extra week of rehearsals for the chorus, there was still no time for a costume parade (at which he could have asked for alterations). Most of the sets were extremely successful but there were complicated changes involving waits, and once again Andreu's headgear was highly fanciful. One critic complained that 'the Trojans were capped like jesters and the Carthaginian priests like chefs'.

Wanting to avoid designating chorus singers by saying 'You, the tall woman in the second row,' John divided them into groups and directed them by giving each group a numbered placard as Noël Coward said he had done in *Cavalcade*. But John was so impressed by their singing at rehearsals he could hardly bear to stop them, and, to make himself heard, he had to blow a whistle. During dress rehearsals, at which the full orchestra was playing, he felt unable to interrupt at all. Instead he kept rushing from the back of the stalls across the narrow bridge over the orchestra pit to correct the positions of singers by moving them physically from one group to another while they sang on apparently unperturbed.

Blanche Thebom, who sang Dido, was an accomplished actress, but after giving Amy Shuard (Cassandra) a number of moves to break up her long love duet with Choroebus, John was pained to find that she sang her way through the scene at the dress rehearsal standing firmly downstage. 'Oh, my dear, I know the music of course but I don't know the words. I've got to keep close to the prompter's box.'

There is a lovely but lengthy clarinet passage in the second act during which Andromache crosses the stage with her little son. In the original production John used a dancer in this non-singing part but in the 1960 revival he persuaded Diana Wynyard to appear as Andromache and she was incomparably more moving.

He solved the problem of the Trojan Horse by having it constructed in four sections so that it could be turned slightly in the wings when it was hauled on by the chorus. The audience saw only the legs, underbelly and tail of the horse, which therefore seemed gigantic. John's mother, who was now eighty-eight and very short-sighted, came to a dress rehearsal and stayed for an hour. After the horse had been dragged across the scene she said 'I liked it so much when the ship came on.'

45 Shakespeare and Graham Greene

For the 1957 production of *The Tempest* at Stratford, Peter Brook directed, designed the sets and costumes and composed the musique concrète. Alec Clunes was Caliban. Patrick Wymark played Stephano in a fisherman's sou'wester and a George Robey bowler hat. The Duke of Naples carried a muff and Brian Bedford was an Ariel too 'robust and spiv-like' to please Philip Hope-Wallace.

The shipwreck scene was simply and imaginatively staged with lamps and bowsprit swinging, shouts from the lurching sailors and swaying ropes. Later, one of the most effective scene changes came when a stage full of vines dissolved into an empty cavern. There was another breathtaking transformation just at the end, when the ship materialized out of nothing, as if it had never been wrecked, and Prospero strode upstage, standing with his back to the audience, apparently at the prow.

For his characterization of Prospero, John wanted to do something more striking than his turbaned conjuror of 1931 and his cross old gentleman of 1941. Peter Brook suggested the idea of a hermit, which John developed, helping to design his own costume – as a quasi-biblical anchorite with cropped, greying hair. Peter Brook devised an enormously effective climax when Prospero was dressed by Ariel in a magnificent blue robe, black skull cap and coronet, holding a sheathed sword on his arm.

As John has said, 'I tried to play it with strength and passion – as a revenge play, which I think it is. The whole action of the play is Prospero's gradually being convinced that hatred and revenge are useless. It's the agony of a tortured saint. Not that Prospero himself is a saint, of course, but a recluse.'

The Times critic gave a clear description of this Prospero,

> clean-shaven with the grizzled hair of a virile middle age and half bared to the waist, rather like the symbolic figure of a workman about to strike the anvil. He is in some sort removed from all about him. He is a hard man determined that his magic shall exemplify Bacon's dictum that man commands Nature by obeying her. The speeches of harsh intemperance are more characteristic than those which give rein to his parental and human tenderness. It is clear that Sir John Gielgud's purpose in emphasizing the impassioned elements in Prospero's nature is to introduce a suggestion of dramatic conflict which is necessarily lacking in an action moving at the will of an omnipotent being.

The disadvantage of this approach was that 'John Gielgud takes little joy in his magic powers. He is an angry and embittered aristocrat speaking his tortured thoughts as though they disgusted him.'

It was John's only part in the 1957 Stratford season but at the beginning of December the production transferred to Drury Lane, empty for a few weeks before the long run of *My Fair Lady*. It was the first Shakespeare play to be staged there since Ivor Novello's

Henry V in 1938 and the first *Tempest* since Macready's in 1833, but to everybody's surprise it played to full houses for 61 performances.

John received a letter from his old employer Basil Dean. 'The inalienable magic of Shakespeare returned from too frequent exile whenever you spoke – especially those closing passages. Magnificent ... I felt I was back with giants.' And a note arrived in Ralph Richardson's familiar handwriting headed 'Fan Letter – No Reply Please.' 'It is a very great achievement, simple and noble, and with tear-bringing poetry. I am sure that W.S. would be delighted with it. It is the best Shakespearean acting I have seen.' The generosity of this is all the more touching in view of the way John had reacted to Richardson's Prospero in 1952. 'I didn't like you in it, Ralph.' 'Didn't you, Johnny?' 'I think I disliked you more in the first half than I did in the second.' 'Why was that?' 'Because there's more of you in the first half.'

Graham Greene's play *The Potting Shed* had first been offered to John in 1956 but much as he admired Greene and much as he wanted to appear in another modern play, he had not really liked it. 'I thought it was an unhappy sort of play for me.' It was first staged in New York, where Robert Flemyng played the lead in a successful six months' run, and John was given a script to re-read just before Christmas 1957. He liked it better now and though he would only have three months free in between the end of *The Tempest* and the Wolsey he was committed to play in Shakespeare's *Henry VIII* at the Old Vic, he accepted the part. Only to be very embarrassed when he happened to meet his old friend Flemyng on holiday in Majorca.

Lewis Casson and Sybil Thorndike had acted with Flemyng in the New York production. They were now on tour in Australia but Casson took the trouble to cable John 'Do find the original third act we discarded.' John took his advice and the version of Act Three finally used was a combination of the two, but still not altogether satisfactory.

Michael MacOwan directed a cast that included Irene Worth, Gwen Ffrangcon Davies and Walter Hudd. Unlike T. S. Eliot, Greene seemed to be quite content to have a non-believer in his leading part, provided he could give a convincing performance. He was too shrewd not to see that John had misgivings about the part and was grateful to him for not allowing them to prevent him from playing with great sincerity. When John said 'I hope you'll write another play for me one day,' Greene's reply was

'If I do, I hope you'll like the part in it better than you did this one.'

John was still playing Prospero in the evenings while rehearsing *The Potting Shed* and he found it fascinating to work alternately on the two kinds of dialogue. Unlike Shakespeare, Greene did not make his characters' inner lives emerge directly in what they said. John told Richard Findlater* that this made it all the more enjoyable 'to work with short phrases and half sentences. And it's particularly curtly written, this play.' It was not easy to arrive at the right style for speaking the lines. 'If you play it to throw away, the audience can't hear.'

Directing him, Michael MacOwan found that the best results were achieved when John concentrated his nervous energy by keeping still instead of diffusing it by moving about. Rehearsing the scene of listening to the priest's story, MacOwan persuaded him to do absolutely nothing. Redmond Phillips, who was playing the priest, was so good that involuntarily tears started to pour down John's cheeks. In performance he found it easy to repeat the effect at the same point each evening.

The ability to shed tears at will is one of John's inherited gifts. Ellen Terry is said to have been able to amuse the other actors by playing the fool during a pathetic scene with tears streaming down her cheeks. Like all the Terrys, John's mother was very emotional when watching a play or reading aloud but surprisingly stoical in a crisis. In Shakespeare John has always had difficulty in restraining tears in both his eyes and voice but, properly controlled, the facility has been of great value to him not only as Hamlet, Leontes and Richard II, and in *The Potting Shed* and David Storey's *Home*, but in comedies like *40 Years On* when a sudden onset of emotion was required.

Cecil Wilson of the *Daily Mail* commended *The Potting Shed* 'for one moving moment alone: Sir John Gielgud's genuine tears as the hero's uncle, another of Mr Greene's shambling whisky priests, lays bare his whole dread childhood secret'. In fact there were several equally moving moments in the same scene, especially when John twice put out a hand to touch the pathetic old priest, but both times his fingers failed to make contact.

In costume, as in stance, manner and gesture, John had to do the opposite of what he had been doing in his long post-war line of classical parts – to make himself look as insignificant as possible, while leaving room for sufficient attack and sufficient varia-

* In an interview printed in the *Sunday Dispatch* on 9 February 1958.

tion to retain his hold on the audience. For John Barber he did not succeed: 'Though Gielgud's chilled face and taut lips wrung my heart, I got tired when that taut look never changed.' Derek Granger too found that 'His playing all through suggested a convulsing inner struggle kept under rigid control and nothing that he does is without a sense of tautness and strain.'

Tynan's review consisted of a dialogue, set ten years into the future, between a psychiatrist and a whisky critic who had his faith taken away from him ten years ago at the Globe Theatre. 'John Gielgud was in the play. Very wrought up he was, very curt and brusque – you know how he used to talk to other actors as if he was going to tip them.'

About this time, George Devine invited him to play in Beckett's *Endgame* (which was produced in October at the Royal Court) but John did not see how Hamm could hold an audience wearing dark glasses and confined to an armchair. He did not understand Beckett and had already dissuaded Ralph Richardson and Alec Guinness from accepting parts in *Waiting for Godot*. 'When I saw Godot, I felt there was no communal experience at all. The audience was glum and miserable and in *Endgame* there's nothing but the first striking effect of the mise-en-scène and then the loneliness and despair.'

Henry VIII was the last of the thirty-six plays in the Shakespeare First Folio to be produced at the Old Vic in Michael Benthall's Five Year Plan. Harry Andrews was to play Henry VIII and John had agreed to play Wolsey on condition that Edith Evans was Katherine. Michael Benthall directed and he remembers that at rehearsals he often saw John 'bursting in a corner'. He would always ask him what his idea was and incorporate it if possible, in the production.

It was a part John had always wanted to play because he knew how effective the scene of Wolsey's downfall could be, but physically he is very odd casting for the fleshy son of an Ipswich butcher, and on the first night he played the part without much attempt at physical disguise. Afterwards he wore padding under his clothes and a more florid make-up. In his characterization he went for the hardness and calculating ambition in Wolsey, doing nothing to prepare for the change of heart at the end. As with Angelo, the softening is all the more effective if totally unexpected. This is how T. C. Worsley described John in the downfall scene. 'The beast goes down but then rises to his feet for the last time and in a stance that completely dominates. And holds it still,

perfectly still, out-facing them even from defeat. It is the first time
we have had the chance to see and feel the greatness of the lamb.'
But John never cared for the play, finding it episodic and lacking
in variety.

46 'The Ages of Man'

John's Shakespearean one-man show, *The Ages of Man*, origina-
ted out of an invitation from the Arts Council to give a recital in
Lady Astor's old house in St James's Square, with interludes on
the lute by Julian Bream. George Rylands had recently published
his Shakespeare Anthology, *The Ages of Man*, and, much taken
with this, John borrowed both the title and the basic idea of
dividing the Shakespearean excerpts into three sections – youth,
maturity, and old age. At first there was no question of any public
performances, though an invitation to give one at Malvern soon
followed.

In preparing his recital, John found he had two main kinds of
problem: he had to come as near as possible to perfecting each
individual speech or sonnet in itself, and he had to find the right
place for it in a pattern that would both be satisfying for the audience, providing variety and the right spacing of the emotional
climaxes, and be feasible for himself, placing the most effective
passages at peak moments, preceded and followed by more lyrical
speeches, contrasting in pace and style. In speeches by youthful
or lighter characters – like Romeo and Oberon – he indicated
without impersonating, only acting full out as Leontes, Richard
II, Hamlet, Macbeth and Lear. This was what Ellen Terry had
done in her recital, *Shakespeare's Heroines*, which John had seen
at the Haymarket as a boy. She acted full out in certain dramatic
peaks (in the Potion Scene from *Romeo and Juliet* for example)
touching in other parts only lightly – Rosalind, Portia and Beatrice. She linked the excerpts together with personal comments
spoken to the audience like intimate asides.

In August 1957 John accepted an invitation to perform the
programme at the Edinburgh Festival, speaking excerpts from

seventeen of the plays. This was a great success, and coming away from the performance at the Freemason's Hall, one festival-goer was overheard saying 'That was a whole orchestral concert in itself.' As Michel St Denis said later, John had devised a programme in which he could present himself in three ways: as an actor, as a director indicating how the various roles ought to be played and as a man talking directly to the audience between the excerpts.

In October he took the programme to Berlin, playing at the Charlottenburger Schloss by candlelight and then on to Paris, where he appeared once at the University and once at the Atelier Theatre, then to Milan and to the Holland Festival.

In August 1958 his mother died in her ninetieth year. Unselfish to the end, she had tried to prepare him some months before by telling him not to come and see her so often. She was an adorably warm-hearted woman, with whom he had enjoyed a close and loving relationship for over fifty years. All through her life she had been dependent first on her father and then on her husband, but when he died, she seemed to discover, at the age of eighty-one, a new independence. She had never even had a dress allowance, and to the end she lived very simply. She always took great pride in John's career, and she was tactful but firm in dealing with the fans who attached themselves to her in the hope of hearing intimate gossip about him. She was always surrounded by a mass of photographs of John and when she stopped laying them out on the big table in her bedroom she must have known the end was near.

In the middle of September John set off to perform *The Ages of Man* on a thirteen-week tour of Canada and the United States, accompanied by Henry Ainley's daughter, who was to act as his secretary during the tour. His sister Eleanor had been working as his secretary since the beginning of 1946, but she hated flying and was still involved in the depressing job of clearing up at home after her mother's death.

In Toronto there were two press conferences and a television interview at which John spoke so fluently and so fast that though they had carefully prepared their questions, the interviewers hardly had a chance to ask them. For the performance there John rearranged the first part of the programme and added John of Gaunt's dying speech to the last. The whole evening went very well.

At Kingston, Ontario, there were thirty-eight churches and three penitentiaries, but no porters at the station and hardly any restaurants open on the Lord's Day. At Ottawa, an audience of over 2000 people was kept waiting because the High Commissioner had been held up in a traffic jam. In Montreal John was very enthusiastically received, except by a strange woman who came backstage: 'Where is Sir John Gielgud? No you are not he. I have a good memory for faces.' After stubbornly refusing either to listen to reason or to go, she wandered off saying 'I am bitterly disappointed.'

In Corning, he gave a performance in the Glass Centre, contending against the air conditioning and the noises from a nearby bowling alley. Invited home afterwards by the daughter and son-in-law of some friends, he was embarrassed when, in compliance with the request Patsy Ainley had made before the performance, they gave him a large steak on a tray, but offered only drinks and peanuts to the large circle of people who were congratulating him and asking questions.

Audiences were varied in their reactions. Playing in a church in the South, John had the audience on their feet and in tears at Lear's death scene, but in some places the reaction was undemonstrative, though it was not always easy to judge the feeling behind it. In another church, belonging to the Agnes Scott College for Ladies, there was no applause at all, though it seemed afterwards that the girls and teachers had enjoyed themselves immensely.

The constant travelling became a great strain, together with the press conferences, the interviews and photographs, and the need to be polite to innumerable strangers. In thirteen weeks, he travelled 18,000 miles, giving eighty-one performances in sixty different towns, constantly rearranging his programme to find the ideal format. Sometimes he played to an audience of 5000, sometimes to one of only a few hundred, but he never had less than thirty visitors afterwards, mostly complete strangers. In one town a twelve-year-old girl, hustled into his dressing room by her formidable mother, greeted him, 'Gee Sir Gielgud, you're phenomenal.'

He now had a week's rest including two days in Cuba for Christmas. With no other tourists, the place seemed strangely quiet. Next day the revolution broke out. Most of his time in Havana seemed to be spent at the Embassy, arranging for a re-entry permit to the U.S., which he had forgotten to obtain before leaving.

He arrived back in New York to open at the 46th Street Theatre, which holds 1300 people. For the first time in his career he had solo billing above the title. Previously, both in New York and in London, though his name had almost always come first, he had invariably shared the honours with his leading lady, even in his various appearances as Hamlet.

The first night audience was studded with American stars and John received a standing ovation led by Lillian Gish, Marlene Dietrich, Katherine Hepburn and Mary Martin. There had been a six-week newspaper strike, but luckily it ended a few hours before the performance and the first papers carried rave notices for John. 'This program is a masterpiece,' Brooks Atkinson declared. 'It is a Shakespeare event of first importance.' 'He frequently blinks his eyes,' Walter Kerr reported, 'as if he were trying to see something. What he sees, we share – the fusion of mind and manner is perfect.'

John also received a huge fan mail. 'Your perfection, John,' Basil Rathbone wrote, 'is the ultimate – I never expected to hear anything like it again . . . we both wept with you over Richard II.' And John Steinbeck confessed himself 'moved and uplifted in a way usually set off by great music, which of course this is, and a great musician. It takes both.'

The season was extended for two weeks, a smash hit which no one had expected. There was soon a busy black market trade in tickets.

47 Acting on Television

Before leaving for a fortnight's holiday in Morocco, he played Andrew Crocker-Harris, the part Rattigan had originally written for him, in *The Browning Version* for C.B.S. television. Like so many of John's modern parts, the character is a failure – a schoolmaster with an unfaithful wife and disrespectful pupils. It was his first part on American television and at first he found it very distracting to have the director (John Frankenheimer) following him closely around during the performance, sometimes standing only a few inches away from his face. But when the programme was transmitted on 23 April 1959 it was a triumph for John. Not a single review was hostile and many of them featured words like 'brilliant', 'superb', 'superlative', 'impeccable' and 'masterpiece'. One critic called it 'the performance of the year'. And on 27 April Sir Laurence Olivier, who was filming in Hollywood, penned a note to John at six o'clock in the morning before going off to the studio. 'Your old friend was bursting with pride and admiration – your performance was quite flawless and dreadfully moving, it haunts me still. Bravo, dearest Johnny, it's just fascinating and most inspiring the way you seem still to find room for improvement all the time.'

At the end of March, John was to make his debut on English television. It was extremely important to choose the right play, especially as Sir Laurence Olivier had only had a moderate success in *John Gabriel Borkman* and Vivien Leigh had failed in the television production of *The Skin of Our Teeth* after being so successful in it on the stage. John wanted to play a modern part, and his first choice was *The Potting Shed*, provided that Alec Guinness played the priest. When he turned out to be unavailable, John stuck to his condition. 'The actor who plays the priest is bound to walk off with the play. I would not mind Alec's doing that, but I was hanged if I'd let anyone else do it.'

Finally he decided to appear in his old part in N. C. Hunter's *A Day by the Sea* and Gladys Cooper flew seven thousand miles from California to play the part of the mother, which Sybil Thorndike had created. ITV claimed an audience of 22,000,000 and Nancy Spain wrote that because he had chosen a family chronicle, John succeeded where both the Oliviers had failed. But John himself was not happy with the result. The action depended on the interplay between a number of characters, all equally important at the same time – and particularly in these ensemble scenes, forced by the size of the television screen to work mostly in close-ups on a single face, the director had to treat the play not so much in terms of interaction as of a series of separate reactions.

48   The Gielgud Voice

In June, John played his *Ages of Man* at Gian-Carlo Menotti's Spoleto Festival and in July he performed the programme in the

West End for the first time. The Queen's Theatre had been destroyed by a bomb in 1940 and it was with *The Ages of Man* that the new building was now opened, with a bust of John as Hamlet (by a Negro sculptor Raymond Barthé) in position on the stairs leading down to the stalls. The reviews were good and Marguerite Steen, who was writing a book on the Terrys, said 'There has been nothing like it since Ellen.' The dissentient opinion came from A. Alvarez, then drama critic of the *New Statesman*. 'The Gielgud voice is always the Gielgud voice, no matter whether the man who produces it is supposed to be Hotspur or Leontes, Oberon or Angelo. There is always the same lengthening of the open vowels and nasals, the same faint tremolo on the stressed word, a quiver that is not so much excess of feeling as an unvarying trick of speech . . . the deeper, the more mature the emotion, the less Gielgud seems to be with it.'

It is true enough that John's voice is always recognizable: it lacks the malleability of Guinness's and the power and range of Olivier's. But, quite apart from its beauty, John's voice is the most expressive of any in the English theatre. It is not a big voice, but without being a mimic or a master of accents and dialects – he has hardly ever needed either – he has developed great versatility. Without ever losing his characteristic manner-isms, he most often manages to adapt them till we accept them as characteristic of the character, and in *The Ages of Man* he was not so much trying to produce a maximum of differentiation between the Shakespearean characters – this could be done quite superficially – as to interpret each of them as deeply as possible.

The interview John gave to *The Times* provides an accurate index of the extent to which he had disciplined his use of his voice since his youthful emotional extravagance.

> When I was young I enjoyed colouring the words . . . Now I try to shut the phrases, so to speak, in rat traps. I try not to sing, not to elongate the a-o syllables and vowels. As in a musical phrase, you should try to do no more than exactly what the text demands. I try now to exert a rigid discipline, above all not to indulge. As Leontes or Wolsey, I weep at the same point for exactly the same amount of time each night, and no longer. When I hold any mood or tone too long, I am aware of the fact and try to change it. Poetry has a beginning, middle and end, held in a kind of arc which must not be broken, although inside it there can be many variations. Like a Gothic arch. Within it there can be elaborations, but the arch remains intact.

Behind this formulation, as behind John's **actual** use of his voice, the influence of Granville Barker is still to be discerned. But by now it had been absorbed so deeply that John had made it utterly his own.

49   Benedick in the States

In August 1959 he played *The Ages of Man* in Boston before opening there in *Much Ado about Nothing* with his third Beatrice, Margaret Leighton. Her characterization was more stylish and sophisticated then Peggy Ashcroft's. She was witty and radiant, but although John had to adapt his performances to hers, as previously to Diana Wynyard's at the Phoenix, he was surprised both times to find how easy it was to make the adjustments.

The Boston theatres were still closed and the play was staged for a so-called Summer Festival in a huge tent twelve miles outside the city. When it rained, the drumming on the canvas made the actors almost inaudible. The dressing-rooms were inadequate and the heat almost tropical. Distractions piled up irritatingly. This is how John has described some of them.*

A bulldozer breaks a water pipe which is laid on for our water supply, and we can neither drink nor wash (on a matinee day too, when we are in the place for a full eight hours). After a great deal of confusion, the local fire brigade arrives to pump in a supply out of the river.

I am asked to sign autographs between the performances for a visiting party of blind people, and demur, as there will be little time to rest. The curtain then rises on the matinee to a half-empty house. Ten minutes later the blind people arrive and are escorted to their seats. This done, the usherettes sink wearily into the empty chairs in the front row and yawn at us and buff their nails. People whose seats are in the direct rays of the sun, shining remorselessly through the gaps in the canvas sides, move about, changing their chairs to get into the shade. The actors keep escaping out of their dressing-rooms to gasp for air on the river bank, some half-naked, some half in costume. The girls' elaborate dresses are soiled as they drag their trains in the long grass,

* *Stage Directions*, pp. 101–2.

and people cannot be found and miss their entrances. One of the actresses slips in front and outrages me by trying to photograph the play from the front in a scene in which she does not appear herself . . .

A cloudburst descends during the last act, and the open passage behind the stage is deep in water. We pick our way from dressing-rooms and battle on with the final scene, not a word of which can be heard, as the rain is crashing down on the sagging top of the roof where it drums and reverberates unceasingly and drips through the gaps in the canvas. The aisles are running with water, and the audience sit, with their feet tucked under them, preparing to plunge out at the earliest opportunity, with umbrellas at the ready.

Despite minor rearrangements, the production, still basically the same as in 1949, was becoming stale and old-fashioned. The scenery from Stratford and the Phoenix had been badly copied by the American painters and was poorly lit. Understandably, Brooks Atkinson liked John's performance better than his production, which struck him as traditional. 'As an approach to Shakespeare, it lacks a sense of freshness now. But Mr Gielgud's Benedick is as fresh as creation. Perhaps, in fact, it is the Benedick that Shakespeare had in mind.' But Tynan, who was now reviewing for the *New Yorker*, was not convinced: 'Beatrice's sudden "Kill Claudio" was greeted with a wide-spread titter, it being quite clear that this Benedick would hesitate before swatting a fly . . . he had civilized the character so completely that it was impossible to think of him as a soldier. His Benedick is suave, prim and haughty, saved from comparisons with Malvolio, whom in other respects he much resembles, by the suggestion that he is mocking himself throughout.'

But if Henry Hewes of the *Saturday Review* is to be believed, Tynan's account of the "Kill Claudio" moment is unfair and the laugh was intentional. 'Gielgud allows this bitter line to have its effect for just an instant before he gets a laugh by drawing back and making a gesture with his hand.' This does seem more plausible. It is very unlikely that, conscious as he was of the danger of the moment, and with all the experience he had by now had both of controlling audience reaction and of playing Benedick, John would have got a laugh he didn't want.

When John read the first draft of Enid Bagnold's new play, he thought the first act effective but said he did not want to play in it, though it would interest him to direct. But in January 1960 the papers announced that he was going to play the lead. The title was not yet decided. It was later called *The Last Joke* and Glen Byam Shaw directed it. In the second act John had to dress up as a Persian in a red fez. His character was a mixture of Cocteau and Firbank – a sophisticated Roumanian prince who lived in Chiswick Mall and fell half in love with easeful death. As a Levantine millionaire, Sir Ralph Richardson had to change his trousers on stage. Both men were very unhappy about the play. Generally the first act had interesting possibilities but the second and third only mystified and bored the audience. Endless revisions on the road had done almost nothing to make the play more convincing and the settings (by Felix Kelly) were more successful than the scenes played in front of them.

The critics were almost unanimously hostile but Tynan conceded 'By sheer neurotic energy, Sir John keeps the first act tingling with promise.'

In February he went back to New York to direct a play by his friend Hugh Wheeler, *Big Fish, Little Fish*, with Jason Robards and Hume Cronyn. Perhaps the progress of rehearsals can best be summed up with a few quotations from Hume Cronyn's diary.

7 February	Rehearsals begin. No introductions, no explanation, just 'Shall we read it?' Everybody stiff and nervous but half way through Act One, someone lets go with an uninhibited fart. Everybody seems relieved.
8 February	Johnny G. seems to have sixteen new ideas a minute. Write and erase, write and erase. Script covered with lunatic markings.
28 February	He expects his actors to do a great deal of work for themselves, which is perhaps a reflection of his own superb powers as an actor. At the same time he is better

able to do those things for an actor that no actor can be expected to do for himself and that lie purely within the realm of 'direction' than any other director I have ever worked for.

51 Othello and Gaev with the Royal Shakespeare Company

'Tomorrow I pack it up with considerable relief,' John wrote to a friend on 28 November 1961 before his last performance of Othello at Stratford-on-Avon, 'though I wouldn't have missed the study and execution of the part for anything. It is rather a long time to spend on a near miss but one never expects to succeed in a masterpiece the first time unless all the circumstances are incredibly fortunate.'

It was generally agreed that his Othello was a failure. What is not generally known is how very near he came to succeeding and that the circumstances were almost incredibly unfortunate. He was happy to be back at Stratford and to be working with Franco Zeffirelli, whose Old Vic production of *Romeo and Juliet* had been so exciting the year before. Charming, exuberant and dynamic, Zeffirelli got on well both with John and with Dorothy Tutin, who was playing Desdemona. Rehearsals started promisingly enough, though it was rather a disadvantage that Zeffirelli had never seen John on the stage, except in *The Ages of Man*.

Zeffirelli's approach was engagingly anti-traditional. It was not going to be a romantic *Othello* but realistic and anti-heroic. He stressed Othello's vanity. John was unwilling to accept this but began to develop a very interesting characterization – middle-aged, restrained, unrhetorical and shy. Peggy Ashcroft, who was playing Emilia, thought it was going to be the greatest of all John's performances.

He had implicit faith in Zeffirelli. At some of the early rehearsals he was asked to sit in the stalls and speak the lines, watching Zeffirelli mime the action on stage, which he did very well, though this method of production, suitable enough for opera singers who needed to be taught how to act, was hardly suitable for John. When he saw the designs, he thought them beautiful, but the costumes and the sets turned out to be extremely damaging. Othello was dressed after a Titian portrait as a Venetian in doublet and hose of a dull purple colour, and his armour and cloaks were so heavy John could hardly carry them. After the first night he went to the wardrobe, looked out the costumes Anthony Quayle had used and wore them instead.

What mattered even more was that the scenery interfered with his performance. The decor was magnificent but far too operatic. There were big steep steps in the Cyprus scene leading improbably down from the top of the stage and the epilepsy scene was set in an elaborate armoury. Everything was huge, even the bed, which was set at the bottom of a great staircase to provide an effective tableau at the end of the play. An underplayed performance would have been lost in this grandiose set – John was forced to resort to the rhetorical declamation he had worked so hard to avoid. The predominant colours in the set were dark, and it was very badly lit, so that John, with his dark face and dark costume, was often almost invisible. Zeffirelli also placed him too far upstage, and his movements were restricted by the bulky furniture. In the jealousy scene he was trapped in a massive armchair on the upstage side of a huge table, with Iago sitting six feet away from him in profile.

Zeffirelli had divided the rehearsal time unequally, spending more on the earlier parts of the play than on later more important scenes. He was late with his designs, too, and as there was already scenery for five other productions hanging on the grid, so much time was spent hanging and storing the *Othello* decor that conditions became chaotic. The actors panicked, knowing there was not going to be enough time for the dress rehearsals they so badly needed. Photographers swarmed in, wasting more precious time, and Stratford was besieged by distinguished visitors from all over Europe. In John's place, almost anyone else would have refused to go on, but he steeled himself and tried to act as a steadying influence on the others. The only full-scale dress rehearsal went on till 5.30 in the morning and the scene changes were so complicated that they had to stop without rehearsing the end of the play.

It was one of the most disastrous first nights that had ever been known at Stratford. Despite two half-hour intervals and long delays at each scene-change, the set was unstable and a pillar tottered when John leaned against it. The actor playing Iago was overwrought with nerves and kept forgetting his lines. At one point he announced that Cassio was dead, hesitated and corrected himself – 'No I mean Cassio is not dead.' John kept as much control as he could over his own performance, but he too was in trouble with his heavy clothes and his beard, which came loose during one of the big scenes with Desdemona. The curtain finally fell four and a half hours after it had gone up.

In spite of everything, Irving Wardle announced in *The Times* that John had given 'a remarkably fine and moving performance'. T. C. Worsley said that Iago had misjudged the size of the theatre. 'But this threw all the more into relief the firm ringing voice which Sir John Gielgud brought to the Moor. The fear with Sir John was that physically he would be too small for a part that we always conceive of as on the scale of a bull. But in those first scenes he seemed to be in such perfect voice that he would soon dispel such fears. As the evening wore rather slowly on, those promises were not fulfilled.'

The original plan had been to bring *Othello* to London for the Royal Shakespeare Company's first season at the Aldwych Theatre. Peter Hall still wanted to, offering to redirect the production himself, but John firmly refused, in spite of Zeffirelli's cabled reassurance that it could still be made into a success. But he kept to his agreement to play Gaev in Michel St Denis's production of *The Cherry Orchard*, which was to open at the Aldwych in December with Peggy Ashcroft and a set by Abd-El-Farrah. St Denis had seven and a half weeks for rehearsal, almost as long as he had had for *Three Sisters* in 1938, but this time he did not succeed in generating such an exciting atmosphere. Nevertheless John contributed a delightful performance. He was developing a new faculty for investing sentiment with self-parody, so subtly interwoven that he was identifying almost fully with the character, at the same time as mocking it as gently and as tenderly as if he were mocking himself. The Headmaster in *40 Years On* must have had his roots in Gaev's address to the cupboard in the 1961 *Cherry Orchard*.

Although there were some keen billiard players in the cast, John did not take advantage of their offers to coach him in the exact movements Gaev ought to make with the imaginary cue. Always clumsy with his hands and reluctant to wield a hammer either in a play (like *Noah*) or in private life, he knew he could manage with an approximation, and he did. As Robert Muller put it, 'Sir John makes of . . . the monumental bore Gaev a more endearing individual than I would have thought possible. His silences are pregnant with memories; time passes, passes visibly, behind his closed eyelids; his fading world has no more use for the Gaevs of this world, and Gaev knows it and suffers – absurdly.' Even Tynan admitted 'Gaev is exactly right.'

52 'The School for Scandal' Again

Since 1937, when he played Joseph Surface so successfully in *The School for Scandal*, John had seen only one of the seven London revivals of the play – Olivier's with Vivien Leigh at the New in 1949. For his new production at the Haymarket, John had thought of bringing the action thirteen years forward, as Guthrie had done to 1790, when costumes were in many ways more attractive than in 1777, but deciding that the Directoire style would make the production look too much like the Scarlet Pimpernel, he stuck to the authentic period, which was consistent with his instinct to avoid glamorizing the production with elaborate dances, pretty pages, sedan chairs and sculptured ceilings. Recoiling from his memories of Guthrie's fidgety impressionism, John wanted to simplify the visual framework, using painted drop scenes, wings and a few historically accurate accessories. He found a clever young designer, Anthony Powell, and they worked happily together on the production.

Another temptation he resisted was to introduce a modern alienation of Sheridan's dialogue. His portrayal of the contemporary world of high fashion was already delicately satirical. To satirize his dialogue in the performance could only blunt the precision of his highly pointed lines. John had a high respect and a strong feeling for Sheridan's style, though he was to find it anything but easy to impose even an approximate consistency on a company of such mixed ages and backgrounds. Some had experience of the classics: Anna and Daniel Massey had won their spurs in light modern comedy, and Howard Goorney (Moses) was a graduate of Joan Littlewood's Theatre Workshop.

After two weeks at Oxford and Liverpool, the production opened at the Haymarket on 5 April 1962. Some of the critics thought Sir Ralph Richardson insufficiently irascible as Sir Peter Teazle. By making him so likable, he made Lady Teazle (Anna Massey) appear rather cruel. Generally, the various characterizations were held to be inadequately integrated and the production was found lacking in sparkle and pace. But the first week set up a new box office record at the Haymarket of £5,500.

The play had been scheduled to close on 13 October but when an American tour was arranged, the run was extended for five weeks, though with some cast changes. John himself took over from Richard Easton, who had succeeded John Neville as Joseph Surface, while Easton replaced Daniel Massey as Charles Surface. Gwen Ffrangcon Davies and Geraldine McEwan succeeded Margaret Rutherford (Mrs Candour) and Anna Massey. Almost all the critics who revisited the production agreed that it was improved both by the changes and by the passage of time, which had eased the other actors into their roles. The Screen Scene, with John and Richardson collaborating in a succession of expertly timed comic points, was now a superb climax.

It was twenty-five years since John had played Joseph Surface, but what he lacked in youth he made up in polish and precision. As T. C. Worsley wrote, he has an 'instinctive feeling for the kind of civilized sharpness which lies not so much in the wit as in the shape of Sheridan's lines. While others make one conscious of the lack of substance in some of the repartee, Sir John makes every sentence seem to carry twice its weight by phrasing it so perfectly. It is the very model of how this should be spoken; and yet the control is so perfect that the artificiality can be broken at will to make a human point, as when, meeting the supposed poor relation, the most delicate pauses between the "Mr" and the "Stanley" can convey the deadliest of insults. Add to this an elegant artificiality of carriage that is itself a weapon, and you have a performance in the high artist class.'

In America the production got off to a bad start in Philadelphia at the end of November. It was a big theatre with poor acoustics and, for an American audience, Sheridan's language and the English accents were both difficult to follow, particularly for the people at the back of the crowded house, and many walked out. But after this, the pace of the speaking was modified and the remaining performances went better. In Toronto (where the public was not expected to be interested in Sheridan) the production was so popular that although they had to play in the O'Keefe Centre, which holds 2,700 people, tickets were completely sold out.

The seven week season on Broadway was equally successful. A newspaper strike prevented reviews from circulating, but the season was already almost sold out on the day after the opening, despite a broadcast by Walter Kerr, who said that the evening 'has a convalescent air about it, as though all of the wags and witches of eighteenth-century London were just getting over colds and couldn't possibly think of going out for a couple of days'.

Before leaving New York John celebrated his fifty-ninth birthday by giving a charity preview of his revival of *The Ages of Man*, which was to open the following day for a run of nine performances at the Lyceum. Reviews were good but box office business was disappointing after his previous Broadway success. The right moment had passed – the novelty had worn off.

53   Two Lean Years

John's next choice of a new play for London was Jerome Kilty's dramatization of Thornton Wilder's *The Ides of March*, in which he was going to play Julius Caesar in modern dress. The novel is written largely in the form of letters showing Caesar's relationships with the young Cleopatra, with the poet Catullus, with Clodia Pulcher and with Brutus, who is assumed to be Caesar's illegitimate son. Jerome Kilty had previously had a big success with *Dear Liar*, bringing some of Shaw's correspondence with Mrs Patrick Campbell to the stage. But instead of limiting himself as he had then, to showing the protagonists speaking extracts from their letters, Kilty introduced an admixture of dialogue, which upset the convention. In his first version of *The Ides of March* he used a narrator outside the action, but later it occurred to him that the actor who played Caesar could take over the narration, stepping in and out of the character of Caesar, donning and discarding a laurel wreath and toga, worn over a modern suit. When the play was staged in Berlin with O. E. Hasse (who played Shaw in the German version of *Dear Liar*) as Caesar, John and Beaumont went over to see it. Without understanding German, they both had the impression that the letter convention was working less successfully than in *Dear Liar*, but John was hoping to persuade Thornton Wilder to collaborate on a new script. All Wilder in fact contributed was a few fragments of dialogue that did not fit the play, and after feeling uncertain all through rehearsals, John became convinced on the pre-London tour that something was basically wrong with the whole conception.

As he had expected, the reviews were unfavourable and the play only had a short run. But the failure did not kill John's interest in the idea of combining historical costumes casually with modern clothes. Soon afterwards he was experimenting with it again in his production of *Hamlet* for Richard Burton. This was based on the notion of getting the actors to play as they would in a rehearsal, using only the odd pieces of costume they might pick up to help them into the feeling of a scene. As John said, '*Hamlet* offers such a great challenge that the artist playing the role can be considered to be engaged in a permanent rehearsal'.

The production was conceived in July 1963 when John was touring in Newcastle with *The Ides of March* and Burton offered him the small but effective part of Louis VII of France in the film of *Becket*, which he was making on location there with Peter O'Toole. Burton had already played Hamlet at the Old Vic in 1953. John did not like the performance and carefully avoided commenting on it in Burton's dressing room. They were going to have supper together but so many people kept coming in that Burton was slow in changing. Growing restive, John finally asked 'Shall I go ahead or shall I wait until you're better? – I mean ready.'

Apparently the faux-pas had an effect on Burton's performance. When Michael Benthall, the director, went to see it again a few nights later, he found Burton giving an imitation of John's Hamlet, reproducing all John's mannerisms but failing to hold the audience because there was no emotional backing to the façade.

1964 was the 400th anniversary of Shakespeare's birth but no approaches were made to John to star in or direct a play for the occasion. His temperament is basically very resilient but it was altogether a dispiriting time. Despite his success as Gaev, his experience with the Royal Shakespeare Company had been blighted by the failure of his Othello and John was thinking that his career as a leading actor might be over. 1963 was a fairly lean year with *The Ides of March* and his small part in the film of *Becket*. He accepted an invitation to tour *The Ages of Man* in Australia and New Zealand, but he had the feeling that he would no longer be able to follow the movement of theatrical fashion. He had been looking forward to playing Lear again but after Scofield's success under Peter Brook's direction it would be pointless to risk another production for several years. Brecht, seven years after his death, seemed to be dictating the style in which Restoration and eighteenth century plays would be pro-duced, while Osborne's *Luther* seemed to herald a new fashion in Brechtian costume drama. The rising generation of young actors belonged to a completely different type from John and since 1956, when the Berliner Ensemble paid its first visit to London and *Look Back in Anger* had its first production at the Royal Court, many critics, following Tynan's lead, had been attacking John as if he had been personally responsible for excluding working-class subjects from British Drama and working-class actors from the profession. The name Gielgud was constantly being attached to the 'old' style of acting which the 'new', more-or-less Brechtian style seemed to be displacing. Even in parts like Hamlet or Prince Hal, the casting of actors like David Warner and Ian Holm was putting a Brechtian emphasis on what Shakespeare's royal heroes have in common with the Common Man. John could never play a working-class character and he made matters worse for himself with some widely publicized animadversions about the avant-garde theatre. For seven years his career had hardly been affected by the change of fashion but now it began to be. Sir Laurence Olivier had been appointed Director of the National Theatre, and had invited Sir Michael Redgrave into the company. But for John there seemed to be no place. Since 1958 he had been responsible for several major London productions, including Terence Rattigan's *Variations on a Theme*, Peter Shaffer's *Five Finger Exercise*, Graham Greene's *The Complaisant Lover* and Benjamin Britten's opera *A Mid-summer Night's Dream* at Covent Garden. His future as a director appeared to be less in jeopardy than his acting career, but altogether the future was extremely uncertain.

During the filming of *Becket*, Burton and O'Toole did what they could to cheer him up. He was not bad-tempered but unusually silent and withdrawn. When he asked Burton what he would be doing for the 1964 Shakespeare celebrations, the immediate reply was that he'd do *Hamlet* again if John would direct him. Half-jokingly, John agreed, thinking nothing would come of the idea, but Alexander Cohen offered to present the production in New York. So they were soon laying plans. Burton disliked acting in doublet and hose and John's idea of staging the play as a rehearsal immediately appealed to him. He remembered watching John in one of the final London rehearsals of *Richard II* before he took it to Bulawayo. The costumes had already been sent on to Africa and the actors rehearsed in their own clothes. John was wearing a torn old white dressing gown over a shirt and white trousers. Burton described this rehearsal as one of the finest things he had ever seen.

John held auditions for *Hamlet* in New York during the last week of October. It was particularly hard to find a good Ophelia. He had to listen to hundreds of girls who all insisted on doing the mad scene. He asked them to read the long verse speech "Oh what a noble mind is here o'erthrown", but they would say they hadn't studied that bit. Some of them wore weird clothes and produced grotesque props. Arriving at the theatre, one girl changed into a kind of nightgown and writhed about on the stage giving birth to a doll, which she finally produced from underneath it.

Eileen Herlie played the Queen, George Voskovec was the Player King and George Rose was the First Gravedigger. Most of the other actors were American. Alfred Drake played the King, with Hume Cronyn as Polonius. The final choice for Ophelia was Linda Marsh. John himself recorded the part of the Ghost on tape. It was represented on stage by a great overhanging shadow.

From the point of view of publicity and box office business, the production was an enormous success; from John's point of view it was a failure in that he failed to stimulate the imagination of the actors and the audiences in the way he wanted to. His basic idea for the production derived from the knowledge that actors were often at their very best in the final run-through of a play before the first dress-rehearsal – miming or improvising props and accessories without being limited by the set, costumes and lighting. As he said at the first rehearsal,* 'One sees an actor pick

* For a detailed account of these rehearsals, see Richard Sterne's book *John Gielgud*

up a piece of material to use as a cloak and fling it over his shoulder convincingly, and he seems to do this more unself-consciously than when he has the final costume. Actors seize on things that they need. If they suddenly think they must have a cloak, a dagger or a sword, they will snatch a substitute from somewhere or even pretend to do so.' Deeply interested himself in the ways actors have of easing themselves into a characterization, he tried to create a similar interest in his company. He invited the actors to dress for rehearsals in clothes that helped each of them not so much to look the part as to feel it. The costume designer was instructed to watch very carefully what clothes people chose for themselves, so that the final selection would include whatever was most effective, while colours could be chosen for the principals 'so that they will stand out in exactly the same way that the royal family in England take care to stand out when they appear in public'. But the actors were generally unresponsive to this freedom of choice and would obviously have preferred to wear period costumes.

For the background, John wanted something like the glamorous clutter of flats and properties that are often stacked at the back of the stage in the old English theatres when one set has been struck and another play is in rehearsal. But he did not realize that in American theatres everything is always cleared away, leaving only the bare white walls. His designer, Ben Edwards, produced a set which looked like an empty stage with double dock doors in the centre of the back wall and weights hanging from the grid. But somehow it did not look beautiful as Sally Jacobs's very similar set did in Peter Brook's production of the *Marat-Sade*.

Burton's attitude to Shakespeare is very different from John's. He wanted people to feel they were seeing *Hamlet* for the first time. 'And if the verse had to be mauled and brutalized a little, then mauling and brutalization should go on.' Even in the early rehearsals he tended to resist John's suggestions about the phrasing, to shout in the emotional climaxes, and to make Hamlet more athletic than John wanted him to be. When it came to the final run-through, John urged the actors to forget the fact that audiences knew the play so well, to believe in the Ghost, and to remain ignorant of Claudius's guilt until the action revealed it. 'Find the *line* of the play and experience it as it develops. This

directs Richard Burton in Hamlet, Heinemann Educational Books, 1968. They are also described in William Redfield's book *Letters from an Actor* (Cassell).

will give the impression of real occurrence, and contemporary occurrence.' He must have been remembering his Indian tour of *Hamlet* and the way his war-time performances had affected the troops in the Far East.

After highly enthusiastic reviews in Boston, the production opened in New York on 9 April 1964. The crowds around the theatre were so dense that first-nighters had to show their tickets to the police in order to get through the cordon. The reviews were mixed. The *New York Post* and the *New York Times* were favourable, but in the *Herald Tribune*, Walter Kerr wrote 'Richard Burton is one of the most magnificently equipped actors living . . . He places on open display not only all of his own reverberating resources . . . but also all of the myriad qualities which the man Hamlet requires. All except one. Mr Burton is without feeling.'

The first night in New York was the last night John saw the production. Despite the mixed reviews, it ran for 138 performances, breaking John's own record of 132, which puzzled him, especially when he saw the film which had been made after the hundredth performance. He found that Burton was indulging in all the tricks he had tried to discourage, leaping over tables, imitating the other actors, and obviously enjoying himself thoroughly.

By now John had completed a tour of *The Ages of Man* which took him to Sweden, Denmark, Poland, Finland, Russia and Ireland, returning to Hollywood for the first time since 1952 for Tony Richardson's film version of Evelyn Waugh's *The Loved One*, a bitingly satirical novel about the American Way of Death. The cast included Rod Steiger, Liberace, Vanessa Redgrave and Robert Morley. John played an ageing British filmwriter who had been working in Hollywood and hanged himself early in the film. But thanks largely to Tony Richardson's encouragement, this small part was something of a turning point in John's film career. For the first time since his Hollywood Cassius, he began to feel no self-consciousness in front of the cameras and more able to control his acting. He also struck up a firm friendship with Richardson.

54 Edward Albee and 'Tiny Alice'

In the spring of 1964 Edward Albee approached John about a new play he was writing with a leading part in it for him. As none of the English avant-garde playwrights had ever offered him a part, John was delighted to be approached by an American. But when Albee sent him the first two acts of *Tiny Alice*, though greatly intrigued, he was worried that he was too old for the part and cabled 'How old am I supposed to be?' Albee's reply was that all the characters in the play were meant to be 'around fifty'. John was also apprehensive that the play in general and his role in particular might be considered blasphemous. But he was fascinated by the character of Brother Julian and accepted the role without having read the third act. He asked for Irene Worth to star opposite him as Miss Alice and she accepted enthusiastically.

Neither of them fully understood the play, but, unlike John, Irene Worth was content not to understand. Having played Celia in T. S. Eliot's *The Cocktail Party*, she was used to working with an author who refused to explain meanings. 'Let's skate along. Let's explore it,' she said, while he kept saying 'What does it mean?' To which Albee's reply was 'You can't play the meaning of a play. You have to play the reality of the characters.' This is true but you also have to invest your own physical reality in dialogue which may fail to add up to a coherent character and the result of John's act of faith in *Tiny Alice* has been well described by Gordon Rogoff*:

> While shape and direction are absent from the play, they are never far from John Gielgud's way of acting . . . Paul Scofield, for example, might have brought a darker innocence to Julian and a more youthful sense of vulnerability, but Gielgud is the master of tensile wonder. An actor born to the quest, he is uniquely equipped to skim delicately over surfaces while sinking slowly into the depths. His arms and legs

* In *Plays and Players*, March 1965.

222

seem never to know quite where his head is leading him, but he brings to the role a tone and temperament that give their spasms the lie. His Julian is a spirit vibrating in repose, a shadow, as Yeats said of a Maeterlinck figure, 'sighing at the edge of the world'. It is lucky for the production that Gielgud can provide so much extraordinary belief.

One of the challenges John had to meet was in the seduction scene, which called simultaneously for religious ecstasy and sexual ecstasy. 'The two are very similar,' he said, 'but also very different. On stage they must both be inner emotions. And since I have three ecstatic moments in the play, I must try to make each of them interesting and in some way different.'

He had a good relationship with Alan Schneider, the director, who at the end of rehearsals wrote to him 'I have simply never met anyone like you. All I can do is thank you for your willingness, your trust and understanding . . . Bless you, and you have a disciple for life.'

At most performances in New York there was both cheering and booing. The critics complained about the play's obscurity but John and Irene Worth were both highly praised and the production ran for over 200 performances. But John was never very happy in the part.

55   'Ivanov'

In June 1965 it was announced that John would star in his own production of Chekhov's second play, *Ivanov*, with Yvonne Mitchell as Anna Petrovna and Claire Bloom as Sasha. John made his own adaptation of the play, working from a translation by Ariadne Nicolaeff. The designer he chose was Rouben Ter-Arutunian, an American Armenian who had designed the film of *The Loved One*. John had known the play for forty years: it was the first Chekhov play he ever saw, when Komisarjevsky directed two performances of it for the Stage Society in 1925 with Robert Farquharson as Ivanov. But this would be its first West End production* and John's first appearance in London (except in *The Ages of Man*) for over two years.

Ivanov is a nineteenth-century hollow man who agonizes endlessly over his own emptiness. At thirty-five – John played it as forty-five – he is weary of life and weary of his own weariness. The great difficulty of the part is to engage sufficient sympathy for him, balancing his negative qualities with enough personal attractiveness to explain the love that two women feel for him. He is passive and egocentric from the beginning and so much of the conflict is internal – a battle he fights against his self-disgust – that it is also hard to achieve sufficient variety. For John, there was the additional problem of presenting a middle-aged man who feels himself to be old before his time.

As so often when directing himself, John rather neglected his own performance in favour of the others, and this time he also cut his own lines while building up the smaller parts. The characters in the party scene are not written in depth and individually they have very little to say. Most of Act Two is devoted to satirizing their malicious gossip and none of the characters that the audience has met in Act One reappear until just before the curtain. But instead of moving briskly through the social satire, John slowed it down with movement and elaborate business. Amusing though this was, it emphasized the diffuseness of the action and by cutting his own lines he lost his chance of establishing Ivanov, right at the beginning of the play, as a compulsive talker, full of restless neurotic energy. As Chekhov wrote it, the dialogue is repetitive, but necessarily so.

John also failed to integrate the acting styles of his supporting cast. Edward Atienza's animated cartoon of the Count (Stanislavski's old part) was in a different convention from Roland Culver's amiably inhibited Lebedev, while Richard Pasco's doctor was too unsympathetic and inappropriately modern in his obstreperousness. But as the suffering Jewish wife Yvonne Mitchell was beautiful and affecting.

John found it difficult to modulate from Ivanov's passive melancholy to the highly melodramatic outbursts in the third and fourth acts. He also had difficulty in controlling the oscillations between comedy and melodrama in the last act. When Sasha appeals to Ivanov to run away with her, his answer is

* There had been a club production at the Arts Theatre, directed by John Fernald with Michael Hordern as Ivanov.

'Where could we go?' Probably a laugh here is quite in accordance with Chekhov's intentions but John was determined to kill it. He tried altering the words and even cutting the line altogether but without it the transition to his last lines before his suicide was very awkward and he had to restore the cut.

In any case the production was a considerable success. Many of the critics praised John's performance as one of his best. The play ran for four months and could have run longer, but for the American tour which had already been arranged. For this, Vivien Leigh took over as the wife and Jennifer Hillary replaced Claire Bloom as Sasha.

But the New York critics were mixed in their reactions and generally far less favourable than the London critics had been. They thought it a pity that *Ivanov* had been chosen instead of one of Chekhov's later plays, while the English accents seemed to make the characters even less acceptable to them – as if they were now at two removes from their Russian originals – and to the Americans Vivien Leigh seemed wasted in so small a part. The production played to slowly diminishing audiences for five and a half weeks.

56 The Mock Turtle

Since the television production of *A Day by the Sea*, John had acted in television adaptations of *The Cherry Orchard* and *Ivanov*, only to be very dissatisfied with the results. He now appeared on television in Jonathan Miller's version of *Alice in Wonderland*. Miller had persuaded the BBC to give him a budget of £25,000 for his own production of his own adaptation. Translating all the animals into human terms, he cast John as the Mock Turtle, and Malcolm Muggeridge as the Gryphon, explaining that he saw the two of them 'as a couple of lackadaisical Victorian uncles. They have private incomes and they've lost all the meaning of their lives in late middle-age. They have nothing to do except reminisce about their schooldays.' So John had to dance along a beach near Hastings singing 'Will you walk a little faster?'

while Muggeridge skipped like an elderly Puck between the pools, wearing spats, white side-whiskers and a Victorian panama hat, exaggerating his angular movements as if to dissociate himself from John's more elegantly languid performance.

The cast included Wilfred Lawson, Sir Michael Redgrave, Leo McKern, Peter Sellers and Peter Cook. Many of the reviews were favourable but many regretted Miller's decision to strip the characters of their animal identities. Writing in the *Daily Telegraph*, Morton Cohen, an American don engaged in editing Lewis Carroll's letters, objected that all Miller did was to present the viewer 'with disconnected vignettes, each dominated by a great actor trying, in his own individual style, to create a memorable performance . . . Sir John Gielgud's Mock Turtle is the only successful characterization, rendered in pure and quiet screen poetry, but it lasts only a few moments.'

John himself felt that 'If Miller had introduced Alice and her whole family – at a party or Christmas dinner – at the beginning of the film, the clever but eccentric idea of using them afterwards for the fantasy characters would have been far more effective and comprehensible.'

Seven months later, in March 1967, Miller again directed John on television in *From Chekhov with Love*, a play based on Chekhov's letters, which had been a great success in Moscow. John played Chekhov and Peggy Ashcroft, Wendy Hiller and Dorothy Tutin had important parts. John felt that Chekhov's humour had a poor showing, but the scenes leading up to his death were effective and generally the production was liked.

57   'The Charge of the Light Brigade' and
      'Half Way Up the Tree'

John had not intended to go on playing *The Ages of Man* but in June 1967 he agreed to give a special charity performance at the State Opera House in Ankara while he was filming in Turkey as Lord Raglan, Commander-in-Chief of the Allied Forces in the Crimea, in *The Charge of the Light Brigade*. Many of the other actors in the film came to support him at the opera house. For the first five minutes he was very nervous but he gathered his forces to give one of his best performances. In the scene of Lear's recognition of Cordelia, the words, as one actor put it, 'seemed to hang in the air'.

During the ten weeks of filming in Turkey, John found that what he had learnt from *The Ages of Man* was surprisingly useful, because he frequently had to react to characters and situations which were not physically present. In a play, of course, an actor never needs to do this, but he often does in filming.

John also found it an advantage that he had laid the foundations of the character during the week's filming in London, where the scene in the War Office was shot before the unit went out to Turkey. Some of Raglan's best lines come in this scene, and though John would have liked more time to think about the part before committing any of it to celluloid, he was encouraged by Tony Richardson's approval of his appearance, manner and general characterization, which he went on developing in Turkey.

His performance as the gentle, vague, donnish commander has been very highly praised, and rightly. It is one of the best things in the film. But though it may seem perverse to criticize an actor's performance for being too much in keeping with his director's intentions, John might have done better to play more against the farcical element in the writing and in the production. Raglan's muddle-headedness was exaggerated to the point where it became impossible to believe in him as a man who could have retained command of his forces. Funny and endearing though he was, one wished for a more three-dimensional character. In the performance, as in the whole film, the mixture of naturalism and farce did not quite work. The historical Lord Raglan may actually have forgotten that he wasn't still fighting the French but he also had a thousand other characteristics that were excluded from this characterization, which reduced him to a vignette. But no doubt the experience of creating the part prepared the way for John's Headmaster in *40 Years On*.

Playing a short part in a Hollywood thriller and meeting Peter Ustinov there in February 1967, John read his play *Half Way Up the Tree*. It is one of his slightest comedies, but John was right in guessing it might succeed with the public, though it took over six months to persuade Beaumont to present it. Ustinov is almost the unlikeliest playwright — as John is quite the unlikeliest director – for a play that seriously (however comically) gets to grips with the hippies, but *Half Way Up the Tree* is basically a conventional drawing-room comedy, complete with conventional comic types – sexy au pair girl, distraught wife, platitudinizing vicar and silly-ass scoutmaster, and a happy ending, with the lovers pairing up neatly to get married.

John had wanted Ralph Richardson to play the general who takes to living in a tree, but he was not interested in the part and it was Beaumont who suggested Robert Morley. Himself a playwright, Morley did so much rewriting, especially of his own lines, that John was apprehensive Ustinov might fall out with him, especially after Morley had been very offhand to him at the first reading. Fortunately Ustinov had to leave London to direct the New York production and when he came back to see John's final dress rehearsal, he made no objection to the re-scripting. The results were very popular and the play ran at the Queen's for over a year.

58   With the National Theatre

It had been announced in November 1966 that John would be joining the National Theatre company for the 1967–8 season, to appear as Bishop Nicholas in Ibsen's *The Pretenders* with Sir Laurence Olivier as Earl Skule, in Molière's *Tartuffe* and in Seneca's *Oedipus*, but *The Pretenders* had to be abandoned because of Olivier's illness. Originally the idea had been to do not *Tartuffe* but *Le Misanthrope*, and Jaques Charon had been mentioned as director. But *Le Misanthrope* too had to be abandoned because the Royal Shakespeare Company was planning a production for the Aldwych. John suggested *Tartuffe* as an alternative and Roger Planchon, Jean-Louis Barrault and Jean Vilar as possible directors. None of these were available and so it was Tyrone Guthrie who directed it, with John as Orgon and Robert Stephens as Tartuffe.

Orgon is not a particularly good part, though Molière once played it himself, and Robert Stephens was oddly cast as Tartuffe.

As if to explain why John had not been given the name part, there was a picture in the programme of the thirty-four-year-old Du Croisy, who played it at the 1664 première, and a note explaining that the role was 'later taken over by La Grange, the romantic lead in Molière's company. The tradition of entrusting the role to older actors dates from long after the author's death, and is not substantiated by anything in the text or in Molière's comments on it.'

For any actor of any age, one of the main problems of playing Tartuffe is to convince the audience that he would succeed in hoodwinking Orgon. With John as Orgon, the problem becomes unusually difficult: he does not come across as a man who could be duped so easily. Tartuffe is posing as an impoverished aristocrat but Guthrie gave Robert Stephens a yokel wig, a beetroot face and a thick Mummerset accent. To be taken in, Orgon would have had to be an idiot. Even in appearance, John's Orgon was the more aristocratic of the two characters.

What were Guthrie's intentions? Writing in *Plays and Players*, Martin Esslin suggested that the reason Orgon allows himself to be taken in so easily is that he feels guilty about his own affluence and security.

> He sees Tartuffe's crudeness, his bad manners, his greed and covetousness; but these, being the consequences of Tartuffe's social handicaps, merely strengthen Orgon's guilt-feelings, his pity for the poor fellow, who has been starved for so long that he cannot be blamed for wanting to eat his own fill.

In fact Esslin makes Orgon into a sixteenth-century counterpart to Max Frisch's Biedermann, who co-operates so readily with the arsonists who burn his house in *The Fire Raisers*. This not only imposes a twentieth-century reading on Molière, it ignores his point about Orgon's snobbery, which makes him such an easy prey for Tartuffe. John was able to convey a vague kindliness and something of what Esslin calls 'the blindness that springs from excessive charity', but the production blunted the satire on religiosity. When John's Orgon seemed impressed by Tartuffe's affectations of piety, the effect was one of half-hearted farce, and generally the Guthrie-Stephens characterization of Tartuffe killed any possibility of a convincing relationship between him and Orgon.

That the actors themselves were unhappy with the production was suggested by a hesitant and jerky first night. The most assured performance came from Joan Plowright as a briskly common-sensical young maid, though traditionally the character has been played as an old servant who has worked in the household for years and orders Orgon about like an old Nanny.

Oedipus was a very different experience. As early as 1951, John had been attracted by Sophocles's *Oedipus*, but Olivier's huge success in the part at the Old Vic in 1944 had made him unwilling to risk comparisons, and he had never read Seneca's play.

Seneca's Roman stoicism is already very distant from both Greek and Shakespearean tragedy, and the work Ted Hughes and Peter Brook did on the text substantially increased the distance. Working from a translation by David A. Turner, Hughes rewrote and made additions in rehearsal. He made a lot of changes to the part of Jocasta, which scarcely exists in Seneca's text, building it up for Irene Worth, who had accepted the part out of loyalty to John and Peter Brook.

Peter Brook has said 'The only reason I did *Oedipus* was a real homage to John.' They had not worked together for ten years and Brook had been approached to direct *Oedipus* at the National Theatre shortly after being very moved by John's address at the memorial service held for Vivien Leigh. It immediately struck him that here was an opportunity to build 'a living bridge' between John and some of the best of the younger actors who had 'developed great possibilities of physical expression and emotional freedom, but who are eventually at a disadvantage to John when it comes to what he can do so marvellously in his reading.'

It was a play which depended very much on the word, but Brook developed the relationship between the principals and the chorus in highly physical terms. His aim was 'to evolve a new style that would depend in equal measure on the contributions brought by the different schools of actors and would be a product of the two. And for that we started on this long series of exercises. John threw himself into them on exactly the same level as the others. Not for one second did it occur to him that he had any special position or privilege different from the others. As an artist he was starting from zero and so were they, and he was always at a disadvantage, because every young actor could do physical leaps and turns and twists in a way that obviously he couldn't. Although he suffered embarrassment from this, he didn't in any way use it as a way of making opposition to it.'

There was no punctuation marked in the scripts Peter Brook

issued to the cast, only intervals between the phrases, which the actors tried to follow, as if they were reading a musical score. This method of working helped them into a liturgical, anti-realistic convention and Brook encouraged them to look on themselves as narrators rather than impersonators of their characters. In one of the later rehearsals he made them stand in a straight line and play their lines as fast as they could without gabbling them.

For the first three of the ten strenuous weeks of rehearsal, they worked entirely on body movements, vocal exercises and improvisations, without even seeing a text. But to prepare John for the scenes in which he would have to dominate the action by his stance, Brook made him do exercises to simplify his gait and to achieve a steady balance. Brook would not tell the actors what they would be wearing, how they would be made up, or what the set would be like. Actually he did not make his own mind up till later on.

This is how Irene Worth remembers the rehearsals:

John was really at his humblest and deepest, breaking right away from his classical training of being totally in command of his material. He begged Peter to keep him as open and malleable and free as possible. Because the old technical skills and the old tricks were no use. There was one session when the three of us were in that filthy National Theatre rehearsal room for six hours. Peter was trying to help John to achieve a certain note of pain to make a real spring of truth for the speech. John tried and tried and tried. I've never seen an actor go through so much breaking down. He was like a loaf of bread being broken into small pieces. He worked and worked at it and Peter said no. He went on into hidden and precious parts of himself, digging into himself, which was particularly hard for him, with his pudeur and his fastidiousness. It was terribly painful for him but he dug deeper and he got it. It was the "All is well" speech after the blinding. To maintain it, of course, is different from finding it, and he found it enormously difficult to reproduce technically.

If he did not succeed altogether, he certainly did not fail. Hilary Spurling in the *Spectator* picked out two of John's moments for special praise. One was the pose — 'hands splayed, body twisted, mouth split in a silent scream' — with which John reacted to the revelation of the past. Praising the beauty of the image John presented, she found its simplicity was matched after the description of the blinding when 'Oedipus speaks in a changed voice: "All is well . . . I like this darkness, I wonder which god

it is that I've finally pleased." This faint dry croak is strangely
sweet and yet, like Lear's, it is still a self-deceiving sweetness.
For Oedipus, like Lear and in almost the same words, must leave
his darkness once again to face Jocasta's hideous death. After
which Sir John's slow departure has the exhaustion, both of
Oedipus's ultimate acceptance, and of a great performance finally
concluded.'

The reactions of the critics were mixed. Some, I think rightly,
found that John touched new notes, flexed muscles he had not
used before. Others, also rightly, found that he seemed not
entirely at home in the production. Nevertheless, there were
moments of extraordinary achievement in it. Tony Richardson
wrote to John describing 'the terrifying moment when before the
blinding you become a half man, half beast before us' as 'a
moment of acting in all its richest imaginative and physical
complexity as great as any I've ever seen'.

59 '40 Years On'

Alan Bennett's *40 Years On* was not written specially for John.
In fact Bennett thought the management was being over-
optimistic in sending the script to John. But he was later to say
that no part since Benedick had ever given him such a 'released'
feeling, and when it opened in London in October 1968 the
reviews were the best he had had since *The Ages of Man*.

Though he immediately thought the script very funny he was
worried at the idea of working with twenty-five boys. At his first
meeting with Bennett he suggested that cardboard cut-outs of the
schoolboys might be less distracting than real ones. He was also
worried about the idea of using photographic slides as a background and he thought some of the jokes in bad taste. He was
afraid they might offend audiences (and especially ex-Harro-
vians) who knew that '40 Years On' had been Churchill's favourite
song. When he saw the final draft, he liked the second half less
than the first but he knew that more work could be done on
the script during rehearsals. In any case it was the first good

modern part he had had in London since *Nude with Violin* in 1955 and what made it particularly attractive was the interludes – the Headmaster playing a doddering Edwardian butler and a fantasy judge in the Court of History. In the script, some of the sketches were not allotted to any particular character and it was John who insisted on playing the Butler and speaking the Sitwell pastiche at the end of the first act about the country house. He came to enjoy his speeches to the audience, which had greatly embarrassed him at first and even the Headmaster's improvised prayers.

The pre-London tour opened in Manchester at the enormous Palace Theatre, which had been closed all through the summer. On the first night only a third of the seats were occupied and the audience seemed to lose interest half way through the second act. In the morning, the *Guardian* was hostile, as was one of the other local papers ('a very brittle, long-winded two and a quarter hours'). Two weeks of poor houses made John and Bennett, pessimistic about their chances in London, though they grimly went on rehearsing changes and cuts almost every day.

John asked Bennett whether he couldn't add a Noël Coward parody for the second act. 'You know the sort of thing, lots of little epigrams, smart witty remarks. It wouldn't be at all difficult.' But Bennett thought it would. Someone at a party suggested that the Headmaster should actually leave at the end of the play. Bennett was unenthusiastic, saying he could not find a speech to fit such a dramatic moment. John said 'It doesn't need words. I can just walk off the stage.' He made a simple but very telling exit, pausing on the way out to straighten the tie of one of the boys as he passed.

It was John's gentle self-parody which made his performance so affecting. It was obvious that he sympathized with some of the ideas and attitudes that the play was mocking, but it was also obvious that there was an ambivalence in his sympathy which, luckily, corresponded with an ambivalence in Bennett's own attitude. Bennett too feels an undeniable nostalgia for the Edwardian period and the twenties and thirties, even though he was only five years old when the 1939 war broke out. But from his affectionate patchwork of pastiches and literary jokes about T. E. Lawrence, Virginia Woolf, Buchan, Sapper and the rest, he not only created a highly theatrical atmosphere, he gave the impression of successfully capturing the flavour of this England he never knew.

Altogether the part was unlike anything John had played before, though his concert party experiences during the war had taught him how to use his personality almost as in a revue, playing lines straight to the audience and being very well aware of their reactions. During the run of *40 Years On* he managed to develop his confidence until the blend of self-involvement and self-parody became very subtle indeed.

60 'The Battle of Shrivings' and 'Home'

Peter Shaffer wrote the two massive leading parts in *The Battle of Shrivings* with John and Laurence Olivier in mind, hoping the play would be staged at the National Theatre, where *The Royal Hunt of the Sun* and *Black Comedy* had both been so successful. Olivier liked both the play and the part, but it was impossible to agree dates and after long delays and complicated negotiations, the play was presented in the West End by the Tennent management with Patrick Magee playing opposite John and Peter Hall directing. John himself had secretly harboured some doubts about the play, and when he took a script away on holiday with him after committing himself to playing in it, he kept picking it up to read and finding himself reluctant to go on. But partly because Olivier, Tynan, Peter Hall and Beaumont all thought it a fine and important play, John swallowed his doubts.

The basic idea is an extremely interesting one – a confrontation between an apparently saintlike pacifist, modelled directly on Bertrand Russell, and a destructive ex-pupil, a bohemian poet domiciled in Greece, who is perhaps modelled loosely on Ezra Pound or Robert Graves. In the first act, which culminates in a kind of declaration of total war between the two men, the tension holds fairly well, but it is not sustained in the second and third. Instead of embodying the conflict between the two giants in action, Shaffer indulged in monologues full of self-revelatory rhetoric, and this led him to write an extremely wordy play. Neither he nor Peter Hall was willing to cut it, though John and Beaumont tried to press for cuts, especially towards the end of rehearsals, when it became obvious how long the performance was going to last, and then during the try-out week at Brighton. But it was only after the unfriendly reviews the play received in London that substantial cuts were finally made.

In the first act, John was easily able to win the audience's sympathy as Sir Gideon Petrie, the kindly old philosopher, self-lessly taxing his frail old body on peace marches and Ghandi-like fasts. Given suitable dialogue, John could have been convincing as an intellectual of Russell's calibre, but very few playwrights are equipped to write on this level, and Shaffer was injudicious in his mixing of generalized argument with a complicated exposé of the old man's sexual history. Potentially the battle between the two men is fine theatrical material, especially as the old philosopher is prevented from hitting back both by his own principles and by the conditions of the battle, which stipulate that he will be the loser if he orders the vindictive Mark Askelon out of his house. It ought to have been possible to create a character that develops theatrically under Askelon's relentless assault, but in fact John's role permitted only a schematic and finally unconvincing development. Petrie loses faith in his own humanism while Askelon is apparently converted to it. John was forced into striking the same note of wounded nobility again and again. The long last act was weakened further by a double scene which fatally divided the audience's interest. Askelon was isolated on the upper stage and his soliloquy was awkwardly interpolated into the scene the other characters were playing below him, artificially silenced whenever he spoke. By the end, the audience had lost interest in the sufferings of both men, so that John's Olivier-like howl of despair inevitably counted for very little.

When a play is neither a success nor a complete failure but goes on playing for several months to sparse audiences in a large theatre, the actors are in a highly unenviable position. There is always a small band of loyal supporters who go on maintaining that the critics were wrong and the play is marvellous. There are always sparks of hope when business rallies slightly at the box office, and depression when it sinks back. There are the inevitable, interminable discussions about what went wrong, and futile attempts to patch the damage by altering the timing in one place, adding a new piece of business in another. But it can only be a relief when notice is finally given that the play is to be taken off.

But before the end of the run, Lindsay Anderson had offered John and Ralph Richardson the two leading parts in David Storey's new play *Home*. At first they were both baffled by it. So much of the dialogue consists of exclamations, inconsequential remarks and unfinished sentences, they were at a loss to know how they would ever learn it or how an audience would take it. But if *The Battle of Shrivings* was badly overwritten, *Home* was subtly underwritten in dialogue with a strange quality which immediately fascinated John. Ralph Richardson soon decided that he wanted to play the character who did the card tricks, so John agreed to play Harry, only to become very worried at the first reading when he realized how scanty his dialogue was. There is one sequence where his only reply to a whole barrage of questions and remarks is the one word "Well . . ." so he had to find a different inflection and a different reason for being non-committal each time. Neither of the two characters can confront the experiences which have upset their mental balance, but whereas Jack throws out elaborate verbal smokescreens, Harry is much less talkative. The actor has to express the character's pain partly through short sentences that tail off into nothing, mainly through silences and spasms of unexpected tears. Keith Dewhurst was later to write in the *Guardian* 'Gielgud's weeping is a depth of emotion which he must find entirely within himself, since in the sense of story-line or interaction between the characters there is very little in the play to help him . . . Actors generally need to proceed from one tangible piece of evidence to the next . . . In *Home* the character just interrupts a conversation with tears and the way in which Gielgud does this, the way in which his whole face goes red and his eyes blink with salt, is simply an act of genius: a consummation of his lifetime's integrity.'

All through the first weeks of rehearsal, both actors were uncertain whether they were right to risk their reputations on such an elliptical, unusual play with so little action or suspense, so few moves, no obvious climaxes – nothing to make an actor feel secure. They were also hesitant about appearing at the Royal Court, where neither of them had ever played since the beginning of George Devine's regime in 1956, though Olivier, Scofield and Guinness had all had successes there. For nearly fifteen years it had been regarded as the stronghold of a new style of acting which was proving the Establishment outdated. But now, though they did not yet know it, John and Richardson were to enjoy an extremely warm reception there.

What renewed John's confidence in the play was the experience of going out front during a rehearsal to watch a scene between Ralph Richardson and Dandy Nichols. He immediately saw that there was an extra dimension to the dialogue, which was not apparent to the actors speaking it. After this, he had a much clearer notion of how an audience might respond.

Towards the middle of the rehearsal period, Lindsay Anderson told the actors that whenever they felt the instinct to move, they should inhibit it, making the move either slightly earlier or slightly later. This helped to create a disjointed rhythm, a strangeness in the atmosphere. Otherwise very little was done to make the point that all five characters are mentally unbalanced. The play was written very quickly, in two days, and when he started writing, Storey had no intention of setting the action inside a mental home. He did not know himself where the dialogue was taking place – in a hotel, perhaps, he thought. In the finished script he keeps the audience in the same uncertainty that he was in himself all through the long opening duologue between Jack and Harry, two old English fogies who might be anywhere. It is only when the two women come on that the dialogue reveals all four characters to be borderline cases. Quite late on in rehearsals, John introduced a moment of walking very hesitantly, counting the paving stones, but he was careful not to over-elaborate this and otherwise did nothing to underline Harry's eccentricity. The performance, like the writing, sent out a message of despair which was all the more moving for being so understated.

For twenty years, ever since his Angelo in Peter Brook's *Measure for Measure*, John had consistently done his utmost not to vary his performance from one night to the next. In *Home* he found it seemed right to allow himself a greater margin of variation in his timing and Lindsay Anderson agreed that he should keep this freedom. The main passages of dialogue became set with a musical precision. In his duets with Ralph Richardson, the contrast between their voices was exploited with very careful scoring, but for much of the give and take of the play's deliberately desultory conversations, John found it best to empty his mind of everything except the character, allowing the timing to be determined by the audience and the mood of the moment. At the same time, he found that the play induced an unusual physical relaxation in him. For once there was no need to sit with a straight back and elegantly placed legs or to attack the dialogue athletically. He also found it much easier than in *Oedipus* or *40 Years On* to play lines straight out to the audience.

One of the questions raised by the production is whether the play could have been a success of the same order without two stars of the magnitude of John and Ralph Richardson. When Storey wrote the play he had no idea of what the two men looked like and the finished script allows the director even more latitude in casting the two men than the two women. In any play or film a star brings something of his own image to the character he plays because the audience is never likely to forget who it is they are watching, but in *Home*, as in *40 Years On*, there was a degree of irony in the casting and of self-irony in the playing. Harry and Jack, like the Headmaster, are representatives of a world that is passing, and John's success derived largely from an unreluctant mixture of sharp-eyed satire with genuine nostalgia. By allowing the two to blend so ripely in his performance, and above all by showing what was worthwhile in the values and conventions that are vanishing, he made audiences share something of his own regret at the same time as laughing. But what is most remarkable of all is that suddenly the problem which has bedevilled the whole of his career since the war is a problem no longer. In two years, as well as receiving an ever increasing number of film and television offers and playing a dozen roles in the two media, he has had three modern-dress parts in new plays and two of them have been major successes.

Not a Conclusion

After nearly fifty years on the stage, John is still breaking new ground, so this book cannot end with an attempt to view the whole of his career in perspective. Fortunately it is far too early for that. But it would be wrong to end without stressing something which is often forgotten. It was only in the sixties that London acquired two state-subsidized companies in which actors are paid West End salaries to play the classics in repertoire with long rehearsal periods and long-term contracts. But while

John has no official connection with either the National Theatre or the Royal Shakespeare Company, he did more than anyone else to create the situation into which they were born.

Though Sybil Thorndike and Edith Evans had already played there, it was John who made the Old Vic fashionable. But for his seasons of 1929–31, neither Richardson nor Olivier would ever have gone to the Vic, and our National Theatre could never have emerged out of it. But revitalizing the Old Vic was not John's only contribution to the situation we have today. After Beerbohm Tree's regime at Her Majesty's, which started in 1897, with shorter rehearsal periods than the National and the Royal Shakespeare now have, there were no comparable seasons in London until John's at the Queen's in 1937–8. Together with his Haymarket season of 1944–5 (which was commercially no less successful) this slowly prepared the ground for the two London repertoire theatres we have today.

But his main importance is as an actor and it is as an actor that he has had – and is still having – most influence. If there is a Great Tradition in English acting, it is John who has embodied it from the thirties onwards and it is still alive in him. It is not enough to say that he was the greatest Hamlet of his period or that his Richard II, his Angelo, his Lear, his Cassius, his Leontes and his Prospero were all definitive. Although his Shakespearean style is more musical than the one currently in vogue, the reaction against it has produced no viable alternative, only a series of experiments which can roughly be divided into two categories: attempts to speak the verse flatly, as if it were prose (as Nicol Williamson did in his Hamlet) and attempts to break it up into different rhythms. Paul Scofield, for instance, started playing Macbeth in staccato cadences which had nothing to do with the verse. But he modified his approach during the run of the play and by the last night at the Aldwych (where the production transferred from Stratford-on-Avon) he had settled down into a far more legato performance. Both kinds of experiment are not only fighting Gielgud, they are fighting Shakespeare, who was perfectly capable of writing prose when he felt it was needed. But since his rhythms are always integral to the meaning of his lines, the only satisfactory way to play the verse is to find a rhythm in thinking which corresponds to the verse rhythm. Certainly John may have been inclined earlier on in his career to rely too much on sustained tone, but an excess of staccato is equally damaging. That actors are still resorting to such desperate measures to escape John's influence is indirectly an enormous tribute to him.

It is a huge pity that London audiences have had no chance to see him in a Shakespearean role since his Wolsey of 1958, for there is no other living actor who can speak Shakespeare as well as he can. In his best performances he has produced an almost incredible richness of vocal texture. Granville Barker helped him to develop a sure sense of the architecture of a Shakespearean speech, and far more important than the inherited beauty of his voice is the skill he has developed in introducing variations of pace, colour and tone, without letting the detail blur the structure. This compensates for the limitations of his vocal compass. The speed of the tonal changes follows the quick pulse of his mind, and it is this, together with his natural nobility and stage presence, his emotional intensity, his poetic sensitivity and his technical control – it is all this that makes him such a great actor.

Chronological Table of Parts and Productions
with page references to this book

Jan	Oxford Playhouse	*The Cherry Orchard*	Trofimov	29
Feb	Royalty	*The Vortex*	Understudy	31
Mar	Comedy	*The Vortex*	Understudy; 16 and 17 Mar & 21 Apr Nicky Lancaster	32
Apr	RADA Players (special perf.)	*The Nature of the Evidence*	The lover	
May	The Little	*The Vortex*	Understudy	
May	Aldwych (special perf.)	*The Orphan*	Castalio	35
May	Lyric, Hammersmith	*The Cherry Orchard*	Trofimov	36
Jun	The Little	*The Vortex*	Nicky Lancaster	
Jun	Royalty	*The Cherry Orchard*	Trofimov	
Aug	Oxford Playhouse	*The Lady from the Sea*	A Stranger	
Aug	Oxford Playhouse	*The Man with a Flower in his Mouth*	Title Part	
Oct	The Little	*The Seagull*	Konstantin	37
Dec	Prince's (special perf.)	*L'Ecole des Cocottes*	Robert	

1926

Jan	Savoy (matinees)	*The Tempest*	Ferdinand	37
Jan	RADA Players (special perf.)	*Sons and Fathers*	Richard Southern	
Feb	Barnes Theatre	*Three Sisters*	Tuzenbach	38
Mar	Barnes Theatre	*Katerina*	Georg	39
Jul	Garrick (special perf.)	*The Lady of the Camellias*	Armand	
Jul	Court (300 Club)	*Confession*	Wilfred Marlay	
Oct	New	*The Constant Nymph*	Lewis Dodd	40

1927

Apr	Apollo (special perf.)	*Othello*	Cassio	
Jun	Strand (special perf.)	*The Great God Brown*	Dion Anthony	
Aug	Tour	*The Constant Nymph*	Lewis Dodd	44

1928

Jan	Majestic, New York	*The Patriot*	The Tsarevich	45
Mar	Wyndham's (matinees)	*Ghosts*	Oswald	46
Apr	Arts	*Ghosts*	Oswald	46
Apr	Arts (special perf.)	*Prejudice*	Jacob Slovak	
Jun	Globe	*Holding out the Apple*	Dr Gerald Marlowe	47
Aug	Shaftesbury	*The Skull*	Captain Allenby	47
Oct	Court	*The Lady from Alfaqueque*	Felipe Rivas	47
Oct	Court	*Fortunato*	Alberto	47
Nov	Strand	*Out of the Sea*	John Martin	49

1929

Jan	Arts	*The Seagull*	Konstantin	49
Feb	Little	*Red Dust*	Fedor	49
	Film	*The Clue of the New Pin*		

Apr	Garrick	*The Lady with the Lamp*	Henry Tremayne	49
Sep	Old Vic	*Romeo and Juliet*	Romeo	55
Oct	Old Vic	*Merchant of Venice*	Antonio	55
Oct	Old Vic	*The Imaginary Invalid*	Cléante	56
Nov	Old Vic	*Richard II*	Richard II	56
Dec	Old Vic	*A Midsummer Night's Dream*	Oberon	57

1930

Jan	Old Vic	*Julius Caesar*	Mark Antony	58
Feb	Old Vic	*As You Like It*	Orlando	59
Feb	Old Vic	*Androcles and the Lion*	The Emperor	59
Mar	Old Vic	*Macbeth*	Macbeth	59
Apr	Old Vic	*The Man with the Flower in his Mouth*	Title Part	60
Apr	Old Vic	*Hamlet*	Hamlet	61
Jun	Queen's	*Hamlet*	Hamlet	63
Jul	Lyric, Hammersmith	*Importance of Being Earnest*	John Worthing	65
Sep	Old Vic	*Henry IV, Part I*	Hotspur	67
Oct	Old Vic	*The Tempest*	Prospero	67
Oct	Old Vic	*The Jealous Wife*	Lord Trinket	68
Nov	Old Vic	*Antony and Cleopatra*	Antony	68

1931

Jan	Sadler's Wells	*Twelfth Night*	Malvolio	68
Feb	Old Vic	*Arms and the Man*	Sergius	69
Mar	Old Vic	*Much Ado about Nothing*	Benedick	70
Apr	Old Vic	*King Lear*	Lear	70
May	His Majesty's	*The Good Companions*	Inigo Jollifant	71
Nov	Arts (special perf.)	*Musical Chairs*	Joseph Schindler	73

1932

Feb	OUDS	*Romeo and Juliet*	Director	72
Apr	Criterion	*Musical Chairs*	Joseph Schindler	74
May	Film	*Insult*		76
Jun	Arts (special perf.)	*Richard of Bordeaux*	Richard (and director)	78
Sep	St Martin's	*Strange Orchestra*	Director	76
Oct	Film	*The Good Companions*	Inigo Jollifant	76
Dec	Old Vic	*Merchant of Venice*	Director	77

1933

| Feb | New | *Richard of Bordeaux* | Richard (and director) | 78 |
| Sep | Wyndham's | *Sheppey* | Director | 82 |

1934

| Jan | Shaftesbury | *Spring 1600* | Director | 82 |

Apr	Tour	*Richard of Bordeaux*		83
Jun	New	*Queen of Scots*	Director	83
Jul	Wyndham's	*The Maitlands*	Roger Maitland	84
Nov	New	*Hamlet*	Hamlet (and director)	85

1935

Apr	New	*The Old Ladies*	Director	88
Apr	Tour	*Hamlet*		
Jul	New	*Noah*	Noah	91
Oct	New	*Romeo and Juliet*	Mercutio (and director)	93
Nov	Film	*The Secret Agent*		
Nov	New	*Romeo and Juliet*	Romeo	96

1936

Feb	OUDS	*Richard II*	Director	
Apr	Tour	*Romeo and Juliet*		
May	New	*The Seagull*	Trigorin	97
Sep	Alexandra, Toronto	*Hamlet*	Hamlet	102
Oct	St James's, New York	*Hamlet*	Hamlet	102

1937

Feb	Tour	*Hamlet*	Hamlet	106
Apr	Tour	*He was Born Gay*	Mason, Producer	107
May	Queen's	*He was Born Gay*	Mason, Producer	107
Sep	Queen's	*Richard II*	Richard II (and director)	109
Nov	Queen's	*School for Scandal*	Joseph Surface	111

1938

Jan	Queen's	*Three Sisters*	Vershinin	112
Apr	Queen's	*Merchant of Venice*	Shylock (and director)	113
May	Ambassador's	*Spring Meeting*	Director	115
Aug	Tour	*Dear Octopus*	Nicholas	116
Sep	Queen's	*Dear Octopus*	Nicholas	116

1939

Jun	Lyceum	*Hamlet*	Hamlet (and director)	117
Jul	Elsinore	*Hamlet*	Hamlet (and director)	118
Aug	Globe	*Importance of Being Earnest*	John Worthing (and director)	120
Sep	Tour	*Importance of Being Earnest*	John Worthing (and director)	122

1940

Jan	Globe	*Importance of Being Earnest*	John Worthing (and director)	122
Mar	Haymarket	*The Beggar's Opera*	Director	122
Apr	Old Vic	*King Lear*	Lear	123
May	Old Vic	*The Tempest*	Prospero	128
Jul	Tour	*Fumed Oak*	Henry Crow	
		Swan-Song	Old Actor	
		Hands across the Sea	Peter Gilpin	129
Oct	Film	*The Prime Minister*	Disraeli	131

1941

Jan	Globe	*Dear Brutus*	Dearth (and director)	133
May	Tour	*Dear Brutus*	Dearth (and director)	134
Nov	Apollo	*Ducks and Drakes*	Director	

1942

Jan	Tour	*Macbeth*	Macbeth (and director)	134
Jul	Piccadilly	*Macbeth*		137
Oct	Phoenix	*Importance of Being Earnest*	John Worthing (and director)	138
Dec	Gibraltar	*ENSA Tour*		139

1943

Mar	Tour	*Love for Love*	Valentine (and director)	141
Apr	Phoenix and Haymarket	*Love for Love*	Valentine (and director)	141
Oct	Westminster	*Landslide*	Director	143

1944

Jan	Apollo	*Cradle Song*	Director	143
May	Lyric	*Crisis in Heaven*	Director	143
Jun	Phoenix	*Last of Summer*	Director	
Jul	Tour	*Hamlet*	Hamlet	144
Aug	Tour	*Love for Love*	Valentine (and director)	147
Sep	Tour	*The Circle*	Arnold Champion-Cheney	147
Oct	Haymarket	*Repertoire Season*		147

1945

Jan	Haymarket	*Midsummer Night's Dream*	Oberon	147
Apr	Haymarket	*Duchess of Malfi*	Ferdinand	148
Oct	ENSA Tour of Far East	*Hamlet*	Hamlet (and director)	
		Blithe Spirit	Charles	149

1946

Apr	Haymarket	*Importance of Being Earnest*	John Worthing (and director)	
May	Tour	*Crime and Punishment*	Raskolnikoff	153
Jun	New and Globe	*Crime and Punishment*	Raskolnikoff	154

1947

Jan	Tour of Canada and US	*Importance of Being Earnest*	John Worthing (and director)	155
Mar	Royale Theatre, New York	*Importance of Being Earnest*	John Worthing (and director)	155
May	Tour of US	*Love for Love*	Valentine (and director)	156

Oct	Tour			
Oct	National Theatre, N.Y.	*Medea*	Jason (and director)	157
Dec	National Theatre, N.Y.	*Crime and Punishment*	Raskolnikoff	158

1948

Jul	Haymarket	*The Glass Menagerie*	Director	161
Aug	Edinburgh Festival	*Medea*	Director	162
Sep	Globe	*Medea*	Director	162
Dec	Globe	*Return of the Prodigal*	Eustace	162

1949

Feb	Haymarket	*The Heiress*	Director	162
Mar	Tour	*The Lady's not for Burning*	Thomas Mendip (and director)	163
Apr	Stratford	*Much Ado about Nothing*	Director	165
May	Globe	*The Lady's not for Burning*	Thomas Mendip (and director)	167
Sep	Apollo	*Treasure Hunt*	Director	168

1950

Jan	Lyric, Hammersmith	*The Boy with a Cart Shall We Join the Ladies?*	Director	
Mar	Stratford	*Measure for Measure*	Angelo	168
Jun	Stratford	*Much Ado about Nothing*	Benedick (and director)	171
May	Stratford	*Julius Caesar*	Cassius	173
Jul	Stratford	*King Lear*	Lear	174

1951

Jan	Royale, N.Y.	*The Lady's not for Burning*	Thomas Mendip (and director)	176
Jun	Brighton	*The Winter's Tale*	Leontes	177
Aug	Edinburgh Festival	*The Winter's Tale*	Leontes	178
Sep	Phoenix	*The Winter's Tale*	Leontes	

1952

Jan	Phoenix	*Much Ado about Nothing*	Benedick (and director)	178
	Stratford	*Macbeth*	Director	179
Aug	Film	*Julius Caesar*	Cassius	179
Dec	Lyric, Hammersmith	*Richard II*	Director	183

1953

Feb	Lyric, Hammersmith	*The Way of the World*	Mirabell (and director)	183
May	Lyric, Hammersmith	*Venice Preserv'd*	Jaffier (and director)	184
Jul	Bulawayo	*Richard II*	Richard (and director)	186

Oct	Tour	*A Day by the Sea*	Julian Anson	188
Nov	Haymarket	*A Day by the Sea*	Julian Anson	188
Dec	Brighton	*Charley's Aunt*	Director	

1954

Feb	New	*Charley's Aunt*	Director	
May	Lyric, Hammersmith	*The Cherry Orchard*	Director	188

1955

Apr	Stratford	*Twelfth Night*	Director	191
Jun	Brighton	*King Lear*	Lear	189
Jun	European Tour	*King Lear*	Lear	189
Jul	Palace	*Much Ado about Nothing*	Benedick (and director)	192
Jul	Palace	*King Lear*	Lear	192
Aug	Film	*Round the world in Eighty Days*	Foster	
Sep	European Tour	*King Lear* and *Much Ado*		189
Dec	Film	*Richard III*	Clarence	

1956

Apr	Haymarket	*The Chalk Garden*	Director	193
	Film	*The Barretts of Wimpole Street*	Mr Barrett	
Sep	Tour	*Nude with Violin*	Sebastian (and director)	194
Nov	Globe	*Nude with Violin*	Sebastian (and co-director)	195
	Film	*St. Joan*	Warwick	

1957

Jun	Covent Garden	*The Trojans*	Director	196
Aug	Stratford	*The Tempest*	Prospero	197
Sep	Edinburgh Festival	*The Ages of Man*		202
Sep	Tour	*The Ages of Man*		202
Dec	Drury Lane	*The Tempest*	Prospero	198

1958

Jan	Brighton	*The Potting Shed*	James Callifer	199
Feb	Globe	*The Potting Shed*	James Callifer	199
Apr	Globe	*Variation on a Theme*	Director	218
May	Old Vic	*Henry VIII*	Wolsey	201
Jun	Cambridge	*Five Finger Exercise*	Director	
Sep	Tour of Canada and US	*The Ages of Man*		203
Dec	46th Street Theatre, N.Y.	*The Ages of Man*		204

1959

Mar	TV	*A Day by the Sea*	Julian Anson	206

Apr	CBS TV	*The Browning Version*	Andrew Crocker Harris	205
May	Tour	*The Complaisant Lover*	Director	218
Jun	Globe	*The Complaisant Lover*		
Jul	Queen's	*The Ages of Man*		207
Sep	US Tour	*Much Ado about Nothing*	Director	208
Dec	Music Box, New York	*Five Finger Exercise*	Director	

1960

Sep	Phoenix	*The Last Joke*	Prince Ferdinand Cavanati	210

1961

Feb	Covent Garden	*A Midsummer Night's Dream*	Director	218
Mar	ANTA Theatre, New York	*Big Fish, Little Fish*	Director	210
Jun	Globe	*Dazzling Prospect*	Director	
Oct	Stratford	*Othello*	Othello	211
Dec	Aldwych	*The Cherry Orchard*	Gaev	213

1962

Apr	Haymarket	*The School for Scandal*	Director	214
Oct	Haymarket	*The School for Scandal*	Joseph Surface (and director)	215
Dec	New York	*The School for Scandal*	Joseph Surface (and director)	216

1963

Jan	Majestic, New York	*Seven Ages of Man*		
Feb	TV	*The Rehearsal*	The Count	
Jun	Tour	*The Ides of March*	Caesar (and co-director)	216
Aug	Haymarket	*The Ides of March*	Caesar (and co-director)	216
Sep	Film	*Becket*	Louis VII	217

1964

Apr	Lunt-Fontanne, New York	*Hamlet*	Director	219
May	World Tour	*Seven Ages of Man*		
Aug	Film	*The Loved One*	Sir Francis Hinsley	221
Oct	Film	*Chimes at Midnight*	Henry IV	
Dec	Billy Rose, New York	*Tiny Alice*	Julian	222

1965

Aug	Tour	*Ivanov*	Ivanov (and director)	223
Sep	Phoenix	*Ivanov*	Ivanov (and director)	224

1966

Mar	US Tour	*Ivanov*	Ivanov (and director)	225
May	Shubert Theatre, N.Y.	*Ivanov*	Ivanov (and director)	225
Jul	US TV	*The Love Song of Barney Kempinski*		
Aug	BBC TV	*Alice in Wonderland*	Mock Turtle	225
Aug	BBC TV	*The Mayfly and the Frog*	Gabriel Kantara	

1967

Jan	US Tour	*The Ages of Man*		
Feb	Film	*Assignment to Kill*		
Mar	BBC TV	*From Chekhov with Love*	Chekhov	226
Apr	Film	*Mr Sebastian*	Head of British Intelligence	
Apr	Film	*The Charge of the Light Brigade*	Lord Raglan	226
Oct	Tour	*Half Way Up The Tree*	Director	227
Nov	Queen's	*Half Way Up The Tree*	Director	227
Nov	National Theatre	*Tartuffe*	Orgon	228

1968

Jan	Film	*The Shoes of the Fisherman*	The Pope	
Feb	BBC TV	*St Joan*	Inquisitor	
Mar	National Theatre	*Oedipus*	Oedipus	230
Apr	Film	*Oh What a Lovely War*	Count Berchtold	
Aug	Coliseum	*Don Giovanni*	Director	
Oct	Apollo	*40 Years On*	Headmaster	232

1969

Apr	BBC TV	*In Good King Charles's Golden Days*	King Charles
Apr	BBC TV	*Conversation at Night*	The Writer
Jun	Film	*Julius Caesar*	Caesar
Oct	Film	*Eagle in a Cage*	Lord Sissal

1970

Jan	Lyric	*The Battle of Shrivings*	Sir Gideon Petrie
Apr	BBC TV	*Hassan*	The Caliph
May	ATV	*Hamlet*	Ghost
Jun	Royal Court	*Home*	Harry
Nov	Morosco, New York	*Home*	Harry

Index

References to plays, films and television plays are indexed under 'Plays', etc

ABOUT THE AUTHOR

RONALD HAYMAN is an English writer and editor noted for his wide-ranging interest in the contemporary theater. He has written ten books under the Contemporary Playwrights Series, which include studies of Robert Bolt, Samuel Beckett, Harold Pinter, Edward Albee, and Arthur Miller. He has written a biography of Tolstoy, published in England by Routledge, and a book, *Techniques of Acting,* published by Methuen in London. He has edited *The Collected Plays of John Whiting,* published also in the United States, and he regularly reviews poetry for *Encounter* and novels for *The Sunday Telegraph.* He has also directed for the stage, his most successful production being a one-man show with Max Adrian as George Bernard Shaw.

3